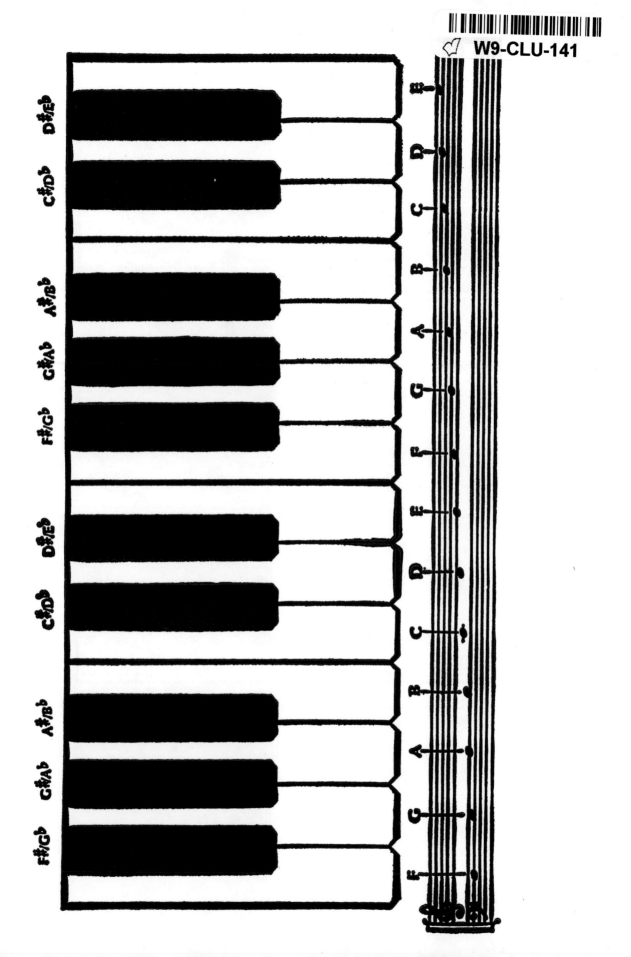

THE Music CONNECTION

T-E
Mu-Si 39
M-7

PROGRAM AUTHORS

Jane Beethoven
Dulce Bohn
Patricia Shehan Campbell
Carmen E. Culp
Jennifer Davidson
Lawrence Eisman
Sandra Longoria Glover
Charlotte Hayes

Martha Hilley
Mary E. Hoffman
Sanna Longden
Hunter March
Bill McCloud
Janet Montgomery
Marvelene Moore
Catherine Nadon-Gabrion

Mary Palmer
Carmino Ravosa
Mary Louise Reilly
Will Schmid
Carol Scott-Kassner
Jean Sinor
Sandra Stauffer
Judith Thomas

RECORDING PRODUCERS

Darrell Bledsoe
Jeanine Levenson

J. Douglas Pummill
Buryl Red, Executive Producer

Linda Twine
Ted Wilson

SILVER BURDETT GINN

PARSIPPANY, NJ   NEEDHAM, MA
Atlanta, GA   Deerfield, IL   Irving, TX   San Jose, CA

ISBN 0-382-26187-9

C · O · N · T

· E · N · T · S

REFERENCE BANK

CONCEPTS

Throughout the world, people have always
felt the urge to make music.

Whether alone or in
groups, people of all cultures play
instruments, sing, or compose. The result
is an immense diversity of musical
performers and styles.

What do all these different styles have in common?
In one way or another, they all make use of the
same basic tools—rhythm, melody,
harmony, tone color, and form.

In this first section of your
book, you will learn about the *concepts*
behind these musical tools. This knowledge
will help you to discover all the
wonderful things
that music has to offer.

section 1

A World of
MUSICAL
Performers

To begin your musical journey, listen to the examples in the montage. Can you match the photographs of the performers with the excerpts?

 Montage of Musical Performers

Whitney Houston

Joan Baez

Arrested Development

Whitney Houston's dynamic, expressive performances as a vocalist have won her millions of fans around the world. Listen to her recording of *The Greatest Love of All*. How would you describe the singer's performance and interpretation?

The Greatest Love of All .... Creed/Masser

A Mexican Mariachi Band

Peter Gabriel

A Symphony Orchestra

Come On In Sit right down

Here's your chance to do some performing of your own, either as a soloist or in a group.

This is a song in the black gospel tradition. What do the lyrics tell you about how it should be performed?

We're Gonna Have a Good Time
from *Your Arms Too Short to Box with God*

Words and Music by Micki Grant

REFRAIN

We're gon - na have a good time. _ We're gon - na have a good time. _ Come on in, __ sit right down, _ Let's have _ a good time.

VERSE

1. Don't be a-fraid to raise _ your voice, _ Let's have _ a good time.
2. When you _ hear me sing __ and shout, _ Let's have _ a good time.

The Lord said make a joy - ful noise, _ Let's have _ a good time.
What's in - side me must _ come out, _ Let's have _ a good time.

Scene from the musical
Your Arms Too Short to Box With God

Solo   C   Gm   C₇   F   C   Chorus   G₇   C

Now   you can   do _ what   you want to, _   Let's have _ a good time.
When the Lord told   me _ to   tes - ti - fy, _   Let's have _ a good time.

Solo   C   Gm   C₇   F   C   Chorus   G₇   C   *D.C.*

But I'm gon - na do   what the Lord said do, _   And have _ a good time.
That's what He meant 'cause the Lord don't lie, _   Let's have _ a good time.

Coda
C   G₇   C   F   C   *rit.*   G₇   F   C

Come on   in, __   sit right   down, _   Let's have _ a good   time. ____

This song is from a movie about a teenage girl whose "slow, glowing dream" is to become a professional dancer. Which phrases in the song's lyrics describe the difficulties and the joys of performing?

Hear the Music

Flashdance ... What a Feeling

Words by Keith Forsey and Irene Cara   Music by Giorgio Moroder

First, when there's noth-ing but a slow, glow-ing dream that your fear seems to hide deep in-side your mind. All a-lone I have cried si-lent tears full of pride in a world made of steel, made of stone.

Well, I hear the mu-sic, close my
I hear the mu-sic, close my

eyes, feel the rhy-thm wrap a-round, take a hold of my heart.
eyes, I am rhy-thm. In a flash it takes hold of my heart.

What a feel-ing. Bein's be-liev - in', I can have it all, now I'm danc-ing for my life. Take your pas-

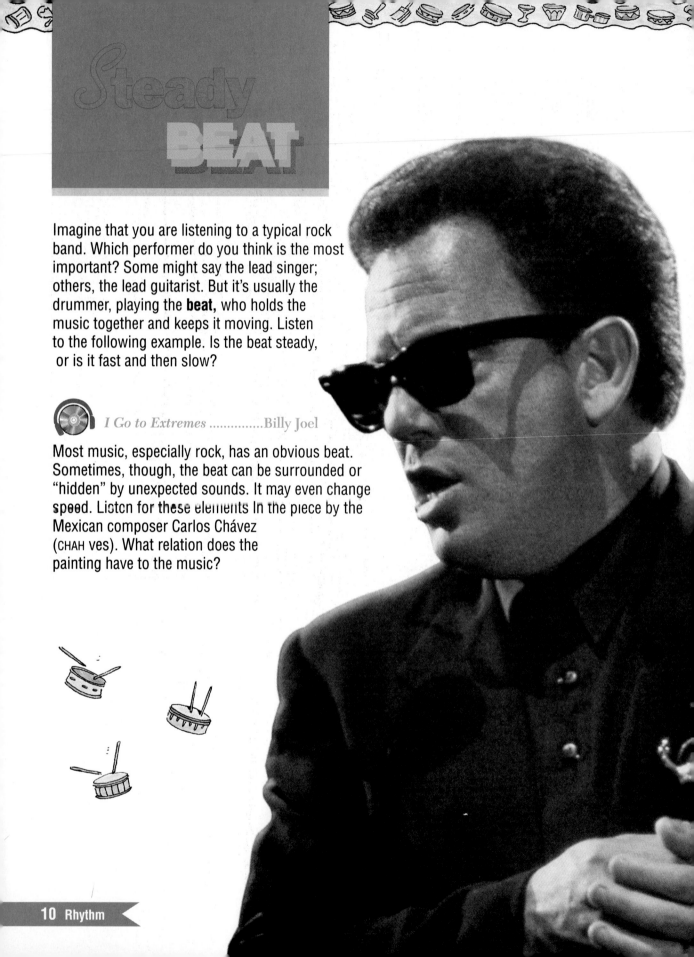

Steady BEAT

Imagine that you are listening to a typical rock band. Which performer do you think is the most important? Some might say the lead singer; others, the lead guitarist. But it's usually the drummer, playing the **beat,** who holds the music together and keeps it moving. Listen to the following example. Is the beat steady, or is it fast and then slow?

I Go to Extremes ....Billy Joel

Most music, especially rock, has an obvious beat. Sometimes, though, the beat can be surrounded or "hidden" by unexpected sounds. It may even change **speed.** Listen for these elements In the piece by the Mexican composer Carlos Chávez (CHAH ves). What relation does the painting have to the music?

Zapatistas   *José Clemente Orozco*

1931 The Museum of Modern Art, New York

 Toccata for Percussion, Movement 3
(excerpt) ....Carlos Chávez

Some music intentionally avoids any feeling of a steady beat. Listen to the following jazz performances. Where does the steady beat occur in each?

 One-Note Samba (excerpt) ....
Laurindo Almeida/The Modern Jazz Quartet

 Also Sprach Zarathustra (2001)
(excerpt) ....Eumir Deodato

TEMPO

Slowly

Slowly the tide creeps up the sand,
Slowly the shadows cross the land.
Slowly the cart-horse pulls his mile,
Slowly the old man mounts the stile.

Slowly the hands move round the clock,
Slowly the dew dries on the dock.
Slow is the snail—but slowest of all
The green moss spreads on the old brick wall.

James Reeves

Read the poem above, then experiment by reciting it at different speeds. Which speed seems most appropriate? Why?

You've probably already noticed that in music, too, the beat can vary in speed. This rate of speed is called **tempo**. Most composers use traditional Italian terms, such as those listed in Call Chart 1, to indicate tempo. (Many composers, however, prefer to use the language of their own country.) Which of these words might you choose to describe the pictures and the poem?

 Call Chart 1

As you listen to examples of these different tempo markings, keep in mind that the terms are not meant to be exact. Descriptions of tempo depend on comparing one piece with another.

1. *Presto*—very fast	**4.** *Andante*—walking tempo
2. *Allegro*—lively	**5.** *Adagio*—slow
3. *Moderato*—moderate	**6.** *Largo*—very slow

Tampering with the Tempo

In each musical example you've heard so far in this lesson, the tempo stays
the same throughout. In some pieces, though, the tempo may get slower
(*ritardando* [ree tahr DAHN doh]) or faster (*accelerando* [ah chel eh RAHN doh]).
The composer Heitor Villa-Lobos (AY tohr vee lah LOH bohsh) used these
devices in this musical description of a journey on a steam-engine train.

*Bachianas Brasileiras No. 2, "The Little Train
of the Caipira"* ....Heitor Villa-Lobos

Are the tempo changes sudden, or are they gradual? Can you guess why,
at certain places, the music slows down and then speeds up again?

*M*eet the *C*omposer

Heitor Villa-Lobos

(1887–1959)

While still a child in his hometown of Rio de Janeiro,
Brazil, Heitor was taught to play the cello by his father.
But instead of continuing with formal training, the
young cellist began playing with local popular musicians in the restaurants and cafes of the city. He eventually studied in Brazil and Paris and soon devoted
himself to composition. Like the piece from *Bachianas
Brasileiras*, many of his compositions were inspired
by the native folk music of Brazil. He wrote more than
2,000 works, including operas, ballets, symphonies,
songs, and piano pieces.

The composer's other great love was promoting
music education in the schools. He enjoyed writing
music especially for young people. At one outdoor
festival, he conducted 20,000 children in singing and
movement activities.

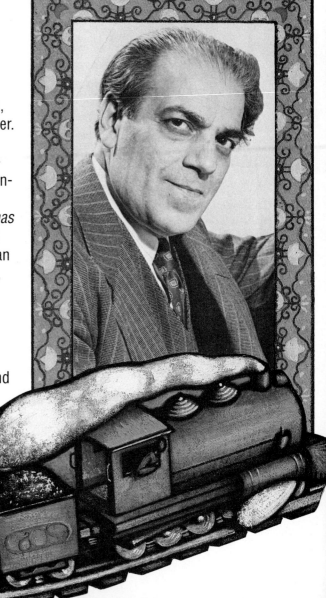

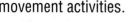

Melody
*O*ut

The **pitches** in a **melody** can move in different ways. Look closely at this melody.

Did you notice that each note is just one *step* away from the note on either side? As long as the notes move from a line on the staff to the next space or from a space to the next line, the melody is moving by step. Try playing the melody on a keyboard instrument to see and hear the stepwise movement.

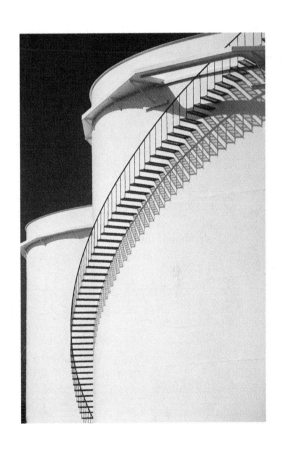

middle C

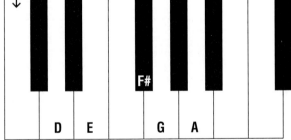

Listen to more of this melody as it is sung by the male soloist. Can you hear where the pitches do *not* move by step?

Symphony No. 9 in D Minor, Movement 4 (excerpt).................Ludwig van Beethoven

Stepping Through a Song

Here is a song that moves mostly by step. After you've learned to sing it, find the places in which the melody (the upper notes) does *not* move by step.

The Swallow (La golondrina)

English Words by Aura Kontra   *Folk Song from Mexico*

Oh, where, oh, where ___ has sum - mer's swal - low flown, ___
¿A - dón - de i - rá ___ ve - loz y fa - ti - ga - da,

So swift in flight, ___ yet wear - y and a - lone? ___
la go - lon - dri - na que de a - quí se va?

Oh, should the wind - y skies lead her a - stray, ___ she'll nev - er
O si en el vien - to se ha - lla - rá ex - tra - via - da bus - can - do a -

find ___ a place where she can stay. ___ As
bri - go y no lo en - con - tra - rá. ___ Jun -

I lie sleep - ing she'll re - turn to me safe -
to a mi le - cho le pon - dré ___ su ni -

ly; Here, she can lin - ger till morn - ing calls her a -
do, en don - de pue - da la es - ta - ción pa -

way. _____ I, too, have wan -
sar. _____ Tam - bién yo es - toy _____

dered, leav - ing home far be - hind _____ me; Since I'm not
en la re - gión _____ per - di - do, ¡Oh! cie - lo

free, _____ I know I'm here to stay. _____
san - to y sin po - der vo - lar. _____

Animal Locomotion, Plate 626   *Eadweard Muybridge*

George Eastman House

To discover another way that melodies move, let's take another look at the Beethoven melody. Play it again, this time leaving out the gray notes.

Do you hear the *leaps* in the melody? When notes move from one line to another line (or further) or from one space to another space (or further), the melody is moving by leap.

Moving On

The melody in this listening selection contains examples of movement by step (shown in blue) and by leap (shown in yellow). As you listen, follow the score to discover one more way that melodies move. (*Hint:* The notes are shown in green.)

Classical Symphony, Movement 3, "Gavotte" ....Sergei Prokofiev

Harmonizing a Melody

Sing or play this well-known melody.

Try it again, this time asking a friend to add another set of notes.

You just created **harmony**, which is simply the sounding of two or more different notes at the same time.

Using the same procedure, learn the melody of the song "How Sad Is True Love." Then add the harmony part. How does the harmony affect the sound and the feeling of the song?

How Sad Is True Love

Love Song of the Maori

How sad is true love, dear-est, For when we're part - ed I feel so lone - ly and brok-en - heart - ed; Re - turn to me, dear, I want you on - ly, You know I love you, Oh, come to

From OUR SINGING WORLD: SINGING TEENAGERS. © 1961 Ginn & Co. Used with permission.

The painting *Red Hot* is an example of what is known as colorfield art. In this style, the focus is on the play and interaction of colors. Describe how the different colors "harmonize" with each other to create an overall effect.

Red Hot   *John Eaves*

1986

me. ___   I fear to greet you,   Lest you should turn a - way   and laugh at me, dear,   Be-cause I love you;   Re - turn to me, dear,   I want you on - ly,   You know I love you,   Oh, come to me. ___

Another way to create harmony is to accompany a song with one or more instruments. The following groups of notes, called **chords** (kordz), can be played on a keyboard instrument to accompany the song "De colores." The chord symbols above the music will tell you when the chords should be played. How many different chords are used in this song?

De colores

English Words by Alice Firgau and Samuel Maquí   *Folk Song from Mexico*

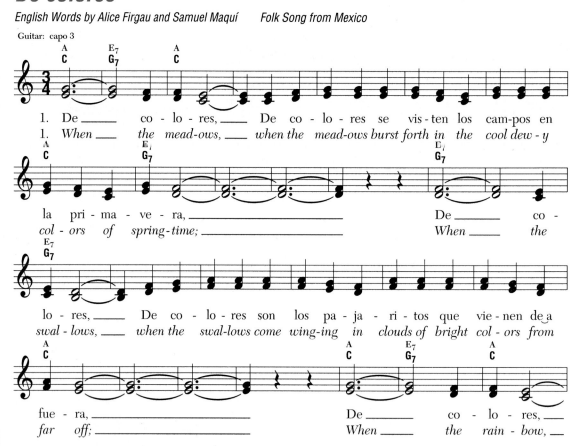

De colores, traditional, arranged, and adapted by Joan Baez © 1974, Chandos Music. (ASCAP)

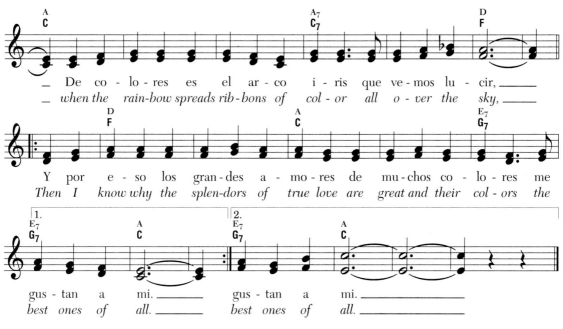

De co - lo - res es el ar - co i - ris que ve - mos lu - cir, _____
when the rain-bow spreads rib-bons of col - or all o - ver the sky, _____

Y por e - so los gran - des a - mo - res de mu - chos co - lo - res me
Then I know why the splen-dors of true love are great and their col - ors the

1.
gus - tan a mi. _____ **gus - tan a mi.** _____
best ones of all. _____ _best ones of all._ _____

2. Canta el gallo, Canta el gallo con el
    quiri quiri quiri quiri quiri;
   La gallina, La gallina con el
    cara cara cara cara cara;
   Los polluelos, Los polluelos con el
    pio pio pio pio pi,
   Y por eso los grandes amores de muchos
    colores me gustan a mi. *(2 times)*

2. *Hear the rooster, Hear the rooster that calls*
    quiri quiri quiri quiri quiri,
   Hear his lady, Hear his lady sing back
    cara cara cara cara cara,
   Hear the small ones, Hear the small ones call out
    pio pio pio pio pi,
   And my favorite folks are the folks who wear colors,
    the colors so pleasant to me. (2 times)

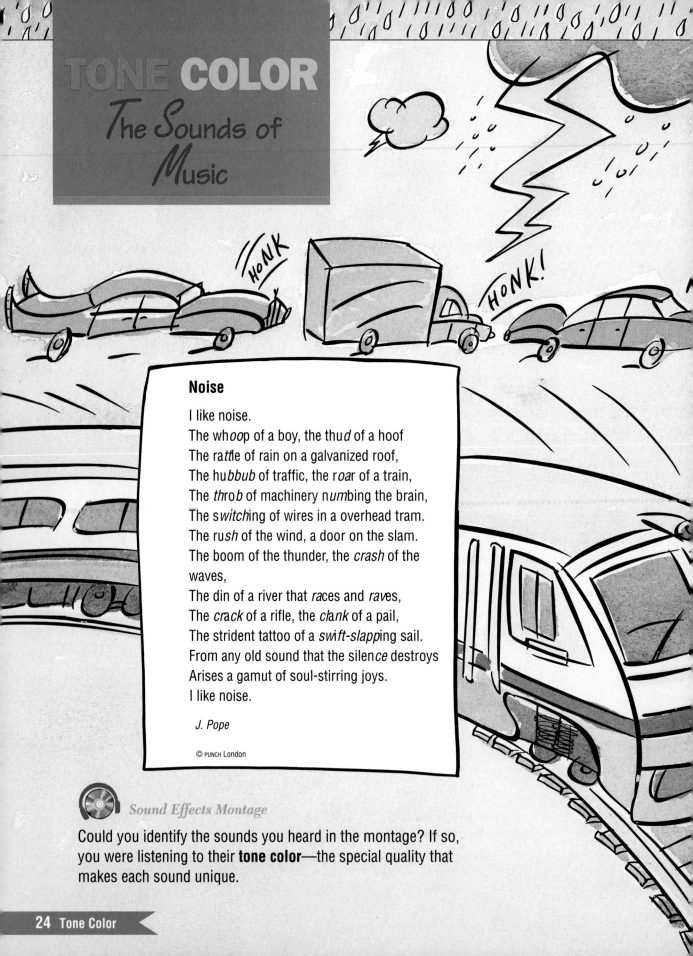

TONE COLOR
The Sounds of Music

Noise

I like noise.
The wh*oo*p of a boy, the thu*d* of a hoof
The ra*tt*le of rain on a galvanized roof,
The hu*bbub* of traffic, the r*oar* of a train,
The *throb* of machinery n*um*bing the brain,
The s*witch*ing of wires in a overhead tram.
The ru*sh* of the wind, a door on the slam.
The boom of the thunder, the *crash* of the
waves,
The din of a river that r*a*ces and r*av*es,
The *crack* of a rifle, the *clank* of a pail,
The strident tattoo of a *swift-slapp*ing sail.
From any old sound that the silen*ce* destroys
Arises a gamut of soul-stirring joys.
I like noise.

J. Pope

© PUNCH London

Sound Effects Montage

Could you identify the sounds you heard in the montage? If so, you were listening to their **tone color**—the special quality that makes each sound unique.

Composing with Sound Effects

Tone colors in music can sometimes come from unusual sources. For instance, the composer of *Dripsody* based the entire piece on the tape-recorded sound of a single drop of water. How do you think the different sound effects were created?

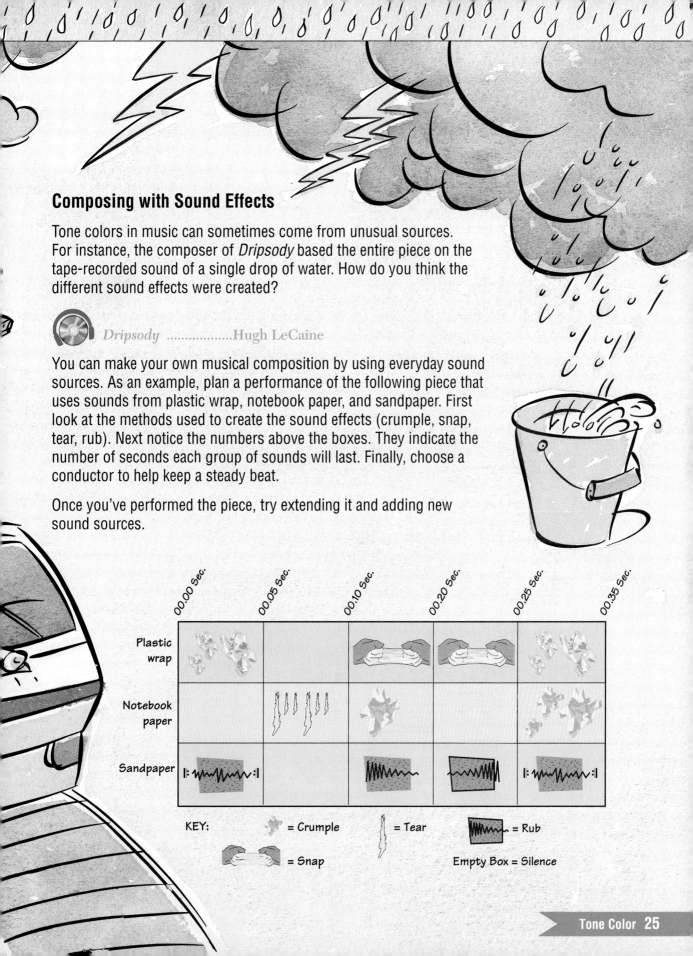

Dripsody ....Hugh LeCaine

You can make your own musical composition by using everyday sound sources. As an example, plan a performance of the following piece that uses sounds from plastic wrap, notebook paper, and sandpaper. First look at the methods used to create the sound effects (crumple, snap, tear, rub). Next notice the numbers above the boxes. They indicate the number of seconds each group of sounds will last. Finally, choose a conductor to help keep a steady beat.

Once you've performed the piece, try extending it and adding new sound sources.

KEY:
= Crumple
= Tear
= Rub
= Snap
Empty Box = Silence

Adding Sound Effects to a Song

In the old days of radio, sound effects were often used to illustrate actions. (Remember, this was before television!) The song "(Ghost) Riders in the Sky" was one of the big "hits" of the time. Once you've learned to sing it, turn to pages 28 and 29 and plan a "dramatic" performance that incorporates the suggested sound effects.

(Ghost) Riders in the Sky *(A Cowboy Legend)*

Words and Music by Stan Jones

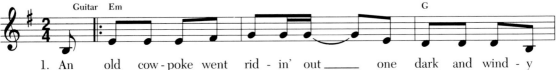

1. An old cow-poke went rid-in' out ___ one dark and wind-y
brands were still on fire ___ and their hooves were made of
fac-es gaunt, their eyes were blurred ___ and shirts all soaked with
rid-ers loped on by him ___ he heard one call his

day, ___ Up-on a ridge ___ he rest-ed as he
steel, ___ Their horns were black ___ and shin-y and their
sweat, ___ They're rid-in' hard ___ to catch that herd but
name, ___ "If you want to save ___ your soul from tor-ture

went a-long ___ his way, ___ When all at once ___ a
hot breath ___ he could feel, ___ A bolt of fear ___ went
they ain't ___ caught 'em yet, ___ 'Cause they've got to ride ___ for-
rid-in' on ___ our range, ___ Then cow-boy ___ change your

might-y herd of red-eyed ___ cows he saw A-plow-in' through the
through him as they thun-dered ___ through the sky For he saw the rid-ers
ev-er on that range ___ up in the sky On hor-ses snor-tin'
ways to-day ___ or with ___ us you will ride A-try'n' to catch the

rag - ged skies _____ and up a cloud - y draw. _____
com - in' hard _____ and he heard their mourn-ful cry. _____
fire, _____ as they ride on, hear their cry. _____
dev - il's herd _____ a - cross these end - less skies." _____

Yi - pi - yi ay, _____ Yi - pi - yi - o, _____

1.,2.,3.

The ghost herd in _____ the sky. _____ 2. Their
The ghost rid - ers in _____ the sky. _____ 3. Their
The ghost rid - ers in _____ the sky. _____ 4. As the
The

4.

ghost rid - ers in _____ the sky. _____

(Ghost) Riders in the Sky

Stan Jones

(Single pair of coconut shell "hoof beats.")
(Introduction)

1. An old cowpoke went ridin' out one dark and windy day,

   (Stop "hoof beats." Sounds of snoring and whistling.)
   Upon a ridge he rested as he went along his way,

   (Large group of "hoof beats," starting soft, getting louder.)
   When all at once a mighty herd of red-eyed cows he saw

   (Continue "hoof beats," then echoes of "hoof beats.")
   A-plowin' through the ragged skies and up a cloudy draw.

   (Continue "hoof beats." Add whooping and howling sounds.)
   Yi-pi-yi-ay, Yi-pi-yi-o, The ghost herd in the sky.

   ("Hoof beats." Sounds of crumpling paper, struck metal.)
2. Their brands were still on fire and their hooves were made of steel,

   (Add slow, heavy panting.)
   Their horns were black and shiny and their hot breath he could feel,

   (Add the single sound of a dropped wastebasket.)
   A bolt of fear went through him as they thundered through the sky

   (Louder "hoof beats." Howling sounds.)
   For he saw the riders comin' hard and he heard their mournful cry.

   (Same as before.)
   Yi-pi-yi-ay, Yi-pi-yi-o, The ghost riders in the sky.

   ("Hoof beats." Quick panting sounds.)
3. Their faces gaunt, their eyes were blurred and shirts all soaked with sweat,

   (Faster, louder "hoof beats." Whooping sounds.)
   They're ridin' hard to catch that herd but they ain't caught 'em yet,

   (Add repeated whispers of the word "forever.")
   'Cause they've got to ride forever on that range up in the sky

   ("Hoof beats." Whooping sounds. Crumpling paper.)
   On horses snortin' fire, as they ride on, hear their cry.

   (Same as before.)
   Yi-pi-yi-ay, Yi-pi-yi-o, The ghost riders in the sky.

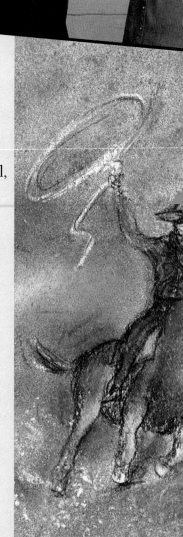

("Hoof beats." One person calls out a name from the class.)

4. As the riders loped on by him he heard one call his name,

("Hoof beats." One person whimpers "Save me.")
   "If you want to save your soul from torture ridin' on our range,

(Add more voices whimpering "Save me.")
   Then cowboy change your ways today or with us you will ride

(Continue all sounds, getting louder.)
   A-try'n' to catch the devil's herd across these endless skies."

(Continue)
   Yi-pi-yi-ay, Yi-pi-yi-o, The ghost riders in the sky.

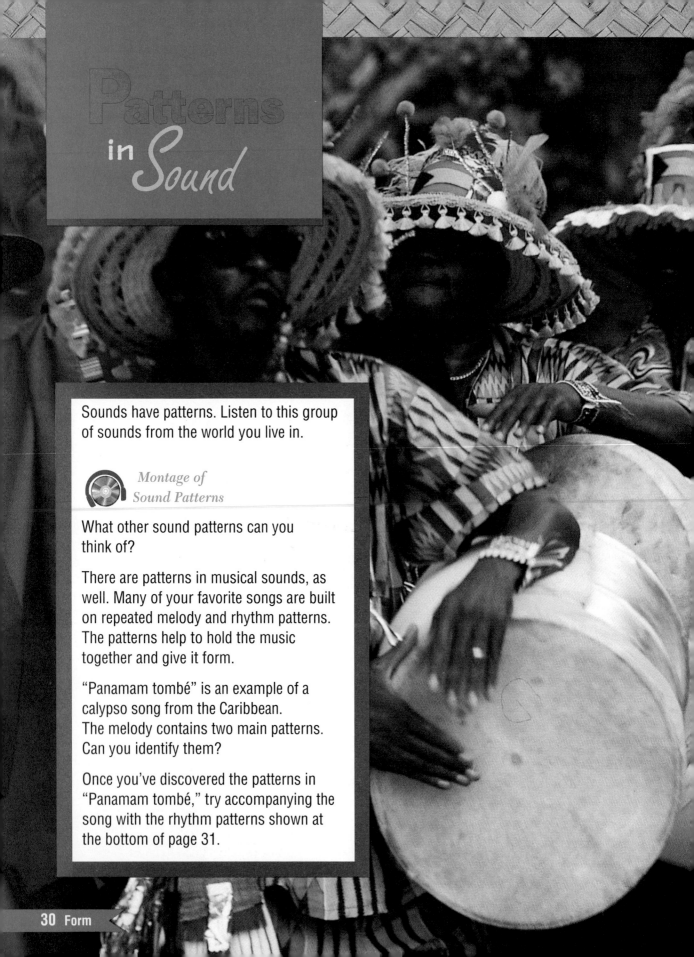

Patterns in Sound

Sounds have patterns. Listen to this group of sounds from the world you live in.

Montage of
Sound Patterns

What other sound patterns can you think of?

There are patterns in musical sounds, as well. Many of your favorite songs are built on repeated melody and rhythm patterns. The patterns help to hold the music together and give it form.

"Panamam tombé" is an example of a calypso song from the Caribbean. The melody contains two main patterns. Can you identify them?

Once you've discovered the patterns in "Panamam tombé," try accompanying the song with the rhythm patterns shown at the bottom of page 31.

Panamam tombé

Calypso Song

Guitar: capo 3

Pan-a - mam _ tom - bé, Pan-a - mam _ tom - bé, Pan-a - mam _ tom -

bé. My Pan - a-ma, Pan-a - mam _ tom - bé. Pan-a - mam _ tom - bé.

Please pick up my Pan - a - ma, _ Pan-a - mam _ tom - bé, When I left the

car - ni - val, _ Pan-a - mam _ tom - bé. Pan-a - mam _ tom - bé, __ Oh! _

By permission of the Carib Singers

Maracas

Claves

Woodblock

Bongos

Cowbell or Guiro

Ostinato Patterns

For centuries, composers have used repeated patterns, called
ostinatos (ah stee NAH tohz), as a way to hold a piece together. Often variations are woven above and around the ostinato. Here is a piece that does just that. The ostinato looks like this.

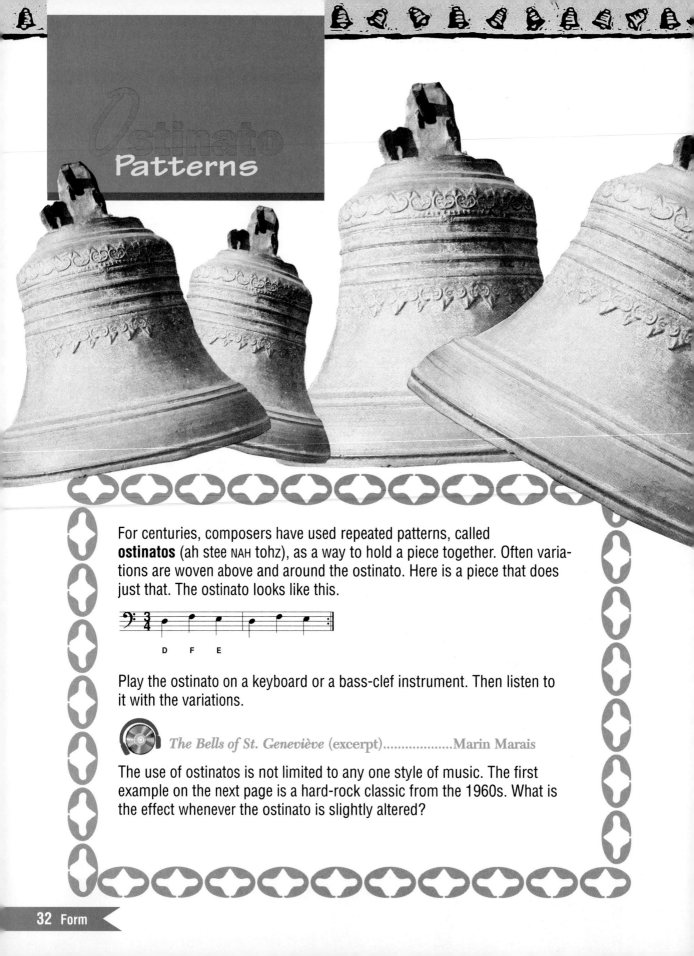

D   F   E

Play the ostinato on a keyboard or a bass-clef instrument. Then listen to it with the variations.

The Bells of St. Geneviève (excerpt).................Marin Marais

The use of ostinatos is not limited to any one style of music. The first example on the next page is a hard-rock classic from the 1960s. What is the effect whenever the ostinato is slightly altered?

 Led Boots................Jeff Beck

Listen to one more example of ostinato. This time, the style is current South African pop. How many different patterns can you hear?

 Alex Jive ....The Boyoyo Boys

Let's take a closer look at this selection. Here is the ostinato, with the chord names.

Plan a performance that combines the ostinato on one instrument with your own keyboard part. Here are the chords in a basic rhythm pattern.
Try improvising new rhythms and melodies to go with the ostinato.

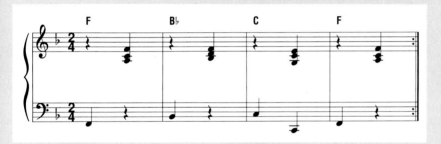

Layering Patterns

Listen to this rap song performed by Arrested Development. See how many different recurring patterns you can pick out.

 Mr. Wendal ....*Speech/Arrested Development*

Did you hear this guitar pattern?

Try creating your own rhythm or melody patterns to accompany the recording.

A River of Patterns

Look at the melody and rhythm patterns below. Sing them or play them on any instrument that has the proper range. They are the patterns for most of the accompaniment of *River*, on the next page. Follow the lyrics as you listen to the recording. The letters beside the lyrics are keys to the patterns that are shown below.

River

Eugene McDaniels

Introduction: A and B

A and B There's a river somewhere,
Flows through the lives of everyone;
And it flows through the valleys and the mountains
    and the meadows of time.

There's a star in the sky,
Brightenin' the lives of everyone;
I know it brightens the valleys and the mountains
    and the meadows of time.

Free improvisation *Solo and Chorus*: Yes, it do.
    with A

There's a voice from the past
A and C Speaks through the lives of everyone;
I know it speaks through the valleys and the mountains
A and C   and the meadows of time.

There's a smile in your eye
A and C Brightens the lives of everyone;
I know it brightens the valleys and the mountains
A and C   and the meadows of time.

Free improvisation *Solo and Chorus*: Yes, it do.
    with C and D

There's a short song of love
C and D Sings through the lives of everyone;
And it sings through the valleys and the mountains
C and D   and the meadows of time.

There's a sweet song of love
C That sings through the lives of everyone;
I know it sings through the valleys and the mountains
C   and the meadows of time.

Free improvisation *Solo and Chorus*: Yes, it do.
    with D

There's a river somewhere,
D Flows through the lives of everyone;
I know it flows through the valleys and the mountains
C and D   and the meadows of time.

There's a sweet song of love
C Sweetenin' the lives of everyone;
And it sweetens the valleys and the mountains
C   and the meadows of time.

Free improvisation *Solo and Chorus*: Yes, it do.

Pattern Building

Some composers have constructed whole pieces from just one or two simple patterns that repeat over and over. One example is *In the Hall of the Mountain King* by the Norwegian composer Edvard Grieg (greeg). The entire composition is based on just two themes, shown below. How are the themes similar?

The trick, of course, is to keep the music interesting. Follow the call chart to find out how the composer does this.

Call Chart 2

Peer Gynt, "In the Hall of the Mountain King"
....................Edvard Grieg

	Instruments	Dynamics	Theme	Tempo
1.	Low strings (basses, cellos) (plucked) - - - - - - - - - - - - - Bassoon, contra-bassoon	Soft	A	Slow
2.	Same as Call 1	Soft	B	Slow
3.	Same as Call 1	Soft	A	Slow
4.	Violins (plucked) - - - - - - - - - - - Oboe, clarinet	Slightly louder	A	Slightly faster
5.	Same as Call 4	Same as Call 4	B	Same as Call 4
6.	Violins (plucked) - - - - - - - - - - - Oboe	Getting louder	A	Getting faster
7.	Strings with full orchestra	Loud	A	Fast
8.	Strings and brass with full orchestra	Loud	B	Fast
9.	?	?	?	?
10.	Full orchestra	Sudden changes	Coda, based on themes	Very fast

Beats in Groups

Meter in 2

What do you notice about these quarter notes?

There isn't much to notice, is there? They're just plodding along. But what happens when we accent (>) every other note?

The beats are now grouped in *twos*— called a meter in 2. Musicians usually put bar lines between groupings.

measure

Look at the conducting pattern for meter in 2. As you practice it, emphasize the downbeat (the first beat of each measure). Then try conducting the listening selection from the ballet *El amor brujo* (el ah moor BROO hoh).

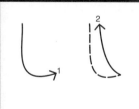

Conducting pattern in 2

El amor brujo, "Ritual Fire Dance"
..................Manuel de Falla

The Time Signature

Have you noticed a pair of numbers at the beginning of most notated music? These numbers indicate the **time signature.** The top number tells what the meter grouping is, and the bottom number tells what note represents the beat. As an example, let's look at the time signature for *Ritual Fire Dance*.

2 = Two beats in each measure
4 = The quarter note (♩) gets one beat

Sometimes other note values represent the beat. For instance, in $\frac{2}{8}$ the eighth note (♪) gets one beat; and in $\frac{2}{2}$ the half note (♩) gets one beat.

*M*eet the *C*omposer

Manuel de Falla

(1876–1946)

Born in Cádiz, Spain, de Falla (FAH yah) remained rooted in the folk music and historical traditions of his country throughout his career. His early works were especially influenced by the music of his native province, Andalusia. Even his piano and orchestral pieces seem to imitate the style of Spain's national instrument, the guitar. In 1939, the Spanish Civil War brought a repressive dictator to power, and de Falla moved to Argentina. There he lived the rest of his life mostly in seclusion.

The exciting premiere of *El amor brujo* ("Love, the Magician") took place in Madrid in 1915. The *Ritual Fire Dance* has since become the composer's most popular work.

Meter in 4

The Photographer, "A Gentleman's Honor" ....Philip Glass

The beats in the piece *A Gentleman's Honor* are grouped in 4, and the quarter note represents the beat. The time signature, then, is $\frac{4}{4}$. What is the difference between this time signature and that of *Ritual Fire Dance*?

Practice the conducting pattern for meter in 4 and then conduct the listening selection. Afterward, learn to sing and conduct "The Rose." The song's time signature is the same as that of the listening piece, but what is different?

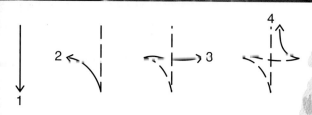

Conducting pattern in 4

Beyond Winter

Over the winter glaciers
  I see the summer glow,
And through the wild-piled snowdrift
  The warm rosebuds below.

Ralph Waldo Emerson

The Rose

Words and Music by Amanda McBroom

1. Some say love, it is a riv - er that drowns _ the ten - der _ reed.

Some say love, it is a raz - or that leaves _ your soul to _ bleed.

Some say love, ___ it is a hun - ger, an end - less ach-ing need. ___

I say love, it is a flow - er, and you its on - ly seed. ____

2. It's the heart a - fraid of break-in', that nev - er _____ learns to dance.
3. When the night has been too lone - ly, and the road _____ has been too long,

It's the dream a - fraid of wak - in', that nev-er ___ takes the ___chance.
And you think ___ that love is on - ly for the luck-y ___ and the ___strong,

It's the one _____ who won't be tak - en ___ who can - not seem to give, ___
Just re - mem-ber, ___ in ___ the win-ter, _ far be - neath _ the win-ter snows _

And the soul a - fraid of dy - in', that nev-er _____ learns to live. ___
Lies the seed that with the sun's _ love, in the

— spring be - comes the rose. _____

Meter in 3

As you listen to this recording of a minuet, try to feel the beats grouped in threes.

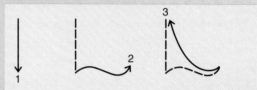

 Le tombeau de Couperin,
"Minuet" ....Maurice Ravel

Here is the conducting pattern for meter in 3. Practice it and then try conducting the minuet.

Conducting pattern in 3

The Minuet Under the Oak Tree   *Louis Joseph Watteau*

1787, Musee des Beaux-Arts, Valenciennes. Giraudon/Art Resource, NY

The two main themes from the minuet by Ravel are notated below. Listen to the recording again as you follow the beats. Which rhythm patterns are repeated most often?

Theme 1

1 2 3 1 2 3 1 2 3 1 2 3

Theme 2

1 2 3 1 2 3 1 2 3 1 2 3

Meet the Composer

Maurice Ravel

(1875–1937)

The French composer Maurice Ravel (rah vehl) wrote the **suite** *Le tombeau de Couperin* ("The Tomb of Couperin") (1914-1917) while serving in the ambulance corps during World War I. Couperin was an eighteenth-century French composer, and Ravel wanted to evoke the style of that period. The reference to a tomb in the title is appropriate, since Ravel dedicated each

movement of the work to a friend who had been killed in battle.

Ravel's compositions were also inspired by a variety of other sources, from Greek myth (the ballet *Daphnis and Chloe*) to American jazz (*Piano Concerto in G*). The composer's two most famous works, *Rapsodie espagnole* and *Boléro*, manage to capture the energy and excitement of Spanish music and dance.

Multi**meter**

What would a song be like if the meter kept changing? In this new setting of an old **folk song**, the arranger altered the meter to give the song an unusual feeling. Notice that the first few measures are in $\frac{3}{4}$, and the *Tumbalalaika* words are in $\frac{4}{4}$. Verse 4 is the tricky part. The time signature is now $\frac{3}{4}\frac{2}{4}$. That means that the beat grouping changes with each measure—from $\frac{3}{4}$ to $\frac{2}{4}$ and back again. The basic beat, though, stays the same throughout the song. All this can be described in one word—**multimeter.**

A Russian balalaika

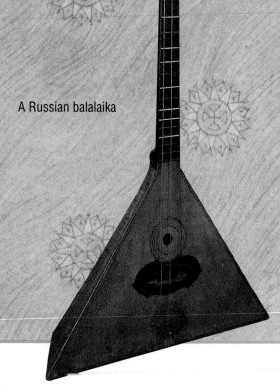

Tumbalalaika

English Words by Margaret Fishback   *Jewish Folk Song*   *Arranged by Lawrence Eisman*

1. Pac - ing, puz - zling all the night long, A
2. "Maid - en, maid - en, can you ex - plain
3. "I - dle lad, you're jok - ing, I know. A

young lad sang a haunt - ing song.
What can grow with - out snow or rain?
stone can grow with - out rain or snow,

"What shall I say to my love to - day, Oh,
What ___ can burn for end - less years, and
Love ___ can blaze and nev - er die, A

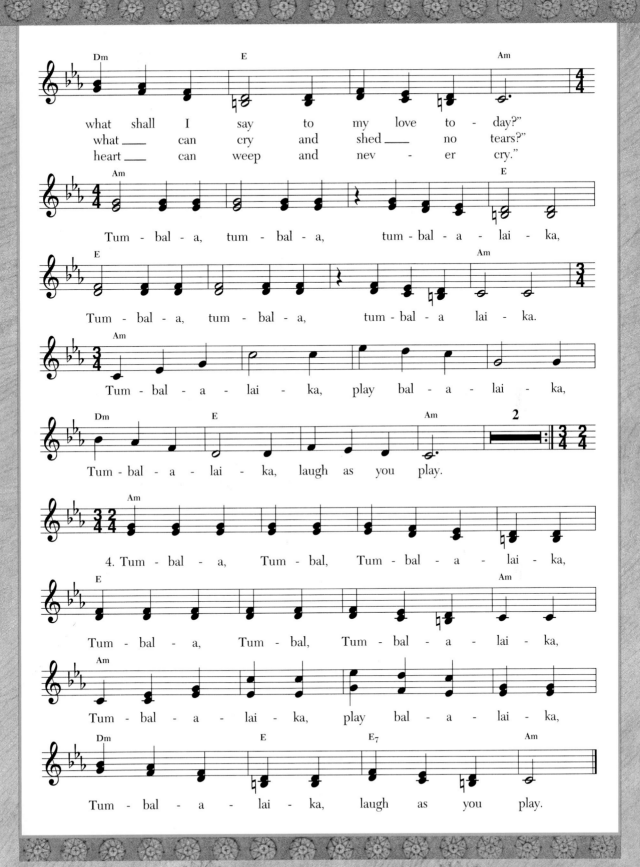

what shall I say to my love to - day?"
what ___ can cry and shed ___ no tears?"
heart ___ can weep and nev - er cry."

Tum - bal - a, tum - bal - a, tum - bal - a - lai - ka,

Tum - bal - a, tum - bal - a, tum - bal - a lai - ka.

Tum - bal - a - lai - ka, play bal - a - lai - ka,

Tum - bal - a - lai - ka, laugh as you play.

4. Tum - bal - a, Tum - bal, Tum - bal - a - lai - ka,

Tum - bal - a, Tum - bal, Tum - bal - a - lai - ka,

Tum - bal - a - lai - ka, play bal - a - lai - ka,

Tum - bal - a - lai - ka, laugh as you play.

A New Meter

Take another look at verse 4 of "Tumbalalaika" on page 45. Do you remember the alternating meter of $\frac{3}{4}\frac{2}{4}$? Now imagine that the bar line between each $\frac{3}{4}$ measure and $\frac{2}{4}$ measure has been removed. What time signature would you now use to describe that larger measure? If you said "$\frac{5}{4}$," you were right. Now follow the "script" of *Dancin'* as you listen to the recording. What do you think its meter is?

 DANCIN' *Sole to Soul* ....Connie Rybak

1	2	3	1	2	1	2
GIRLS					*BOYS*	
On	the	street,	Let's	dance,	Let's	dance,
Feel	the	beat,	Great	chance,	Great	chance,
Twist	and	roll	Clock -	wise,	Clock -	wise,
Keep	con -	trol	Rock -	wise,	Rock -	wise.
BOYS					*GIRLS*	
Try	the	stage,	Up,	down,	Up,	down,
It's	the	rage,	Down -	town,	Down -	town,
Now	that	glide,	Toe -	heel,	Toe -	heel,
What	a	ride,	Un -	real,	Un -	real.
GIRLS					*BOYS*	
When	I	move	Free -	ly,	Free -	ly,
Trou -	bles	soothed,	See	me,	See	me,
Feel	my	best	Danc -	in',	Danc -	in',
Need	no	rest	Pranc -	in',	Pranc -	in'.
BOYS					*GIRLS*	
Add	more	voice,	Hear	ye,	Hear	ye,
It's	your	choice,	Clear -	ly,	Clear -	ly,
Danc -	in's	role,	Real -	ly,	Real -	ly,
EVERYONE						
Sole	to	soul.	(*stamp*,	*clap*	*stamp*,	*clap*)

©1988 Connie Rybak

Did you guess that the meter is in 7? The text of *Dancin'* groups its beats into a pattern of **1** 2 3, **1** 2, **1** 2. Why, do you think, are the beats divided this way and not **1** 2, **1** 2, **1** 2 3 or **1** 2, **1** 2 3, **1** 2? *(Hint:* Look at the way the word accents fall.)

Sing It in 7

If you've ever sung the song "Oh, Susanna," you may have noticed that the meter is in 2. Try singing this updated version of Foster's tune. You can see from the time signature that the meter is in 7. Which of the beat groupings in the box best fits the music?

12, 123, 12
123, 12, 12
12, 12, 123

Oh, Susanna

Words and Music by Stephen Foster   *Arranged by Sol Berkowitz*

Guitar: capo 3

I __ came from Al - a - bam - a with my ban - jo on my
rained all night the day I left the weath-er it was

knee, I'm _ go-in' to Lou'-si-an-a my __ true love for to see. It __
dry, The _ sun _ so hot I froze to death, Su - san - na don't you

1.

2.

cry. ___ Oh, Su - san - na, __ Oh, don't you cry for me, For I've

come from Al - a - bam - a with my ban - jo on my knee, For I've come from Al - a -

bam - a with a ban - jo on _ my knee. ___

Half Steps/
Whole
Steps

You learned on page 15 that notes sometimes move in steps. The lower row of bells in the illustration are arranged in consecutive steps, but are the bells evenly spaced?

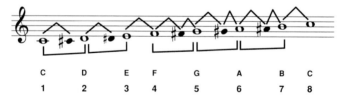

You may have noticed that the space between steps 3 and 4 and between 7 and 8 is not as great as the space between the other steps. That's because the other steps, in fact, have another note between them. (Look at the upper row of bells.) The notes that are as close together as possible are a *half step* apart. The other notes are a *whole step* apart. Let's see what these notes look like on the staff.

⊔ =whole step ∧ =half step

C	D	E	F	G	A	B	C
1	2	3	4	5	6	7	8

The song "Music, Music, Music" uses both whole and half steps. Some of each have been marked for you. Can you find others?

Music, Music, Music

Words and Music by Stephan Weiss and Bernie Baum

Put an-oth-er nick-el in, — in the nick-el - o-de - on, — All I want is lov-ing you — and mu-sic, mu-sic, mu-sic! I'd do an-y-thing for you, — An - y-thing you'd want me to, — All I want is lov-ing you — and mu-sic, mu-sic, mu-sic! Clos - er, _____ my dear, come clos - er, _____ The ni-cest part of an - y mel-o - dy — is when you're sing-ing here with me, — So put an-oth - er nick-el in, — in the nick-el - o-de - on, — All I want is lov-ing you — and mu-sic, mu-sic, mu-sic.

Listen to this excerpt by Franz Liszt (list). The melody is based on a pattern of whole steps and half steps.

Hungarian Rhapsody No. 2 (excerpt) ....Franz Liszt

The Major Scale

Look again at the lower row of bells in the illustration on page 48. Here is that sequence of notes written on the staff.

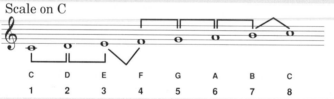

Scale on C

C	D	E	F	G	A	B	C
1	2	3	4	5	6	7	8

The term for a series of notes moving upward by step is *scale*. And the specific type of scale is determined by its pattern of whole steps and half steps. For instance, any scale with a step pattern of whole, whole, half, whole, whole, whole, half is a **major scale**. Is the scale shown above a major scale? How about this scale?

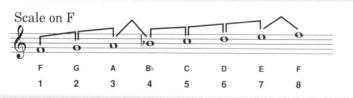

Scale on F

F	G	A	B♭	C	D	E	F
1	2	3	4	5	6	7	8

Yes, they're both major scales. A major scale can start on any note, as long as it follows the same step pattern.

Key Signatures

Look at the F-major scale again on page 50. One flat (B♭) is needed to make the scale follow the major-scale step pattern. Since this flat will appear each time in the music, we simply place it on the staff at the beginning of the line, like this.

This indication of the **sharps** (♯) or **flats** (♭) that are needed to make a scale follow a particular step pattern is called the **key signature.** Now the F-major scale can be shown without having to write the flat sign each time.

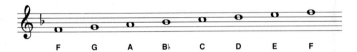

F   G   A   B♭   C   D   E   F

Here is a song in the key of C major. (That means no sharps or flats are needed in the key signature.) Can you find the descending C-major scale in the music?

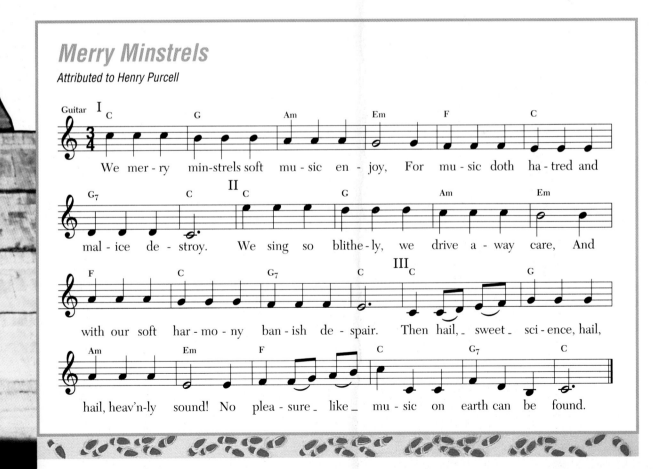

Merry Minstrels

Attributed to Henry Purcell

We mer-ry min-strels soft mu-sic en-joy, For mu-sic doth ha-tred and
mal-ice de-stroy. We sing so blithe-ly, we drive a-way care, And
with our soft har-mo-ny ban-ish de-spair. Then hail, sweet sci-ence, hail,
hail, heav'n-ly sound! No plea-sure like mu-sic on earth can be found.

The Minor Scale

Compare the two scales below. The first one is the C-major scale from the previous lesson. The second one also starts on C, but it's a **minor scale.**

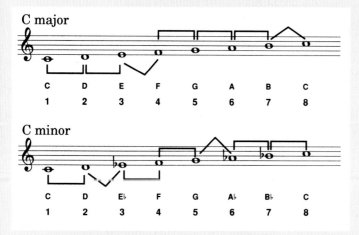

Play the two scales up and down. How do the two step patterns differ? In a major scale (remember?) the half steps occur between notes 3 and 4, and between 7 and 8. In a minor scale, however, the half steps occur between 2 and 3, and between 5 and 6.

"Hatikvah" is based on a minor scale that begins on D, so it is in the key of D minor. (Notice the key signature.)

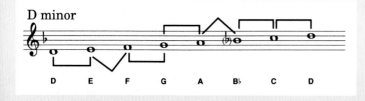

The Pentatonic Scale

Here is a scale with an unusual step pattern. And, unlike the major and minor scales, it has only five different notes. That's why the name given to this kind of scale is **pentatonic** (*penta-*, "five"; *tonic*, "note"). Beginning on C, it would look like this.

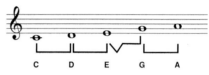

C   D   E   G   A

The Boat Song (Dò Dọc Dò Ngang)

Work Song from Vietnam

From *FROM RICE PADDIES AND TEMPLE YARDS: Traditional Music of Vietnam* by Phong Thuyet Nguyen and Patricia Shehan Campbell. Published by World Music Press, PO Box 2565 Danbury, CT 06813.

Have you noticed the gap between E and G? Have you also noticed that there are no half steps in this scale? These features give the pentatonic scale its special sound.

You can create a pentatonic scale starting from any note. This type of scale is great for inventing good melodies.

Pentatonic scales have been used for centuries, and they play an important part in the music of many Asian countries. "The Boat Song" is an example from the Vietnamese culture. Once you have listened to or sung the song, work out the instrumental accompaniment on the next page.

Chorus   *Solo*   *D.C.*

Khoan hởi __ hò khoan. Sao không __ đồng __ lòng, mang tiếng __ hoài trông.
kwang haw - ee haw   kwang shah o kohng   dohng   lawng mahng tee - eng hwai ee trohng

Coda
All (sing 3 times)

Ta nên ___ vợ ___ chồng. Khoan hởi ___ hò khoan.
tah   nehng   ver   ksohng   kwang   haw - ee   haw   kwang

3. *(Solo)*   Nghe anh một lần.
                nyae ahn moht learng

     (Chorus)   Khoan hởi hò khoan.
                kwang haw-ee haw kwang

     (Solo)   Ta xe chì hồng.
                tah sae ksee hohng
                Kết nghĩa dược chăng?
                kuh(t) nyee-ah dew(k) ksahng
    (Refrain and verse 1)

4. *(Solo)*   Ta nên vợ chồng.
                tah nehng ver ksohng

     (Chorus)   Khoan hởi hò khoan.
                kwang haw-ee haw kwang

     (Solo)   Mai kia dầy dàn.
                mah ee kee-ah day-ee dahng
                Con cháu thiêt dông.
                kawng ksah-oo thee eht dohng
    (Refrain and Coda)

Landscape Near My Home   *Ngo Qúoc Trung, Age 8*

Accompaniment for "The Boat Song"

Part 1 enters after the zither introduction on the recording. Parts 2, 3, 4, and 5 enter one at a time, after every four measures. Once a part enters, it continues to play to the end of the song.

Intervals

In a melody, a leap is just a leap, right? Well, yes and no. The distance between any two tones can be described as a specific **interval**. As an example, play or sing this interval.

E   G

This interval is called a *third*. Why? Let's look at it more closely.

E F G

If you start with the lower note of the interval and count up by each line and space to the higher note, the number you place on the higher note will tell you the interval—a third. Let's look at other intervals. Can you tell what they are by counting the lines and spaces?

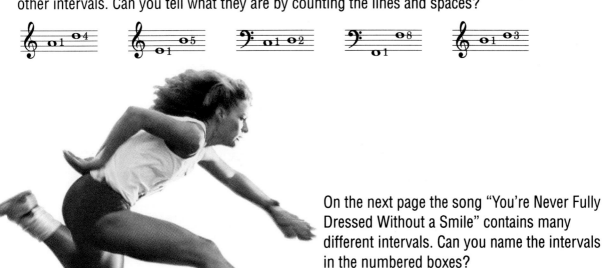

On the next page the song "You're Never Fully Dressed Without a Smile" contains many different intervals. Can you name the intervals in the numbered boxes?

You're Never Fully Dressed Without a Smile *from Annie*

Words by Martin Charnin   Music by Charles Strouse

Hey, ho - bo man, Hey, Dap - per Dan, You both_ got your
Your clothes_ may be Beau Brum - el - ly, They stand_ out a

style,
mile, } But bro - ther, You're nev - er ful - ly ___ dressed with-out a

smile! _____ smile! _____ Who cares what they're

wear - ing on Main Street or Sa - ville Row? It's what you wear from ear to

Scene
from *Annie*

Dm | rall. | Am | D₇ 10. | G | Gm C₇ | F *a tempo*

ear, and not from head to toe that mat - ters; So, Sen - a - tor,

F

So, jan - i - tor, So long for a while, Re - mem - ber, you're

Gm 12. | C₇ | 13. Am | 14. | Cm | D₇

nev - er ful - ly dressed, though you may wear the best, You're

Gm 15. | C₇ | 16. | F

nev - er ful - ly dressed with - out a smile.

Playing with Intervals

The six intervals below are taken from "You're Never Fully Dressed Without a Smile." Once you've played or sung them, name each inter-val. Then try the following activities.

• Repeat each interval as an ostinato, but make up different rhythm patterns for each.

• Create melodies by playing or singing intervals 1 through 5 in different combinations. (Always end on the note F.)

• Write and perform new melodies that are based on intervals 1 through 6, but begin on different notes.

Triads
Triads
Triads

Do you remember playing chords to accompany the song "De colores" on page 22? A chord is made up of three or more notes sounded together. The specific name for a three-note chord is *triad*. To discover how to build the most common type of triad, let's begin with the G-major scale.

G   A   B   C   D   E   F#   G

Beginning on any note of the scale, count up an interval of a third and add the second note. Now count up another third and add the last note.

G   A   B   C   D   E   F#   G

In this way, a triad can be built on any scale tone and in any key.

Look at the three triads below. We're going to put them to work in the song "Hymn of Joy." The first two are taken right from the G-major scale; the third is borrowed from the D-major scale.

G chord   D chord   A chord

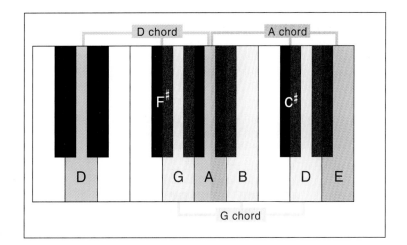

Using a keyboard instrument or a guitar, follow the chord symbols over the music to accompany the song.

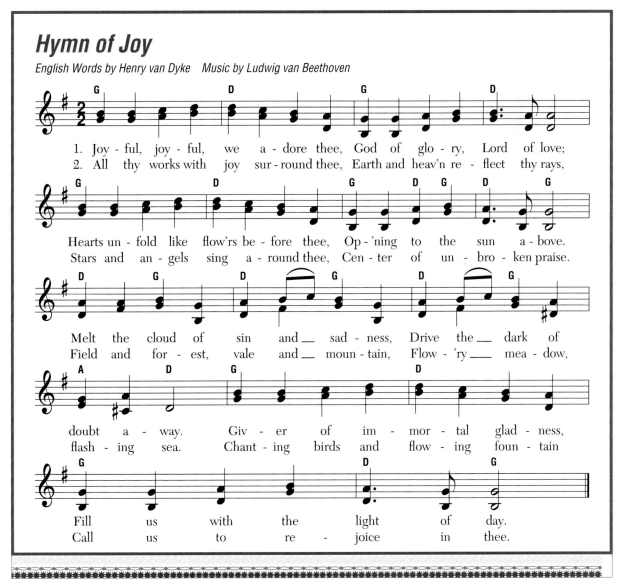

Hymn of Joy

English Words by Henry van Dyke   Music by Ludwig van Beethoven

1. Joy - ful, joy - ful, we a - dore thee, God of glo - ry, Lord of love;
2. All thy works with joy sur - round thee, Earth and heav'n re - flect thy rays,

Hearts un - fold like flow'rs be - fore thee, Op - 'ning to the sun a - bove.
Stars and an - gels sing a - round thee, Cen - ter of un - bro - ken praise.

Melt the cloud of sin and __ sad - ness, Drive the __ dark of
Field and for - est, vale and __ moun - tain, Flow - 'ry __ mea - dow,

doubt a - way. Giv - er of im - mor - tal glad - ness,
flash - ing sea. Chant - ing birds and flow - ing foun - tain

Fill us with the light of day.
Call us to re - joice in thee.

Chord Patterns

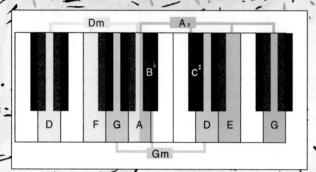

Look at the chord symbols and notes for the song "This Old Hammer." Can you tell on which scale the chords are based?

Before accompanying the song, look at the three different chords you will be using. They are built on the first, fourth, and fifth notes of the scale. (The small *m* means "minor".) Notice that an extra note has been added to the A triad by simply counting up seven steps from the first note of the chord.

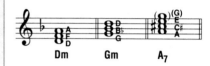

This Old Hammer

African American Work Song

1. This old ham-mer _____ killed John Hen-ry, _____ This old
2. Take this ham-mer _____ to the walk-in' boss, _____ Take this

ham-mer _____ killed John Hen-ry, _____ This old ham-mer _____
ham-mer _____ to the walk-in' boss, _____ Take this ham-mer _____

— killed John Hen-ry, _____ but it won't kill me, _____
— to the walk-in' boss, _____ Tell _ him I'm gone, _____

— no, it won't _ kill me. _____
— Oh, _____ tell him I'm gone. _____

The John Henry Series: John Henry on His Right   *Palmer C. Hayden*

Collection of the Museum of African Art. Armando Solis Photographer.

Now try playing the chords along with the song, using four quarter notes in each measure.

$\frac{4}{4}$ ♩ ♩ ♩ ♩

Did you notice that the chords progress in a repeated pattern? It looks like this.

Dm | A₇ | Dm | Dm | Gm | A₇ | Dm | Dm |

Singin' the BLUES

The blues style goes back to the music of the African American community in the early 1900s. As an example, you'll be listening to a jazz arrangement of an old song by the blues legend Huddie Ledbetter. It's in the key of F, and it uses three basic chords.

The traditional chord progression in this style is called a *12-bar blues*. That just means that the music is usually made up of three **phrases**, each one being four measures long.

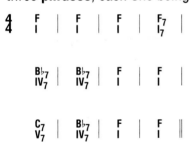

Meet the Musician

Huddie Ledbetter
(1885–1949)

Born in Louisiana, Ledbetter was composing and performing blues on the 12-string guitar by the age of twelve. His life was filled with many difficulties, including serving time in prison, and these experiences were frequently expressed through his music. Ledbetter's tough reputation earned him the nickname Leadbelly. As a performer, he was known for his rough, full-throated singing and his rhythmic guitar playing. Fortunately, many of the 500 or so songs that Leadbelly composed or performed were preserved in the extensive recordings he made for the Library of Congress.

The jazz ensemble that you will hear performing *Shorty George* is made up of piano, drums, string bass, guitar, trumpet, clarinet, and trombone. At each call number, you will hear different combinations of instruments playing the 12-bar blues progression shown on the preceding page. After listening, try improvising along with the recording.

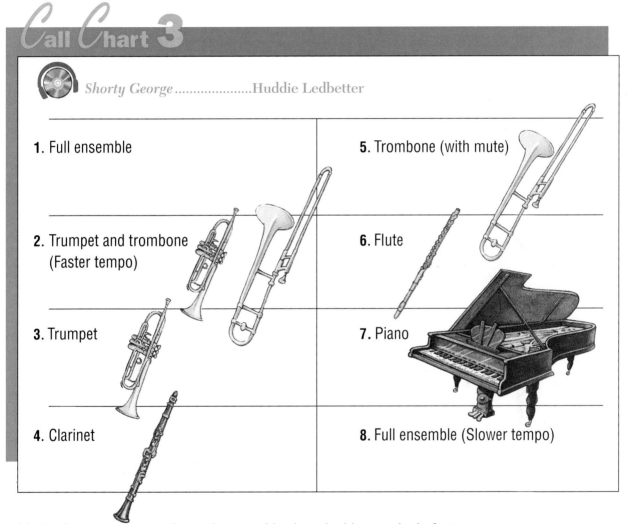

Call Chart 3

🎧 *Shorty George* ....Huddie Ledbetter

1. Full ensemble

2. Trumpet and trombone (Faster tempo)

3. Trumpet

4. Clarinet

5. Trombone (with mute)

6. Flute

7. Piano

8. Full ensemble (Slower tempo)

Much of our popular music can be traced back to the blues style. In fact, the 12-bar blues progression can pop up in some unexpected places. *Going Back to Birmingham* was first recorded by Little Richard, a rock 'n' roll pioneer of the 1950s. Then in the 1970s, the British rock group Ten Years After made this version. The song follows the same chord progression as *Shorty George*, except it's in the key of G. Once you've learned the chords, play along with the recording.

 Going Back to Birmingham ....Penniman/Ten Years After

Rockin' with Chords

"Rock Around the Clock" was one of the first big rock 'n' roll hits of the 1950s. Not surprisingly, its repeated chord progression (shown at the right) fits the basic 12-bar blues pattern. The progression begins with the first verse.

Rock Around the Clock

Words and Music by M. Freedman and J. Deknight

One, two, three-o' clock, four o' clock rock! Five, six, sev-en o' clock, eight o' clock rock!

Nine, ten, e - lev-en o' clock, twelve o' clock rock. We're gon-na rock a-round the

clock to-night! 1. Put _ your glad rags on, join me, hon,' _ we'll have some fun
chimes ring five, six and sev - en, we'll be right

when the clock strikes one, We're gon-na rock a-round the clock to - night, _
in ___ sev - enth heav'n, We're gon-na rock a - round the clock to - night, _

we're gon-na rock, rock, rock 'til the broad day-light, _ We're gon-na rock, we're gon-na
we're gon-na rock, rock, rock 'til the broad day-light, _ We're gon-na rock, we're gon-na

rock _ a - round _ the clock _ to night. _____ 2. When _ the clock strikes two,
rock _ a - round _ the clock _ to night. _____ 4. When _ it's eight, nine, ten,

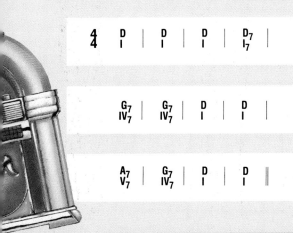

When you're ready, accompany the song with the chord pattern.

Come On, Let's Go!

If you compare this Ritchie Valens song with "Rock Around the Clock," you'll find that *Come On, Let's Go* uses a different chord pattern. In fact, there's a different chord pattern for each of the two sections of the song.

Section Ⓐ

$\frac{4}{4}$ | A(I) | D(IV) | A(I) | D(IV) | A(I) | D(IV) E$_7$(V$_7$) | A(I) | A(I) ‖

Section Ⓑ

$\frac{4}{4}$ | D(IV) | A(I) | E$_7$(V$_7$) | A(I) | D(IV) | A(I) | E$_7$(V$_7$) | E$_7$(V$_7$) ‖

Practice playing the two chord progressions, then try improvising along with the recording.

A   D   E$_7$

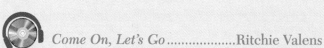

Come On, Let's Go .... Ritchie Valens

Meet the Musician

Ritchie Valens
(1941–1959)

Born Richard Valenzuela, of Mexican Indian parents, Valens spent long evenings as a young boy with family and friends singing lively Mexican songs. With the help of a friend, he quickly became an accomplished guitarist. He even built his own electric guitar while still in junior high school.

About a year after his biggest hit single— *Donna/La Bamba*—made him a new rock 'n' roll star, tragedy struck. While on tour in the midwestern United States, the 17-year old singer flipped a coin with another guitarist for the last seat on their chartered plane. Ritchie won the toss. Minutes later, all on board lost their lives when the plane crashed.

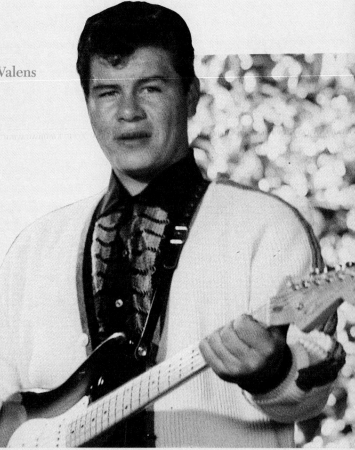

Valens's music, with its Latino strains and subtle African rhythms, went on to influence many later rock musicians.

New Progression/
New Way

Scene from *Grease*

The songs from the musical *Grease* were composed in the style of 1950s rock 'n' roll. Look at one song from the score—"Those Magic Changes," on page 70. The word *changes* in the title refers to another common chord progression.

As you sing the song, follow the repeated chord pattern. (If you need help, just pay attention to the lyrics.) Does the pattern ever change?

For a challenge, let's take the same chord pattern and arrange it using a familiar rhythm from the song.

Now try accompanying the song on a keyboard instrument. Can you create new rhythms for the chord pattern?

Those Magic Changes

from *Grease*

Words and Music by Warren Casey and Jim Jacobs

A Pattern from the Movies

Axel F ....Harold Faltermeyer

In the movie *Beverly Hills Cop*, the lead character (played by Eddie Murphy) was identified with his own theme music. Let's recreate this music from "the bottom up." We'll start with the repeated chord pattern, which is based on the F-minor scale.

Eddie Murphy in
Beverly Hills Cop

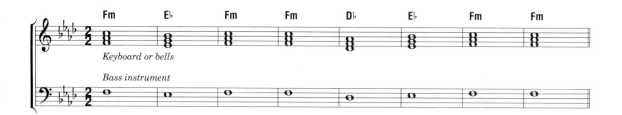

Next this rhythmic figure is added in the bass.

Now for the main ingredient—the melody.

Practice the parts separately and together. Then try playing along with the recording. (For now, take a break during those sections in which the chord pattern changes.) For variety, experiment by playing the chords in different rhythms. For example,

Improvising Parts

Can you create more melody patterns to play above the main chord progression? One idea would be to play separate notes from each chord in a repeated rhythm. Here's an example to start you off.

As you keep adding to your arrangement, don't forget that your voice is an instrument, too!

Repetition and Contrast

Look at the three outfits worn by the models in the photograph. Do any of them seem to have too many different colors? Or too few? Is there an outfit that seems balanced between contrast and repetition?

Balance is important in music, too. Play or sing these melodies. Which has too much repetition? Which has too little? Which is well balanced?

The jazz musician Dave Brubeck used repetition and contrast to both unify and give variety to this piece. As you listen, notice the unusual way he groups the beats. (That's the reason for the term *unsquare* in the title.) How does the meter contribute to the unity and the variety of the piece?

  Unsquare Dance ....Dave Brubeck

You probably realized that it is the metric feel—acting as an ostinato throughout the piece—that is the unifying feature. The piano part that Brubeck weaves over the ostinato provides variety and interest.

Here is the ostinato pattern for *Unsquare Dance*.

1	2	3	4	5	6	7
A	x	G	x	A	x	x
A	x	G	x	A	x	x
D	x	C	x	D	x	x
A	x	G	x	A	x	x
E	x	D	x	E	x	x
A	x	G	x	A	x	x

The letters on beats 1, 3, and 5 show the notes the string bass plays. The *x*'s represent the hand claps. Using a melody instrument, try playing the ostinato by itself, then with the recording.

Meet the Musician

Dave Brubeck
(1920–   )

Now considered one of the most important composers and performers in the mainstream of jazz, Brubeck originally intended to follow his father's career as a rancher and cowboy. It was his mother who convinced him to receive a musical education. Brubeck and his legendary quartet have produced such jazz standards as *The Duke, In Your Own Sweet Way,* and *Blue Rondo a la Turk.* Always innovative, this group was one of the first to issue recordings of live concerts.

Many of Brubeck's larger compositions were inspired by sacred texts and strong social themes. These works include *To Hope: A Celebration, La Fiesta de la Posada, The Light in the Wilderness,* and *The Gates of Justice.*

Creating UNITY

Look at the painting below. What single element unifies the entire canvas?

1958, encaustic on canvas. 30 7/8 x 45 1/2 x 5 inches. Collection of Whitney Museum of American Art. 50th Anniversary Gift of the Gilman Foundation, Inc., The Lauder Foundation, A. Alfred Taubman, an anonymous donor, and purchase 80.32

Three Flags   *Jasper Johns*

A song, too, can be based on a single idea.
Do you recognize this rhythm pattern?

It's the rhythm of "America, the Beautiful," and it's what holds the music together. Find the pattern in the song. How many times does it occur in each verse? Is the <u>melody</u> the same every time?

America, the Beautiful

Words by Katherine Lee Bates   Music by Samuel A. Ward

1. O beau-ti-ful for spa-cious skies, For am-ber waves of grain, For
2. O beau-ti-ful for pil-grim feet, Whose stern im-pas-sioned stress A
3. O beau-ti-ful for he-roes proved In lib-er-at-ing strife, Who
4. O beau-ti-ful for pa-triot dream That sees be-yond the years, Thine

pur - ple moun-tain maj-es-ties A - bove the fruit-ed plain! A -
thor - ough-fare for free - dom beat A - cross the wil-der-ness! A -
more than self their coun-try loved, And mer-cy more than life! A -
al - a-bas-ter cit - ies gleam Un-dimmed by hu-man tears! A -

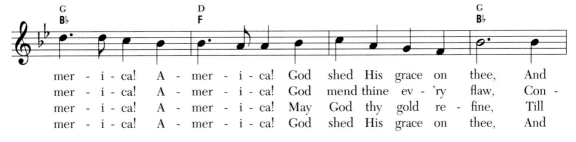

mer - i - ca! A - mer - i - ca! God shed His grace on thee, And
mer - i - ca! A - mer - i - ca! God mend thine ev-'ry flaw, Con -
mer - i - ca! A - mer - i - ca! May God thy gold re - fine, Till
mer - i - ca! A - mer - i - ca! God shed His grace on thee, And

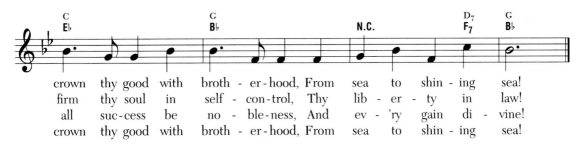

crown thy good with broth - er-hood, From sea to shin - ing sea!
firm thy soul in self - con-trol, Thy lib - er-ty in law!
all suc-cess be no - ble-ness, And ev - 'ry gain di - vine!
crown thy good with broth - er-hood, From sea to shin - ing sea!

Repeated patterns help to give structure to music. Notice the melody and rhythm pattern in the first line of "On My Journey." How does the rest of the song develop from this pattern?

On My Journey

African American Traditional Song   *Arranged by Lawrence Eisman*
New Words and Adaptation by Fred Hellerman, Lee Hays, Ronnie Gilbert, and Erik Darling

want you to weep af - ter me. _____

want you to weep af - ter me. _____

A Minuet Motive

Nearly 300 years ago, Johann Sebastian Bach used a rhythm and melody pattern (called a **motive**) to give structure and unity to this short minuet. You can see the motive in the first two measures of the line score below. Follow the line score as you listen to the recording. The color boxes will help you discover how the composer varied and expanded the motive.

 Minuet.....................Johann Sebastian Bach

Compound Meter

Do you remember learning about $\frac{2}{4}$, $\frac{4}{4}$, and $\frac{3}{4}$ meters on pages 38 to 43? These basic meters are called *simple meters*. To discover a different type of meter, take another look at "Chopsticks." Can you name the time signature and explain what it means?

The $\frac{6}{8}$ time signature means that there are six beats per measure and the eighth note (♪) represents the beat. As you count the beats out loud, try playing or tapping this meter, accenting beats 1 and 4. Now speed up the tempo a bit.

What is happening to the meter? Play the example again, but this time count the beats as indicated by the larger numbers below.

It seems as if each group of six small beats has been transformed into two large beats. In fact, it would be easier to count or conduct this as meter in 2, rather than 6. This "meter-in-a-meter" is called **compound meter.**

Team Up with Your Meter

There are other compound meters besides $\frac{6}{8}$. In fact, any meter in which the basic beat is subdivided into groups of three can be called a compound meter. For another example, look at the meter of *Football Team Chant*, on the next page. The time signature indicates 12 beats to each measure, but what is the overall beat grouping per measure?

First clap the patterns while counting the beats, then chant the team names. Remember to accent the strong beats.

Football Team Chant

Part 1 — Browns, Jets, Browns, Jets,

Part 2 — Tam - pa, Dal - las, Tam - pa, Dal - las,

Part 3 — Rams, Los An-ge-les Rams, Los An-ge-les

Part 4 — New York Gi-ants, New York Gi-ants,

Part 5 — In - di - an - a - po - lis Colts, In - di - an - a - po - lis Colts,

Now try performing *Football Team Chant* with this recording.
Do the meters match?

 Dooji-Wooji ....Duke Ellington

Dooji-Wooji Improvisations

After a four-measure introduction, the chord progression in
Dooji-Wooji follows the type of blues pattern you learned on
page 64. Here are the chords.

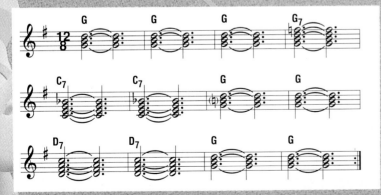

Choosing individual notes from the chords, try singing or playing an improvised part along with the recording. Here are some ideas to get you started.

For a challenge, plan your very own performance of *Dooji-Wooji*. Begin by learning to play these ostinato patterns. If you listen to the recording again, you'll hear them played on the piano with the left hand.

Now follow the chord progression and add as many **vocal** or instrumental parts as you like. See if you can make that compound meter really "swing"!

Meet the Composer

Edward Kennedy "Duke" Ellington

(1899–1974)

Ellington is generally recognized as the most important composer in the history of jazz. His elegant manner and expressiveness inspired respect and earned him the name Duke.

Born in Washington, D.C., Ellington exhibited talent in both music and art during his high school years. His rise to fame began in New York City at the Cotton Club in Harlem. His big band made dozens of recordings and toured throughout the United States and Europe. One of Ellington's many musical innovations was his distinct use of instrumental tone colors.

Some of Ellington's best-known compositions are *Mood Indigo*, *Sophisticated Lady*, and *I'm Beginning to See the Light*. One of his most ambitious works, *Black, Brown and Beige*, is a musical panorama of black history in America.

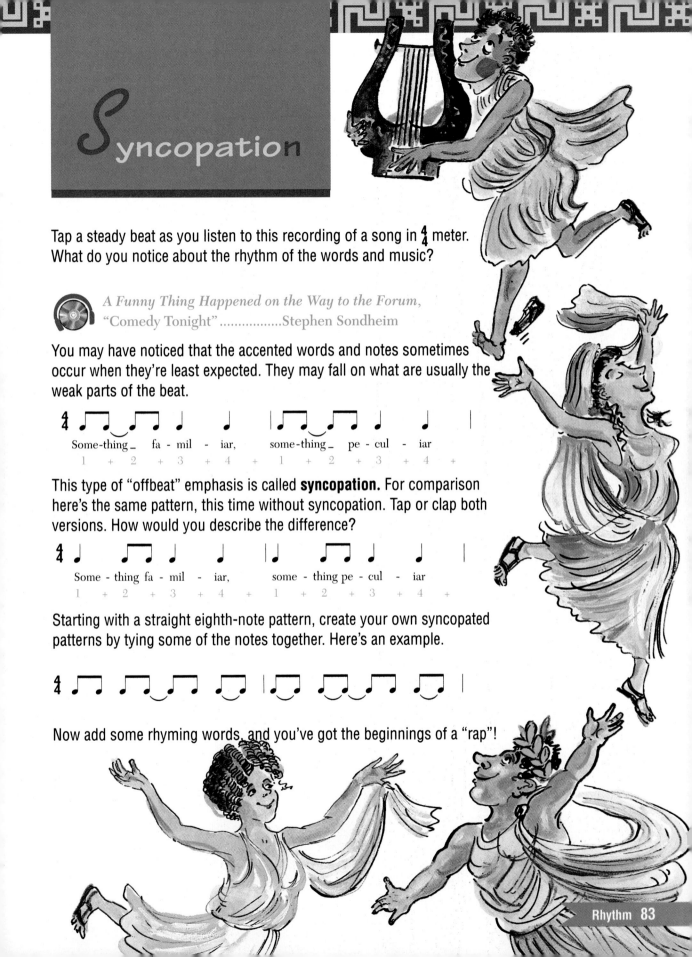

Syncopation

Tap a steady beat as you listen to this recording of a song in $\frac{4}{4}$ meter. What do you notice about the rhythm of the words and music?

A Funny Thing Happened on the Way to the Forum,
"Comedy Tonight" ....Stephen Sondheim

You may have noticed that the accented words and notes sometimes occur when they're least expected. They may fall on what are usually the weak parts of the beat.

Some-thing _ fa - mil - iar, some-thing _ pe - cul - iar
1 + 2 + 3 + 4 + 1 + 2 + 3 + 4 +

This type of "offbeat" emphasis is called **syncopation.** For comparison here's the same pattern, this time without syncopation. Tap or clap both versions. How would you describe the difference?

Some - thing fa - mil - iar, some - thing pe - cul - iar
1 + 2 + 3 + 4 + 1 + 2 + 3 + 4 +

Starting with a straight eighth-note pattern, create your own syncopated patterns by tying some of the notes together. Here's an example.

Now add some rhyming words, and you've got the beginnings of a "rap"!

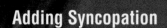

Adding Syncopation

It's fun to take some "square rhythm" songs and "jazz them up" with syncopation. Try it with the familiar round "Row, Row, Row Your Boat." First, in unison, sing it in the usual way. Now sing this jazz version and compare the two styles.

 Row, Row, Row Your Boat (jazz version)

Syncopation is also an important element in most rock music. In this example by the group 'Til Tuesday, listen for the syncopation at the end of the vocal phrases and in the synthesizer fadeout.

 Voices Carry (excerpt) ....Aimee Mann/'Til Tuesday

Aimee Mann

An Offbeat Rhythm

Syncopation can be found in nearly all musical styles and in the music of many different cultures. Follow this short syncopated pattern— ♪ ♩ ♪ — as it makes an appearance in each of the following examples.

This American ragtime "classic" was written about the turn of the twentieth century. The syncopated pattern can be heard in the first section, after the introduction.

 The Entertainer ....Scott Joplin

Here's another piece for piano. Again, you'll hear the same pattern after the introduction. Is there any difference in the feeling?

 Pasquinade, "Caprice" ....Louis Moreau Gottschalk

Meet the Composer

Scott Joplin (1868-1917) is regarded as a pioneer of the piano rag. The son of a freed slave, he was raised in Texarkana, Texas, and was playing the banjo, the fiddle, and the piano before the age of 7. Joplin learned the early jig piano, or ragtime, style as he traveled throughout the Mississippi Valley. He eventually composed more than 50 works for the piano, in addition to songs and the operas *A Guest of Honor* and *Treemonisha*. Four years before his death, Joplin referred to the impact of ragtime in a letter he wrote to the music editor of a magazine: "Ragtime rhythm is a syncopation original with the [black] people . . . But the other races throughout the world today are learning to write and make use of ragtime melodies. It is the rage in England today."

Unfortunately Joplin's music, a forerunner of many of today's jazz and rock styles, was never taken seriously during the composer's lifetime. "The king of ragtime" died in poverty, convinced he was a failure. More than 50 years later, Scott Joplin finally received the acclaim he deserved. His music (including *The Entertainer*) was featured in the 1973 hit movie *The Sting* and won the Academy Award for Best Score. Then in 1976, the composer was awarded a special posthumous Pulitzer Prize for his lasting contributions to American music.

Singing Syncopation

Can you find our syncopated
figure in this song from Mexico?

¡Ay, Jalisco no te rajes!   (Oh, Jalisco!)

Words by Emesto M. Cortázar   Music by Manuel Esperon   English Words by Sandra Longoria Glover

¡Ay!   Ja - lis - co,   Ja - lis - co,   Ja-
Oh,   Ja - lis - co,   Ja - lis - co,   Ja-

lis - co,   tú tie - nes tu no - via que es Gua - da - la - ja - ra.____
lis - co,   your great-est at - trac-tion is Gua - da - la - ja - ra.____

Mu - cha - cha bo - ni - ta,   la per - la más ra - ra de
Beau - ti - ful land,___ the rar - est of pearls___ in

to - do Ja - lis-co, es mi Gua - da - la - ja - ra._____
all of Ja - lis - co,   is Gua - da - la - ja - ra._____

¡Ay! Ja-_____   ¡Ay,_____
Oh, Ja-_____   Oh,

© 1941 by Promotora Hispano Americana de Música, S.A.

"¡Ay, Jalisco no te rajes!" salutes the Mexican region of Jalisco and the city of Guadalajara.

Ja - lis - co no te ra - jes! _____ me sa - le del
Ja - lis - co, don't des - pair, _____ it is from my

al - ma _____ gri - tar con ca - lor, _____ a - brir to-do el
heart, _____ I sing with _ pride. _____ I o - pen my

pe - cho pa'e - char es - te gri - to: ¡Qué lin - do es Ja - lis - co, pa -
heart _ to shout with _ joy, _ Oh, pret - ty Ja - lis - co, the

la - bra de ho - nor! lis - co, pa - la - bra de ho - nor!
land that I love! lis - co, the land that I love!

Building a Melody

"One of Those Songs" is based on a repetition of the following pattern. How many times does the pattern appear?

One of Those Songs

Words by Will Holt   Music by Gerard Calvi

Guitar: capo 5

Begin slowly and get faster to the end

Well, this is one of those songs — that you hear now and then, — you
one of those songs — that can make you re - call — a
one of those songs — that's so eas - y to hear, — you

don't know just where, _____ you don't know just when. — It's
ride in the spring - time, a walk in the fall, _____ A
lis - ten just once, __ then you play it by ear. _____ It's

one of those songs __ that are o - ver and then, ___ it's
day in the coun - try, a night on the town, ___ the
hummed on ve - ran - das and strummed on gui - tars, ___ and

one of those songs _____ that start play - ing a - gain. __
sun com - ing up, _____ or the rain com - ing down. __
all you re - mem - ber is "lah - dee - dah - dah." __

Look at this painting by the French artist Cézanne (say ZAHN). Can you see how the artist used repetition to fill the canvas?

C
F

_ Yes, it's just one of those songs _ that you hear for a while, _ that
_ Or else the eve-ning you part - ed, the morn-ing you met, _ the
_ But lat - er on you'll re - call ___ it in some oth - er year, _ you

C / A₇   Dm
F / D₇   Gm

come in - to fash - ion and go out of style. ___ It's
love of your life ___ you can nev - er for - get. ___ The
may start to smile ___ or you may shed a tear. ___ You'll

Dm   G₇   C   Am
Gm   C₇   F   Dm

one of those songs ___ that you think you for - got, ___ but it's
rea - son is sim - ple, the mem - 'ry be - longs ___ to
find that one part ___ of your life - time be - longs ___ to

|1.,2 ||3.

D₇   G₇   C   G₇   C
G₇   C₇   F   C₇   F

one of those songs _ you can - not! 2. Be - cause it's
one of those won - der - ful songs. 3. Well, this is
one of those won - der - ful   songs. ___

Follow the call chart to discover how these composers used repetition in building and extending their melodies.

Call Chart 4

Melody Building

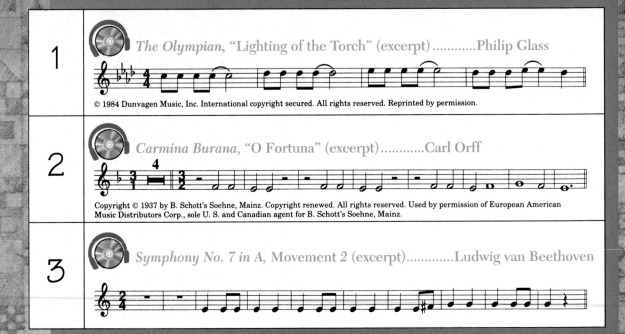

1 *The Olympian,* "Lighting of the Torch" (excerpt) ....Philip Glass

© 1984 Dunvagen Music, Inc. International copyright secured. All rights reserved. Reprinted by permission.

2 *Carmina Burana,* "O Fortuna" (excerpt) ....Carl Orff

Copyright © 1937 by B. Schott's Soehne, Mainz. Copyright renewed. All rights reserved. Used by permission of European American Music Distributors Corp., sole U. S. and Canadian agent for B. Schott's Soehne, Mainz.

3 *Symphony No. 7 in A,* Movement 2 (excerpt) ....Ludwig van Beethoven

Poets make use of repetition, too. How is repetition used in this poem?

How Not to Have to Dry the Dishes

If you have to dry the dishes
(Such an awful, boring chore)
If you have to dry the dishes
('Stead of going to the store)

If you have to dry the dishes
And you drop one on the floor–
Maybe they won't let you
Dry the dishes anymore.

Shel Silverstein

How might you compose and use melodies to reflect the repetition in the poem? For example, here's a melody for the repeated line.

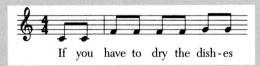

If you have to dry the dish-es

Now use the pentatonic scale that begins on F (F-G-A-C-D) and improvise a different melody for each contrasting line in the poem.

EXTENDING a Melody

Another way a composer can "stretch" a melody is through the use of **sequence**. An example of this device can be found in the song "Music, Music, Music," on page 49. Here is the opening motive.

motive

The motive is then repeated, but this time the pattern starts two steps lower.

sequence

What happens next?

That's right; it's the motive again, starting one step lower.

sequence

Can you find another sequence in the song?

What would happen if a sequence suddenly went "out of control"? The composer of this humorous piece decided to find out.

1712 Overture (excerpt)............."P.D.Q. Bach" (Peter Schickele)

1959, Solomon R. Guggenheim Museum, New York.

Homage to the Square: Apparition   *Josef Albers*

Variation and CoNtRaSt

The artist Kandinsky used the repeated form of a circle as his main theme in this painting. Imagine how boring the work would have been if he made all the figures exactly the same size and color! In a similar way, composers use variation and contrast to make their melodies interesting.

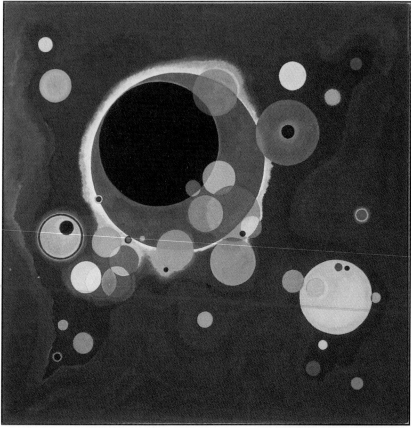

January-February 1926. Solomon R. Guggenheim Museum, New York, Gift, Solomon R. Guggenheim, 1941.

Several Circles,
Wassily Kandinsky

Look at the melody of "This Old Hammer," from page 62.
Notice how variation and contrast help to keep the melody interesting.

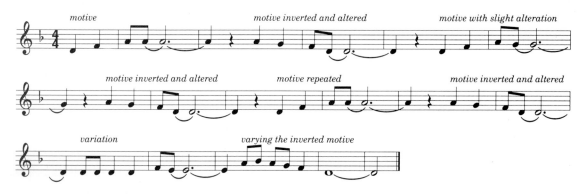

Melodies and Meters

Let's try an experiment to see how varying the meter can change the character of a familiar melody. First sing "Row, Row, Row Your Boat" in its original meter ($\frac{6}{8}$). Then sing it in the other two meters shown. How would you describe the difference?

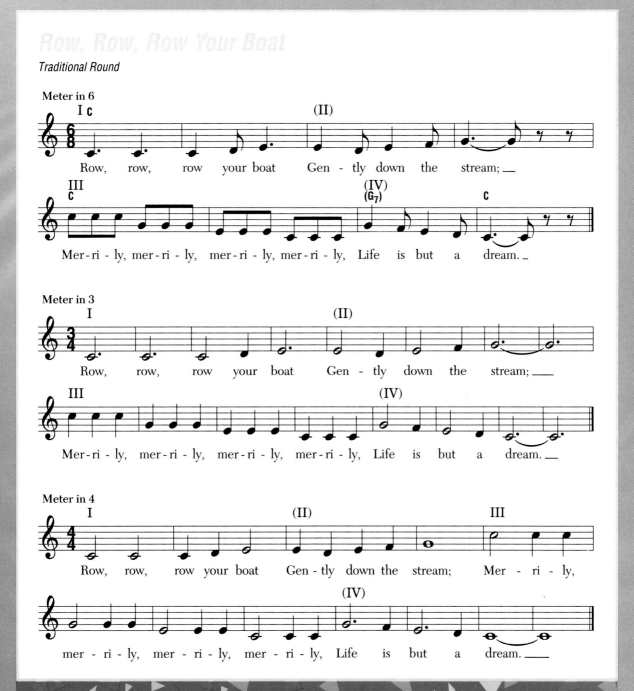

Row, Row, Row Your Boat

Traditional Round

Meter in 6

I C — (II)
Row, row, row your boat Gen-tly down the stream;

III C — (IV) (G7) C
Mer-ri-ly, mer-ri-ly, mer-ri-ly, mer-ri-ly, Life is but a dream.

Meter in 3

I — (II)
Row, row, row your boat Gen-tly down the stream;

III — (IV)
Mer-ri-ly, mer-ri-ly, mer-ri-ly, mer-ri-ly, Life is but a dream.

Meter in 4

I — (II) — III
Row, row, row your boat Gen-tly down the stream; Mer-ri-ly,

(IV)
mer-ri-ly, mer-ri-ly, mer-ri-ly, Life is but a dream.

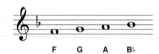

The Reappearing Motive

Varying the rhythm can make a big difference with a motive. Look at this four-note motive, for example.

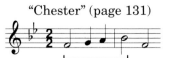

F   G   A   B♭

Now add two different rhythms and see what happens.

"One of Those Songs" (page 88)

"Chester" (page 131)

The same four-note motive makes an appearance in this song.
Can you find it?

This Land Is Your Land

Words and Music by Woody Guthrie   *Countermelody by Ruth Tutelman*

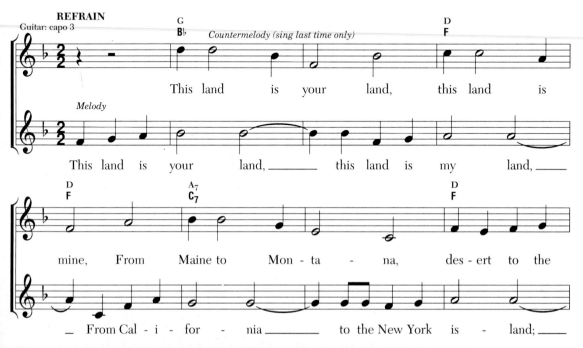

REFRAIN
Guitar: capo 3

Countermelody (sing last time only)

This   land   is   your   land,   this   land   is

Melody

This   land   is   your   land, _____ this   land   is   my   land, _____

mine,   From   Maine   to   Mon - ta - na,   des - ert   to   the

_ From Cal - i - for - nia _____   to the New York   is - land; _____

A *Flight* of **Variations**

The finale of Igor Stravinsky's colorful ballet *The Firebird* is based on three variations of the same melody. Follow the call chart on the next page and you'll discover how the melody builds up to a dramatic ending.

Melody A

Melody B

Melody C

Sketch for the set of "The Firebird"   *Pavel Kusnezov*

Call Chart 5

The Firebird, "Finale" ....Igor Stravinsky

Instrument(s)	Tempo	Melody	Dynamics
1. French horn	Slow	Melody A	Soft (*p*)
2. ?	?	?	?
3. Violins	Slow	Melody A	Soft
4. Violins, flute	Slow	Melody A extended	Moderately soft (*mp*)
5. Violins, woodwinds	Slow	Melody A	Moderately loud (*mf*)
6. Strings, trumpet, woodwinds	Slow	Melody A	Loud (*f*)
7. Brass	Fast	Interlude, then Melody B	Loud
8. ?	?	?	?
9. Trumpet, trombone	Fast	First measure of Melody C twice	Loud
10. Strings, brass	Fast	Melody C extended	Loud
11. Strings, French horns, trumpet	Fast	First measure only of Melody C	Loud
12. Strings, woodwinds, brass	Moderately slow	Melody B	Very loud (*ff*)
13. Strings, woodwinds, brass	Getting slower	Melody B extended	Very loud

Careers in Music– *Composing*

Many people have come to know composer Suzanne Ciani (CHAH nee) through her film scores and deeply affecting instrumental music. From her studio, which is equipped with the latest music-making technology, she has also produced innovations in the areas of sound design for television advertising and arcade games. Listen to this versatile composer as she discusses her life and work.

Careers in Music ....Suzanne Ciani

Suzanne Ciani

Follow That Theme

Before you listen to Ciani's *Composition for Synthesizer*, take a close look at the complete main theme. Can you find the sequence?

Composition for Synthesizer................Suzanne Ciani

Did you notice that, in addition to sequence, the piece also uses such devices as repetition and ostinato? Listen again, then try to describe some of the ways in which the theme is altered.

Manipulating a Motive

You may remember that a motive is a short musical theme that a composer uses to build a piece. Here is the motive for a keyboard composition called *Manipulations*.

Follow the score as you listen to discover how the composer changes the motive.

Manipulations

Sol Berkowitz

Theme and Variations

You've already seen some ways a composer can change and develop a melody to create interest. Here's an example in which one composer takes a **theme** attributed to an earlier composer and uses it as the basis for a set of variations. Listen as the piece opens with a full statement of the theme.

 Variations on a Theme by Haydn (excerpts) ....Johannes Brahms

Theme ("St. Anthony Chorale")

Now let's go to the second **variation**. This short section is based on a repetition of the rhythm and pitches of just the first three notes of the theme. (Your ear may also tell you that the variation begins in a minor key.)

Variation II

In the sixth variation, the composer turns the first three pitches of the theme upside down (inversion). Then he incorporates some of the original notes from the theme, as shown by the color boxes.

Variation VI

The grand **finale** (fee NAH leh) begins quietly with a bass line that is made up, in part, of four notes from the theme. (See the color box.) With extraordinary creativity, the composer spins out a total of seventeen variations over this repeated figure. Can you tell when the full theme finally returns?

Finale

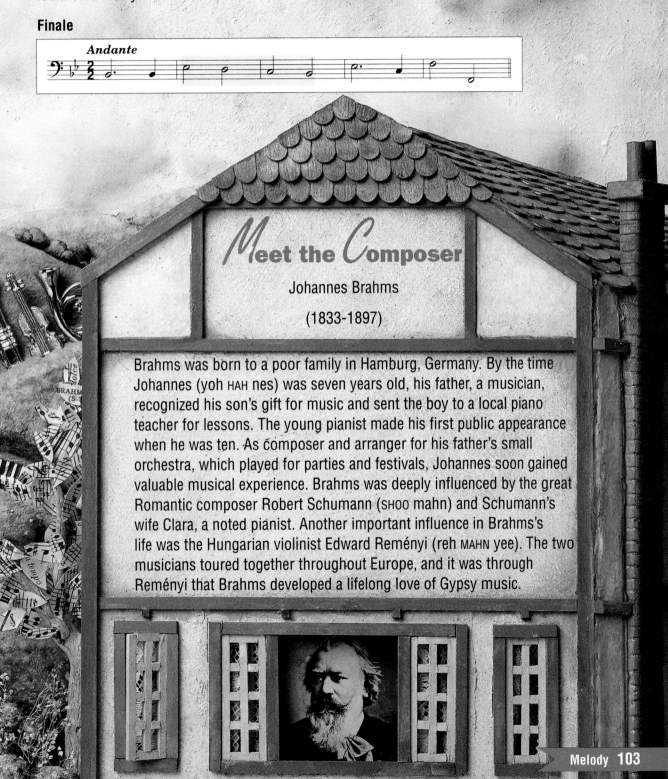

Meet the Composer

Johannes Brahms

(1833-1897)

Brahms was born to a poor family in Hamburg, Germany. By the time Johannes (yoh HAH nes) was seven years old, his father, a musician, recognized his son's gift for music and sent the boy to a local piano teacher for lessons. The young pianist made his first public appearance when he was ten. As composer and arranger for his father's small orchestra, which played for parties and festivals, Johannes soon gained valuable musical experience. Brahms was deeply influenced by the great Romantic composer Robert Schumann (SHOO mahn) and Schumann's wife Clara, a noted pianist. Another important influence in Brahms's life was the Hungarian violinist Edward Reményi (reh MAHN yee). The two musicians toured together throughout Europe, and it was through Reményi that Brahms developed a lifelong love of Gypsy music.

Musical Texture

In music, melody and harmony can interact in many ways. This relationship is called **texture.**

The simplest kind of texture in music consists of a single melody line, without any harmony or accompaniment. It's called **monophony** (moh NAHF uh nee), or monophonic (mahn oh FAHN ik) texture. You'll hear three examples of this texture in *Monophonic Montage*: (1) a **plainsong** of the early Christian Church, chanted by a choir of men; (2) a piece for solo flute; and (3) an American folk song sung by a female soloist.

 Monophonic Montage

Changing Textures

To discover another kind of texture, listen first to this monophonic version of a folk song from South Africa.

 Jikel 'Emaweni (monophonic version)

Now look at the whole score for "Jikel 'Emaweni," on the next page. You'll notice that harmony parts have been added, with all the voices moving in the same rhythm. The texture has been changed to **homophony** (hoh MAHF uh nee), or homophonic (hahm uh FAHN ik) texture. Listen to or sing the song in both textures. How would you describe the difference?

Jikel 'Emaweni

Folk Song from South Africa

Courtesy of The Grail Singers

A Texture of Many Voices

Have you ever heard two or more independent melodies sung or played at the same time? The result is a third kind of texture called **polyphony** (puh LIF uh nee), or polyphonic (pahl ih FAHN ik) texture.

The interweaving of the different melodies (or the same melody played at different times) produces harmony, but each melody can be sung or played independently of the others.

Most **rounds** are good examples of polyphonic texture. In "A Home on the Rolling Sea," each part has its own melodic direction and rhythm.

Swans   *M.C. Escher*

A Home on the Rolling Sea

Words and Music by David Eddleman

I
Give me a home on the roll - ing sea, and let me be a sail - or;

II
Let me ___ a sail - or be;

III
Let me sail off on a ship for a life on the rol - lick - ing sea.

A *Fugue* for **Organ**

Shown is the organ in the Church of St. Thomas, Leipzig, Germany. Behind the pipes that are visible are many additional pipes.

As you learned in the previous lesson, a round is a fairly simple example of polyphonic texture. There is just one melody, and it is repeated exactly as each part enters. A more complex form of polyphony is the **fugue** (fyoog). The main melody of a fugue, called the *subject*, may repeat and overlap as in a round, but it doesn't always start on the same pitch. Also, a new melody, called the *countersubject*, frequently accompanies the subject.

Johann (YOH hahn) Sebastian Bach (bahk) is considered to be the master of polyphonic writing. The call chart on the following pages will guide you through the first section of one of his short fugues for organ. Each call number will indicate when a "voice" enters with the subject, shown in red. Statements of the countersubject, meanwhile, are shown in blue.

This opening section of the fugue, called the *exposition*, ends once all the voices have had a chance at the subject. As the recording continues, listen for more appearances of the subject. How does the composer make the subject sound different each time?

Call Chart 6

 Fugue in G Minor, "The Little" ....Johann Sebastian Bach

Exposition

Voice 4

tr

The Whole Picture

The following chart shows the pattern of the entire *Fugue in G Minor*. The red bars represent entrances of the subject. *Episode* is the term that is used to describe a section of the fugue that contains freely treated material.

Fugue in G Minor "The Little"
(without call numbers)................J.S. Bach

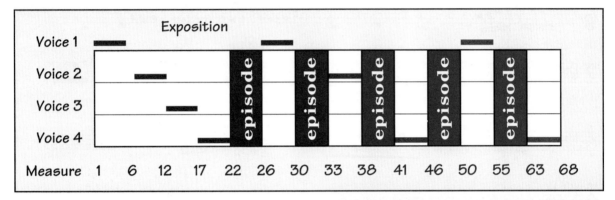

*M*eet the *C*omposer

Johann Sebastian Bach (1685-1750) was born in Eisenach, Germany, toward the end of the Baroque period of music history. Although now considered by many to be the greatest composer who ever lived, he was much better known during his lifetime as a performing musician. At one concert for King Frederick the Great of Prussia, Bach displayed his remarkable musical skills by improvising a fugue in six parts on a theme of his own.

For many years, Bach was organist and director of music at the Church of St. Thomas in Leipzig. (See the photograph on page 107.) It was there that he composed such sacred masterworks as the *St. John Passion* and the *Mass in B Minor*. (His choir school duties, meanwhile, included teaching and gathering firewood.) Bach became almost completely blind in his later years, but that didn't stop his creativity. After his death, the

Bach musical "dynasty" continued, as four of his sons (out of a total of 20 children!) became important composers in their own right.

In German, the word *bach* means "stream." It's been said, though, that Johann Sebastian Bach was not a mere stream but a whole ocean of music.

A Chorus of TEXTURES

George Frideric Handel was born in the same year as Bach (1685) and composed in a similar style. But Handel became famous for his **oratorios**—musical dramas for voices and orchestra that are often based on religious stories. Some oratorios are staged like **operas**, but most are performed without costumes, scenery, or action. Audience etiquette is a bit different, too. It is customary to applaud after each **aria** or **chorus** in an opera but not in an oratorio.

On the next page, you'll see a call chart for the chorus "Hallelujah, Amen" from Handel's oratorio *Judas Maccabaeus.* The music uses all the textures that you have studied so far—monophonic, homophonic, and polyphonic. Can you recognize them?

Judas Maccabaeus   *Taddeo di Bartolo*

Palazzo Pubblico, Siena, Italy. Scala/Art Resource, NY.

Judas Maccabaeus, "Hallelujah, Amen"
..................George Frideric Handel

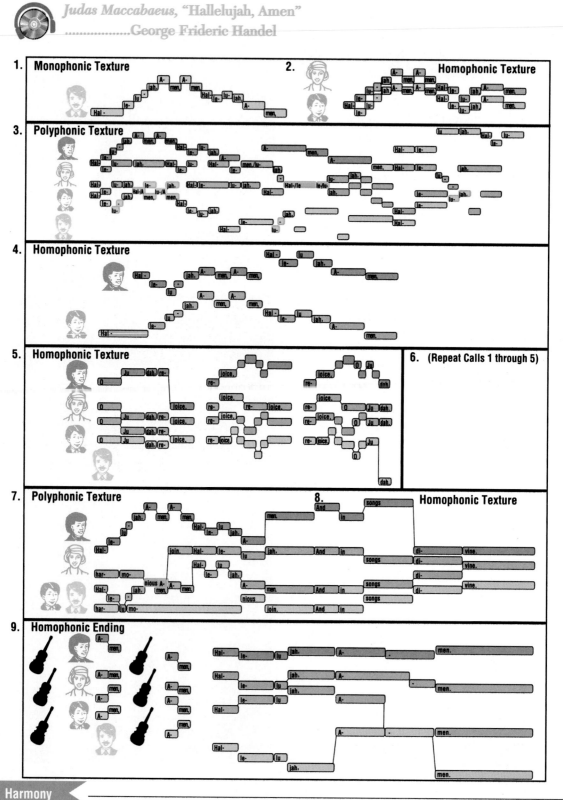

1. **Monophonic Texture**
2. **Homophonic Texture**
3. **Polyphonic Texture**
4. **Homophonic Texture**
5. **Homophonic Texture**
6. (Repeat Calls 1 through 5)
7. **Polyphonic Texture**
8. **Homophonic Texture**
9. **Homophonic Ending**

Instrumental Tone Color

You know that the primary colors are red, yellow, and blue. All other colors are made by combining these three colors in many different ways.

Music has color, too. In addition to the various vocal colors, there are four basic color categories, or families, into which instruments fall. Listen to these examples of music specially written for each group of instruments.

Brass

Brass Quartet "In Honorem Paul Hindemith," Movement 1 ....David Eddleman

trumpets   French horn   trombone

Woodwinds

La cheminée du Roi René, Movement 1 ....Darius Milhaud (mee yoh)

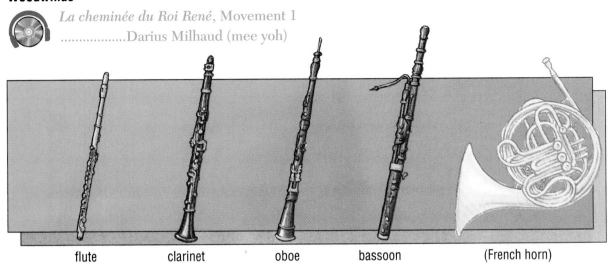

flute   clarinet   oboe   bassoon   (French horn)

Strings

Suite for String Orchestra, Movement 3,
"Badinerie"................Corelli/Pinelli

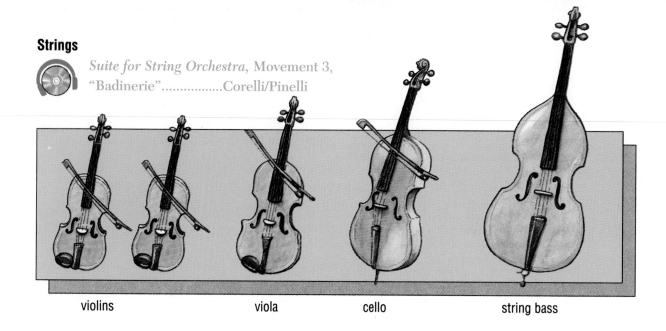

violins   viola   cello   string bass

Percussion

The Aztec Gods, Movement 1................Gardner Read

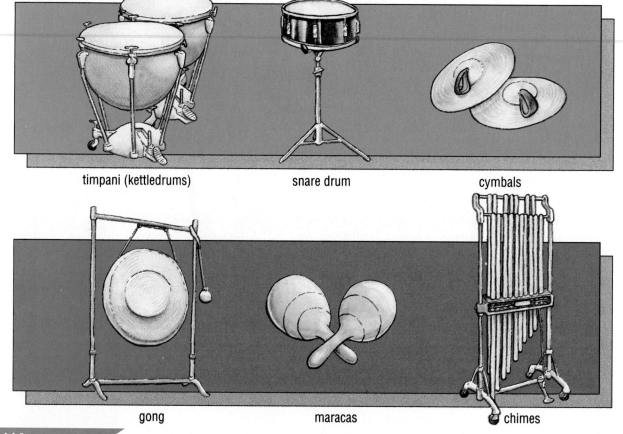

timpani (kettledrums)   snare drum   cymbals

gong   maracas   chimes

A Sense of Color

Sunflowers   *Vincent van Gogh*

1888, Van Gogh Museum, Amsterdam, Art Resource, NY.

What do you notice first about the two paintings on this page? Well, they're both depictions of the same subject: sunflowers. But something is different. The artists used color, among other variables, to give each painting its own particular appearance and "feel."

In this recording, you'll hear the same composition played by each of the four instrumental families. How would you describe the effect of each version?

Tales from the Latin Woods
.................Eddleman

1. Brass group

2. String group

3. Woodwind group

4. Percussion group

Did you guess that the composer of *Tales from the Latin Woods* originally had the tone colors of the woodwind family in mind when he wrote this piece? But since music is an art, not a science, you may very well have preferred another instrumental group.

Bouquet of Sunflowers   *Claude Monet*

The Metropolitan Museum of Art, Bequest of Mrs. H.O. Havermeyer, 1929.
The H.O. Havermeyer Collection. (29.100.107)

Listen to how one composer uses different combinations of instrumental colors in this rousing dance from a ballet. The call chart will help you recognize the instruments.

Call Chart 8

The Red Poppy, "Russian Sailor's Dance" ....Reinhold Glière

		Instruments	Tempo	Dynamics
1.	Introduction	Full orchestra	Fast	*ff*
2.	Theme	Low strings, low brass	Slow	*f,* then *mf*
3.	Variation I	Clarinet, strings, tambourine	Slow	*mp*
4.	Variation II	Clarinet and piccolo solos, strings accompany	Slow	*mf*
5.	Variation III	Horns, woodwinds, tambourine	Fast	*f*
6.	Variation IV	Strings, tambourine, brass	Slow	*ff*
7.	Variation V	Oboe, clarinet, low strings plucked (pizzicato)	Slow	*mp*
8.	Variation VI	Woodwinds, strings, brass, percussion	Very fast	*ff*
9.	Variation VII	Full orchestra, brass section predominates	Fast	*ff*
10.	Coda	Full orchestra	Very fast	*ff*

Meet the Composer

Reinhold Glière

(1875-1956)

Glière (glee AIR) was born of Belgian ancestry in the city of Kiev, the capital of Ukraine. His father was a maker of wind instruments, and young Reinhold probably grew up surrounded by these musical sounds.

Glière composed in the Russian Romantic tradition. His operas, ballets, and symphonies are noted for their expressive melodies and colorful orchestrations. Many of the composer's works make use of the folk music he collected during his extensive travels through Europe and Asiatic Russia. Unlike some other composers in the former Soviet Union, Glière rarely ran afoul of the government. This was perhaps due to his interest in national styles and his "politically correct" popular works.

The Red Poppy ("Krasnïy tsvetok" in the original Russian) was completed in 1927. The sailors in the ballet are ending an evening of celebration in which many dances have been performed, culminating in the wild performance you just listened to.

It's All in the Family

Here's your chance to become an active participant in one of the four instrumental families. The percussion **ensemble** piece below calls for pitched and nonpitched instruments. What other percussion instruments might you like to add?

Beating the Blahs

Mary E. Hoffman (Adapted)

Finger Cymbals

Soprano Glockenspiel

Resonator Bells

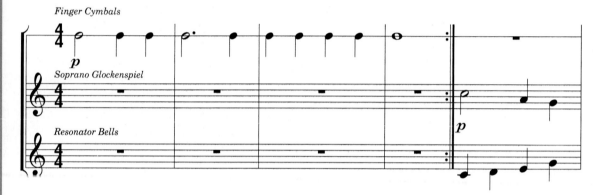

Take claves

claves

Take finger cymbals

Finger Cymbals

ritard.

ritard.

ritard.

Faster

Take tambourine

Take finger cymbals

Finger cymbals

Tambourine

p let sound die away

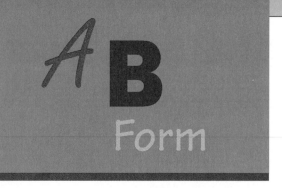

A B Form

In music, as in all the arts, there must be a balance of like and unlike elements. The organization of similar and contrasting ideas partly determines the **form** of a composition.

Listen to or sing the song "One Tin Soldier," then compare the melody of the verse with that of the refrain. Are the two melodies the same, or are they different?

The form of "One Tin Soldier" can be diagramed by assigning a letter to each major section of the song. For instance, if we label the verse *A*, the contrasting refrain would be labeled *B*. Using this method, how would you diagram a complete performance of the song?

One Tin Soldier

Words and Music by Dennis Lambert and Brian Potter

Guitar: capo 2   **VERSE**

1. Lis-ten, chil-dren, to a sto-ry that was writ-ten long a-go,
2. So the peo-ple of the val-ley sent a mes-sage up the hill
3. Now the val-ley cried with an-ger, "Mount your hors-es! Draw your sword!"

'Bout a king-dom on a moun-tain and the val-ley folk be-low;
Ask-ing for_ the bur-ied treas-ure, tons of gold_ for which they'd kill._
And they killed_ the moun-tain peo-ple so they won_ their just re-ward._

On the moun-tain was a treas-ure bur-ied deep be-neath_ a stone,
Came an an-swer from the king-dom, "with our broth-ers we_ will share
Now they stood_ be-side the treas-ure on the moun-tain, dark_ and red,

The Generals

Said General Clay to General Gore,
"Oh must we fight this silly war?
To kill and die is such a bore."
"I quite agree," said General Gore.

Said General Gore to General Clay,
"We could go to the beach today
And have some ice cream on the way."
"A grand idea," said General Clay.

Said General Clay to General Gore,
"We'll build sand castles on the shore."
Said General Gore, "We'll splash and play."
"Let's leave right now," said General Clay.

Said General Gore to General Clay.
"But what if the sea is closed today?
And what if the sand's been blown away?"
"A dreadful thought," said General Clay.

Said General Gore to General Clay.
"I've always feared the ocean's spray,
And we may drown!" "It's true, we may.
It chills my blood," said General Clay.

Said General Clay to General Gore,
"My bathing suit is slightly tore.
We'd better go on with our war."
"I quite agree," said General Gore.

Then General Clay charged General Gore
As bullets flew and cannons roared.
And now, alas! there is no more
Of General Clay or General Gore.

Shel Silverstein

And the val - ley peo - ple swore __ they'd have it for __ their ver - y
All the se - crets of our moun - tain, all the rich - es bur - ied
Turned the stone __ and looked be - neath __ it, "Peace on earth" __ was all it

B REFRAIN

own.
there." Go a-head and hate your neigh - bor, __ go a-head and cheat __ a friend.
said.

Do it in the name of heav - en, __ jus - ti - fy it in __ the end. There

won't be an - y trum-pets blow - in' __ come the judg - ment day; On the

blood-y morn-ing af - ter __ one tin sol - dier rides a - way. __

ABA Form

As you listen to the recording of the song "Sentimental Journey," ask yourself the following questions.

- How many major sections are there?

- Are any of the sections alike?

- Which section is different?

- How might this song be diagramed?

ABA is one of the most commonly used forms in music. The call chart on the next page will help you to identify the ABA form of an orchestral piece from the Romantic period.

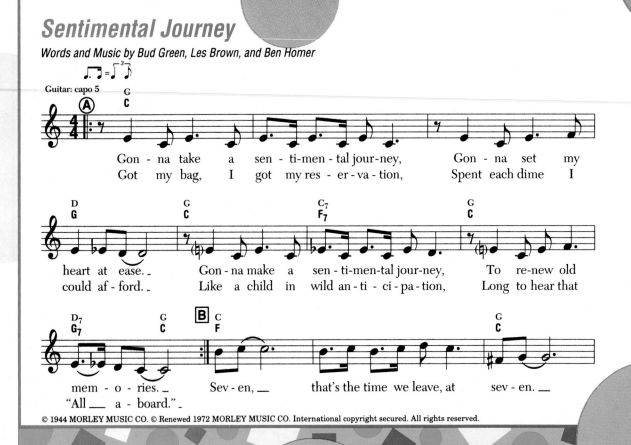

Sentimental Journey

Words and Music by Bud Green, Les Brown, and Ben Homer

Guitar: capo 5

A

Gon - na take a sen - ti-men-tal jour-ney, Gon - na set my
Got my bag, I got my res - er-va-tion, Spent each dime I

heart at ease._ Gon - na make a sen - ti-men-tal jour-ney, To re-new old
could af - ford._ Like a child in wild an - ti - ci-pa-tion, Long to hear that

B

mem - o - ries._ Sev - en, __ that's the time we leave, at sev - en. __
"All __ a - board." _

Norwegian Dance No. 2 in A ....Edvard Grieg

	Section	Instrument(s)	Tempo	Dynamics
1.	A	Oboe solo	Moderate	Soft (*p*)
2.	A	Flutes, clarinets, violins	Moderate	Soft
3.	B	Full orchestra	Fast	Loud (*f*)
4.	B	Full orchestra (theme played higher)	Fast	Loud
5.	A	Oboe solo	Moderate	Soft
6.	A	Flutes, clarinets, violins	Moderate	Soft

I'll be wait-in' up for Heav-en, ___ Count-in' ev-'ry mile of

rail-road track _ that takes me back. _ Nev-er thought my heart could be so "yearn-y."

Why did I de-cide to roam? _ Got-ta take this

sen-ti-men-tal jour-ney, sen-ti-men-tal jour-ney home. _

Rondo Form

Like a boomerang properly thrown, the main theme in rondo form always returns. Listen to this famous march. After a short introduction, you'll hear the main theme. How many times does this theme recur during the remainder of the piece?

 Colonel Bogey March
..................Kenneth Alford

In between the statements of the main theme, you heard different, contrasting themes. As you listen again to the march, this diagram will help you follow the rondo form.

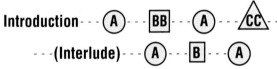

Introduction - - - (A) - - - BB - - - (A) - - - CC -
- - - (Interlude) - - - (A) - - - B - - - (A)

Some contemporary composers find new ways of using rondo form, as you'll hear in this modern piece for harp and small orchestra.

Call Chart 10

 Concertino for Harp and Orchestra, Movement 3, "Rondo" ....Germaine Tailleferre

1	(A)		4	(A) (FRAGMENT)	
2	(A)		5	B	
3	B		6	(A) (FRAGMENT)	

Meet the Composer

Germaine Tailleferre

(1892-1983)

Born in a small town near Paris, France, Germaine Tailleferre (zher mehn   ta yuh fehr) was still a young girl when she began to compose. With her mother's support (and against her father's wishes), she entered the Paris Conservatory when she was only twelve years old. There, the young student not only earned many first prizes but also developed an interest in the works of the young artists and poets of the time. Even after World War I disrupted her studies, Tailleferre continued to grow as a composer. Throughout her long, successful career—and despite many difficulties and self-doubts—she produced works of fresh, endearing beauty.

7 ⚠C	🎻 → 🎻 → 🎻 → 🎻 → *tutti*		11 Ⓐ (FRAGMENT)	// 🎻🎻
8 Ⓐ	🎵		12 B	🎺
9 Ⓐ	// 🎻🎻 🎺		13 Ⓐ (FRAGMENT)	🎷 🎵
10 B	🎵 🎺		14 CODA	🥁 → *tutti*

THEMES and STYLES

What type of music did people listen
to 200 years ago?

What is the musical result when
two very different cultures meet and interact?

What are some of the roles music
plays in our lives?

In exploring these and other questions
in this section of your book, you'll discover that
music knows no boundaries
of time or place.

Along the way, you'll be meeting
some interesting people,
including a poor milkman named Tevye,
a composer who was also a hero,
a rock star, and even
a cat named Mr. Mistoffelees.

section 2

Style Conscious

What is style? Visually, **style** is the appearance of an object such as a painting, a building, a suit of clothes, or even the look of a certain dance. Everything has style. Recognizing and describing style comes down to making comparisons. In order to determine the styles of different time periods, you should focus on identifying differences and similarities. As an example, look at the illustrations on this page. A piano is the subject of each. How would you describe the characteristics of each depiction?

Yale University Art Gallery. Gift of Collection Societe Anonyme.

Metropolitan Museum of Art, NY.

Grand Piano, ca. 1840,   *Erard & Co.*

In music, style is based on sound, not visual appearance. Both of these **concertos** feature a solo piano accompanied by an orchestra, but they represent two contrasting styles from different historical periods. One was written in the twentieth century, the other, in the eighteenth century. By focusing on the musical elements of rhythm, melody, harmony, and tone color, can you tell which example is which?

 Concerto No. 21 in C Major for Piano and Orchestra, Movement 2 (excerpt) ....Wolfgang Amadeus Mozart

 Concerto for Piano and Orchestra, Movement 1 (excerpt) .... Arnold Schoenberg

Each composer uses similar instrumentation, and each piece has a clear melody and an accompanying harmony; but the very different sounds of each of these elements help us to define the differences in style. Mozart (MOH tsahrt) wrote in the eighteenth-century Classic style. Schoenberg (SHUHRN behrg), on the other hand, wrote in a modern, twentieth-century style.

From the Department of prints and drawings of the Zentralbibliothek Zurich.

Same Song
Different
Styles

In music, a composer will sometimes use an existing piece as the starting point for a new work in a completely different style. On the following pages, you will see two versions of a song from the American Revolution. The chart below will help you compare them. What other similarities or differences can you name?

	"Chester"	"NonChester"
RHYTHM, BEAT	Steady beat and rhythm	Steady beat
METER	$\frac{2}{2}$ unchanging	Meter changes $\frac{3}{4}$ $\frac{5}{4}$ $\frac{4}{4}$ $\frac{7}{8}$
FORM	Four equal phrases	AB(A variation)
NOTE VALUES	Mainly	
MELODY STEPS	Many steps	Few steps
LEAPS	Few leaps	Many leaps
SINGING VOICE	All sung	Partly sung
SPEAKING VOICE	No speaking voice	Partly speaking voice
UNUSUAL VOCAL SOUNDS	None	Many

The Battle of Lexington at the Beginning of the Combat   *A.Doolittle and J.W. Barber*

Chester

Words and Music by William Billings

1. Let ty-rants shake their i - ron rod,
2. What grate-ful off-ring shall we bring,

And slav-'ry clank her gall - ing chains;
What shall we ren - der to the Lord?

We fear them not, We trust in God;
Loud hal-le-lu-jahs let us sing,

New Eng-land's God for-ev - er reigns.
And praise His name on ev - 'ry chord.

Meet the Composer

William Billings (1746-1800) is considered to be the outstanding American-born composer of the eighteenth century. He was largely self-taught and spent most of his life in the Boston area teaching singing in the churches. At age 24, in 1770, he published *The New England Psalm Singer*, which was the first completely American collection of music by an American composer. Billings's fame grew in the 1780s, and he was hailed as "the rival of Handel." A devout patriot, Billings was as important a force in the American Revolution as the Boston Tea Party. Through courage and determination, Billings overcame serious physical disabilities (one of which was a rasping, unmusical voice). Sadly, the composer's popularity declined rapidly, his death went largely unnoticed, and his grave site is unknown.

Frontispiece to Billings's *The New England Psalm Singer*

NonChester

Words by William Billings   *Music by Mary E. Hoffman*

The Symphony Orchestra: Then and Now

An eighteenth-century concert at a private house   (France)

Listen to these two symphony movements written for **orchestra.** They, like "Chester" and "NonChester," are also in different styles. Decide which column in the chart on page 134 best describes elements in the Mozart piece and which column best describes those in the Shostakovich (shah stuh KOH vich) piece.

Symphony No. 40 in G Minor, Movement 3
.....................*Wolfgang Amadeus Mozart*

Symphony No. 5 in D Minor, Movement 2
.....................*Dmitri Shostakovich*

Mozart, as you know, lived and composed during the eighteenth century. Shostakovich was a twentieth-century composer. Both men used the same musical building blocks—pitch, rhythm, meter, tone color, and so forth. But the different ways they put these building blocks together created the composers' different styles.

	COLUMN 1	COLUMN 2
TONE COLOR	Full orchestra (Classic)	Full orchestra (modern)
METER	Meter in 3	Meter mostly in 3
RHYTHM	Steady beat and rhythm	Shifting accents
MELODY	Singable	Not very singable
HARMONY	Little dissonance	Some dissonance
DYNAMICS	Few changes between loud and soft	Frequent changes between loud and soft

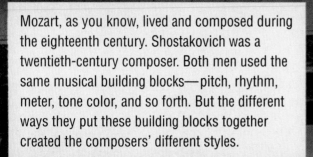

Meet the Composer

Wolfgang Amadeus Mozart   (1756-1791)

Born in Salzburg, Austria, Mozart was only three when his father discovered that his son had unusual musical talent. Young Wolfgang was soon playing the harpsichord and, later, the violin and the organ. Not satisfied with playing other people's music, he began writing pieces of his own when he was five. (By the age of 12, he had composed several sonatas, symphonies, and an opera.) At the age of six, his father took him on a concert tour of the great cities of Europe. The young prodigy performed brilliantly, and he continued to tour for the next 10 years.

Unfortunately, Mozart struggled with financial difficulties throughout his adult life. Ironically, the composer who came to represent the Classic period at its finest died in poverty at the age of 35 and was buried in a pauper's grave.

Meet the Composer

Dmitri Shostakovich   (1906-1975)

Shostakovich was born in St. Petersburg during the early stirrings of the Russian Revolution. Many feel that he is the finest symphony composer of the mid-twentieth century. His fifteen symphonies show not only a great deal of depth but a struggle to be fresh and original without overstepping the bounds laid down by the government of the former Soviet Union. The Soviet government insisted that composers write within a style of "socialist realism"—a style that demanded folk or folklike elements, little dissonance, straightforward rhythms, simple harmonies, a patriotic element, and so forth. To do otherwise, especially during the Stalin regime, could literally have meant death. That Shostakovich was still able to write works of immense depth and originality is a tribute to his genius.

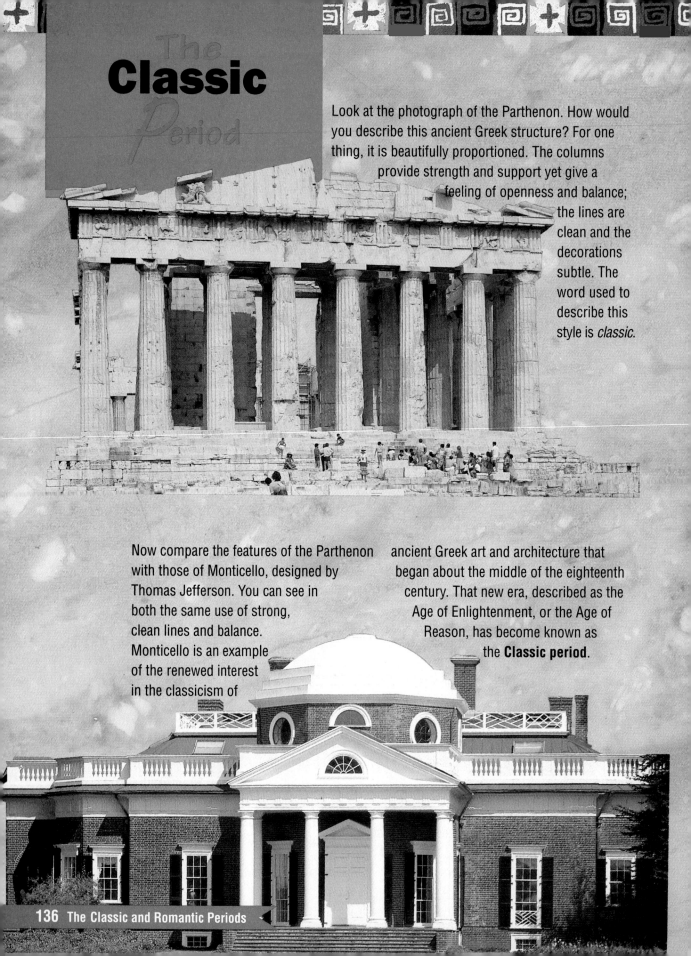

The Classic Period

Look at the photograph of the Parthenon. How would you describe this ancient Greek structure? For one thing, it is beautifully proportioned. The columns provide strength and support yet give a feeling of openness and balance; the lines are clean and the decorations subtle. The word used to describe this style is *classic*.

Now compare the features of the Parthenon with those of Monticello, designed by Thomas Jefferson. You can see in both the same use of strong, clean lines and balance. Monticello is an example of the renewed interest in the classicism of ancient Greek art and architecture that began about the middle of the eighteenth century. That new era, described as the Age of Enlightenment, or the Age of Reason, has become known as the **Classic period**.

Paris, Louvre. Giraudon/Art Resource, NY.

The Oath of the Horatii   *Jacques-Louis David*

Painting in the Age of Reason

As you look at the painting by David (dah VEED), notice how this Classic artist composed the work. Much importance is given to the number three: a group of three women at the right of the painting, and three men at the left; triangles formed by the swords and by the legs of the men; three archways in the background. An overall sense of balance is created by the positions of the figures. Even the colors are balanced: red clothing in the center and at both ends, and light-colored clothing at both ends. This painting clearly illustrates the key elements of proportion and balance in the Classic style.

Classic Balance

Composers during the eighteenth century also wanted to use the Classic elements of proportion and balance in their work. Their efforts resulted in music with a sound and style all its own. Let's put some Classic music together bit by bit. Start by singing or playing this short melody fragment.

The melody doesn't sound finished, does it? It's unbalanced as it is—and Classic music is all about balance and symmetry. Sing or play the following three melody fragments, and then decide which of these best balances Example 1 when added to it.

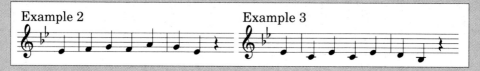

Examples 2 and 4 don't work as well as Example 3 does. If we're looking for symmetry and balance, Example 3 is the right choice. Its melodic contour is the same as that of Example 1, but Example 3 is one pitch lower. If we add them both together, as shown in Example 5, we can hear and see how nicely they complement each other.

Example 5

We now have a good melodic contour, but have you noticed that the duration of every note is the same? Let's add some interest to the rhythm with this bright little pattern.

Example 6

For balance, let's add a second phrase having the same length as the first. Up to now the general direction has been downward, so we'll make our answering phrase move upward while keeping the new rhythm pattern. Notice that the second phrase itself is balanced by a downward movement at the end.

Phrase 1

Phrase 2

Have you also noticed that the rhythm pattern not only has become the most memorable feature but also is the element that holds the phrases together?

Adding Harmony

Our Classic piece is in the **key** of B♭. That means that the notes in it are based on the B♭-major scale. On the **staff**, the B♭-major scale looks like this.

Harmony can be created by grouping the first, third, and fifth notes of the scale . The result is a triad. We'll call the B♭ triad *triad I*, since it is built on the first step of the scale.

The B♭ triad can be nicely balanced by building on its top note, F (the fifth note of the scale), to make an F triad *(triad V)*.

Try playing the B♭ and F triads in this sequence.

Now reverse the sequence to balance the pattern. The entire pattern so far looks like this.

It shouldn't surprise you to find that this balancing harmony fits beneath our well-balanced melody from page 139. Try adding the harmony to the melody.

This is all the harmony you will need to know for the first section (A) of our song. To harmonize the second section (B), you will need a new chord—one that balances the F triad. Do you remember that we balanced the B♭ triad by building a triad on its top note? Now let's do the same with the F triad. The result is a C triad.

The new triad is needed because the song changes to a new key, from B♭ to F. A change of key is called **modulation**, and it is another characteristic of the Classic style.

Finishing Touches

Have you noticed that balanced shapes often occur in threes? In our song so far, we have the opening section followed by a contrasting second section. What do you think will happen next? Of course! The opening section will return in order to balance the whole piece.

Over the last few pages, we have been reconstructing a song by Wolfgang Amadeus Mozart, a master of the Classic style. It is an aria from his opera *The Marriage of Figaro*. If you have learned to play the chords on pages 140 and 141, you can accompany the whole song, which appears on the next page.

Amphora with geometric design, Greek

5th c BCE. Louvre, Paris. Erich Lessing/Art Resource, NY.

In the Army from *The Marriage of Figaro*

Music by Wolfgang Amadeus Mozart

About the Music

The Marriage of Figaro is set in Seville, Spain, during the eighteenth century. The story relates the comic events that involve a host of assorted characters. In the scene leading up to the aria *Non più andrai* (the original title of "In the Army"), Cherubino (keh roo BEE noh), a young servant, has been caught flirting with some of the maids and with the countess. In order to get rid of him, the count tells him he has to join the army. In the aria, Figaro, Cherubino's friend, tells him that his flirting days are over and that he must now turn to more serious matters.

The house pictured to the right, in Vienna, Austria, is where Mozart wrote *The Marriage of Figaro*, one of his finest operas. You can still visit the dwelling and stand in the very room where the composer produced "In the Army," one of the hit songs of his day. In one of his letters, Mozart wrote of how delighted he was to hear the delivery boys whistling the melody as they went about their work in the streets of Vienna.

Ludwig *van* Beethoven

A Beethoven Time Line

1770   Ludwig van Beethoven is born in Bonn, Germany.

1775   The American Revolution against British rule begins.

1776   The Declaration of Independence is ratified in Philadelphia.

1782   Beethoven has his first music published.

1789   The French Revolution begins.

1790   The Industrial Revolution begins.

1791   The Bill of Rights becomes part of the Constitution of the United States of America.

       Mozart dies at age 35.

1795   Beethoven gives his first public piano recital.

1797   Franz Schubert (composer) is born near Vienna, Austria.

1801   Beethoven writes the *"Moonlight" Sonata* for piano.

1802   Beethoven learns he has incurable deafness.

1803   The Louisiana Purchase doubles the size of the United States.

1804   Napoleon Bonaparte crowns himself emperor of France.

       Nathaniel Hawthorne (America's first great novelist) is born in Salem, Massachusetts.

       Americans Lewis and Clark begin exploration of Louisiana Purchase.

1805   Beethoven publishes his *Symphony No. 3* ("The Eroica").

1807   Beethoven completes his *Symphony No. 5*.

1809   Abraham Lincoln is born in Kentucky.

1810   Beethoven completes the *Egmont Overture*.

1812   The War of 1812, between the United States and Great Britain, begins.

1815   Napoleon is defeated at the battle of Waterloo.

1819   Victoria (queen of Great Britain) is born.

       Walt Whitman (American poet) is born in New York.

1824   Beethoven, now totally deaf, completes his final symphony, *Symphony No. 9* ("The Choral").

1827   Beethoven dies in Vienna from pneumonia.

A Servant Class

In Beethoven's time, musicians were of the servant class. They usually served as church musicians or as "house" composers and conductors in the palace homes of the aristocracy. Beethoven's father and grandfather had served the elector, or ruler, Franz Joseph. Everyone expected that young Ludwig, learning the viola and piano with his father as his teacher, would follow his elders into the elector's service. (But Beethoven, believing that all people should have control over their own lives, had other plans.) From that beginning he became one of the greatest composers in history.

"A Chamber Concert at Sans Souci"

Beethoven performing before Prince Louis Ferdinand of Prussia

Beethoven's Youth

Beethoven's early years were unhappy. His alcoholic and overbearing father made a habit of waking young Ludwig in the middle of the night and making him practice on the violin, on the viola, and at the piano until sunrise. The boy was even discouraged from writing his own music.

In spite of his father, young Beethoven managed to develop his considerable talent. He became an assistant organist and a violist in the local court chapel and orchestra, positions that helped him to learn about the major composers of his time and about the instruments of the orchestra. Before long, Beethoven became famous as a concert pianist and a composer.

A Musical Hero

Beethoven was born at a time when the heroic ideas of brotherhood, equality, and liberty had begun to affect the way people lived their lives. The composer admired the great deeds of such people as Napoleon and the British naval hero Admiral Nelson. But Beethoven's own heroic struggle was against deafness, a condition that caused the composer much anguish. Instead of being defeated, though, Beethoven committed himself to the principles of personal freedom and brotherhood among all peoples.

Call Chart 11

 Egmont Overture.....................Ludwig van Beethoven

1. Introduction and opening theme,

   followed by answer in woodwinds.

2. Similar to beginning; opening theme played by full orchestra.

3. New theme, played by strings and woodwinds.

4. First appearance of Egmont's theme.

5. Repeated pattern, played by violins;

   gradual crescendo.

6. Egmont's theme, played *f* by high strings.

The Duke of Egmont

Beethoven's love of freedom drew him to a play by Goethe (GUHR tuh), the great German poet, playwright, and novelist. The play, entitled *Egmont*, tells the true story of the Duke of Egmont, a sixteenth-century Dutch nobleman, who fought against the Spanish invaders of his country, the Netherlands. Although he was captured, tortured, and executed, his heroic deeds inspired the Dutch people to rise up and win freedom for themselves.

Beethoven wrote incidental music for *Egmont*. Listen to the Overture, which sets the mood for the play, as you follow the call chart.

7. New theme, played by strings,

followed by answer in woodwinds;

Gradual build-up of instruments; crescendo; ascending scales.

8. Fragmentation of Egmont's theme.

9. Repetition and variation of Calls 4, 5, 6, and 7.

10. Key changes to major; meter changes to $\frac{4}{4}$; fast tempo; gradual crescendo to "victory" theme.

11. New theme, introduced by low strings and woodwinds, gradually taken up by full orchestra;

Brass flourish, leading to final cadence.

The Romantic Period

"I'm an individual, and I'm going to do my own thing."

"When I compose, I want to use more instruments and write for the largest orchestra ever!"

"The piano is my instrument of choice. I'll write piano music of technical brilliance!"

These were sentiments of composers who lived in the nineteenth century, an era known as the **Romantic period**. During this time, the whole music vocabulary was dramatically expanded. Harmony became thick, and new chords and dissonance began to play more expressive roles. Melody and form became more loosely structured. How different all this was from the Classic period, with its emphasis on balance and keeping things neat and precise!

Listen to this piano piece by Liszt (list). How many Romantic characteristics can you hear in this work?

Transcendental Etude No. 8 in C Minor ("Wild Hunt") ....Franz Liszt

Markisches Museum

Piano recital by Liszt

Meet the Composer

Franz Liszt   (1811-1886)

Hungarian-born Franz Liszt was one of the first solo concert performers. He dazzled audiences throughout Europe with his piano virtuosity. His passionate playing (usually of his own compositions) and flamboyant, controversial behavior evoked strong emotions wherever he went. It was a lifestyle that we associate today with many movie stars and rock stars. Yet, Liszt also had a religious need that led him to take minor holy orders in the Roman Catholic Church. To the end of his life he was called Abbé (Father) Liszt.

Much of Liszt's music (including the etude [ay tood] you listened to) was inspired by literary or artistic ideas or by images from nature. Such descriptive pieces are called **program music.**

A Nationalist Composer

During the nineteenth century, national sentiment was an important factor in the political and social development of many countries. Romantic composers frequently expressed love of country through their music. This tribute to a nation's people, using folk elements and patriotic references, is called **nationalism**.

The composer Antonín Dvořák (an toh NEEN d'VAWR zhahk) was born in Bohemia, a Slavic country that is now part of the Czech Republic. His *Slavonic Dances* are based on native folksongs and dances and were said to have sprung "directly from the soul of the people."

 Slavonic Dance in G Minor ....Antonín Dvořák

Twentieth Century— and Beyond

The twentieth century has seen many changes in such areas as architecture, clothing styles, and, especially, technology. As the eighteenth century became known as the Age of Reason, the twentieth century might well become known as the Age of Technology.

Everything in our society has been touched by the rapid technological developments over this century. One stamp below commemorates Wilbur and Orville Wright's first "flying machine" in 1903 (the term *airplane* did not appear until several years later). In an amazingly short amount of time, this grand achievement led to the event commemorated by the other stamp, the landing of a man on the moon on July 20, 1969.

Changes are happening so fast we can hardly keep track of them. How many performing groups can you name from the Top 40 charts of three years ago? Of last year? Of last month? Things are happening fast in music, too.

Rhythms Today

The opening of the twentieth century saw a revolutionary burst of activity in rhythm. Listen to part of Stravinsky's **ballet** *The Rite of Spring* to hear how this twentieth-century composer makes "new" use of strong accents and shifting meters. When this music was first played, in Paris in 1913, it caused a riot in the theatre.

The Rite of Spring, "Finale" (excerpt) ....Igor Stravinsky

A strong sense of twentieth-century rhythm is not limited to music. What elements give this painting a feeling of active rhythm?

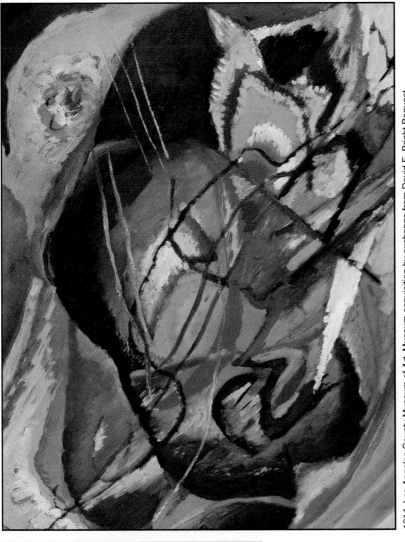

1914. Los Angeles County Museum of Art. Museum acquisition by exchange from David E. Bright Bequest.

Untitled Improvisation III   *Wassily Kandinsky*

A Percussion Piece

The simple percussion piece notated below shows some of the ways a twentieth-century composer might vary an uncomplicated rhythm:

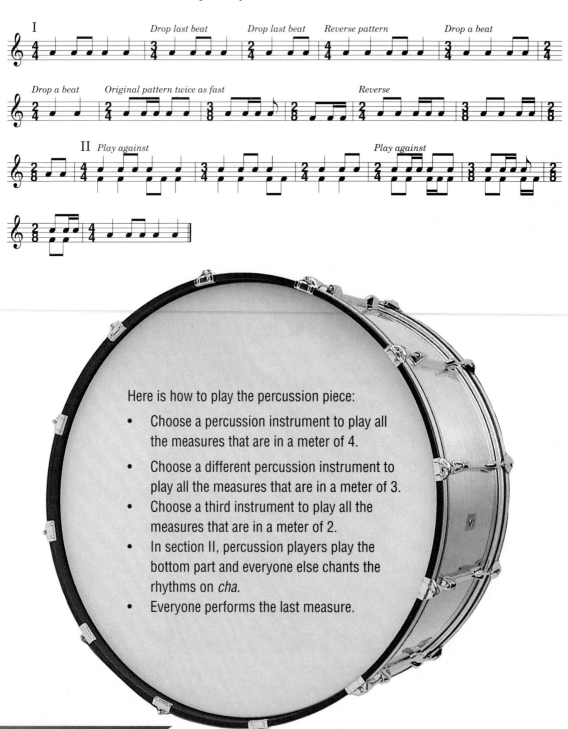

This rhythm is subjected to certain changes. Yet the resulting new rhythms still retain the basic character of the original rhythm.

Here is how to play the percussion piece:

- Choose a percussion instrument to play all the measures that are in a meter of 4.
- Choose a different percussion instrument to play all the measures that are in a meter of 3.
- Choose a third instrument to play all the measures that are in a meter of 2.
- In section II, percussion players play the bottom part and everyone else chants the rhythms on *cha*.
- Everyone performs the last measure.

Twentieth-Century Melody

Melodies of the twentieth century are hard to pin down. Some of them are singable in a Classic or Romantic way, and others are so unusual that they are difficult to follow.

All of these twentieth-century pieces feature the flute. How would you describe the melody of each?

 Listening for Melodic Styles

Interpolations for Flute (excerpt)
.............Haubenstock-Ramati

Irlandaise (excerpt)
.............Claude Bolling

Opus Vetrinus (excerpt)
.............Eddleman/Roberts

Sonata for Flute, Movement 2 (excerpt)
.............Paul Hindemith

Or (excerpt) ....Robert Dick

Twentieth-Century Harmony

In the twentieth century, harmony—like every other element of music—evolved into something very different sounding. Compare the harmonies in these two pieces. The first is a Classic composition, and the second, a twentieth-century piece. How do the harmonies differ?

 Minuet in G ....Beethoven

 Mikrokosmos, "Wrestling" ....Béla Bartók

Tone Clusters

Many twentieth-century composers reject the standard triad structure of chords. (See page 60.) Some have experimented with building chords by grouping notes into clusters. You can create your own **tone clusters** by using these methods.

- With a ruler or your forearm, depress as many piano keys as you can at one time.

- Put two or more mallets in each hand and play tone clusters on a xylophone, glockenspiel, or metallophone.

- Hold down one note on an electronic keyboard. At set time intervals, add adjacent notes, one at a time, until you cannot hold down any more.

The composer of this piece used string clusters to create an eerie effect. As you listen, examine the last page of the **score.** You can see the solid blocks that stand for the tone clusters in this all-strings work.

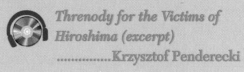

Threnody for the Victims of Hiroshima (excerpt)
.................Krzysztof Penderecki

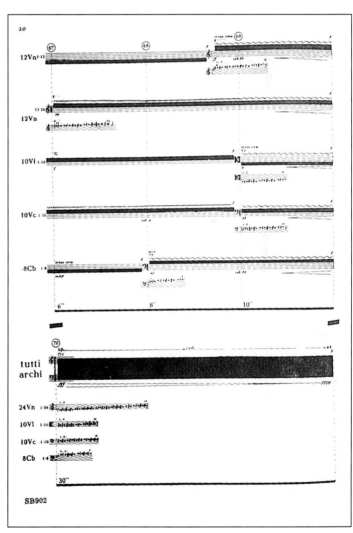

Twentieth-Century *Tone Color*

The twentieth century has brought music and technology together in a perfect marriage. There is hardly a rock group around that doesn't make use of a variety of synthesizers and other electronic instruments, many of which are combined with computers. Curiously, it was "serious" composers who first experimented with this technology. They manipulated the basic **wave forms** produced by the early machines and created different-sounding musical compositions. Listen to some of these wave forms.

 Wave Forms

a. Sine wave (low)—very pure sound
b. Sine wave (high)—very pure sound

c. Sawtooth wave—a nasal sound

d. White noise—not an actual wave form but a mixture of all frequencies sounding at once; sounds like a hiss

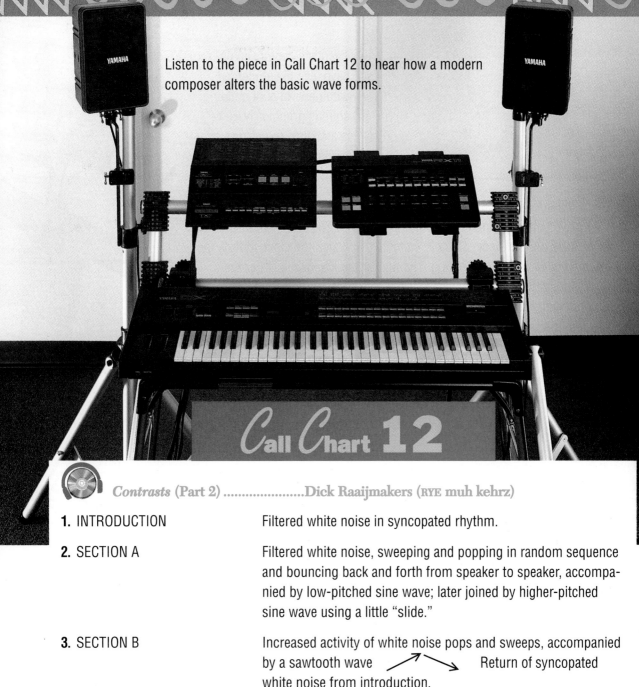

Listen to the piece in Call Chart 12 to hear how a modern composer alters the basic wave forms.

Call Chart 12

Contrasts (Part 2) ....Dick Raaijmakers (RYE muh kehrz)

1. INTRODUCTION   Filtered white noise in syncopated rhythm.

2. SECTION A   Filtered white noise, sweeping and popping in random sequence and bouncing back and forth from speaker to speaker, accompanied by low-pitched sine wave; later joined by higher-pitched sine wave using a little "slide."

3. SECTION B   Increased activity of white noise pops and sweeps, accompanied by a sawtooth wave ⟶⟶ Return of syncopated white noise from introduction.

4. SECTION A   Similar to Call 2.

5. CODA   Low-pitched sine wave with sawtooth wave.

Here is an example of how the synthesizer can be used in a completely different style.

Dervish D (excerpt) ....Vangelis

A *Graphic* Score

Twentieth-century composers have also experimented with new ways of notating sounds graphically. Here is a chance to perform a modern piece that is written in **graphic notation**.

"See Sharp" calls for four kinds of vocal or mouth sounds and for one pitch (C#) to be played on the piano or any other instrument. The class can form four sections to work out the piece. There is no meter, so watch the clock to time the sections. If a box is empty, do nothing. The thicker the line or the larger the symbol, the louder the sound. If a line is wavy, make the sound with a wide **vibrato** (vih BRAHT oh). If a line or dot is high in the box, make a high sound; if it is low, make a low sound. Are you ready?

See Sharp

Mary E. Hoffman

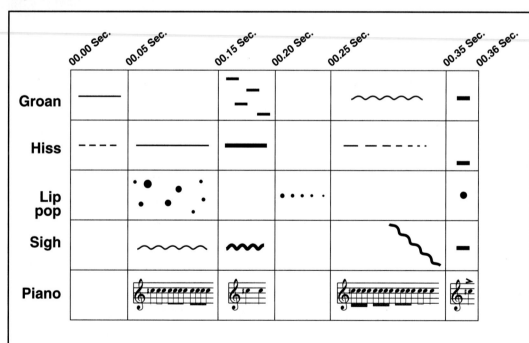

Try It Yourself

You can create your own piece by using graphic notation. With your classmates, make up a vocal or an instrumental sound for each symbol shown below. Put the symbols on the board in a specific order, then perform the piece. For a more interesting effect, try layering three or four different voices or instruments.

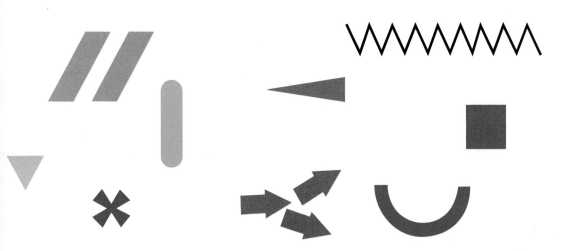

African Roots

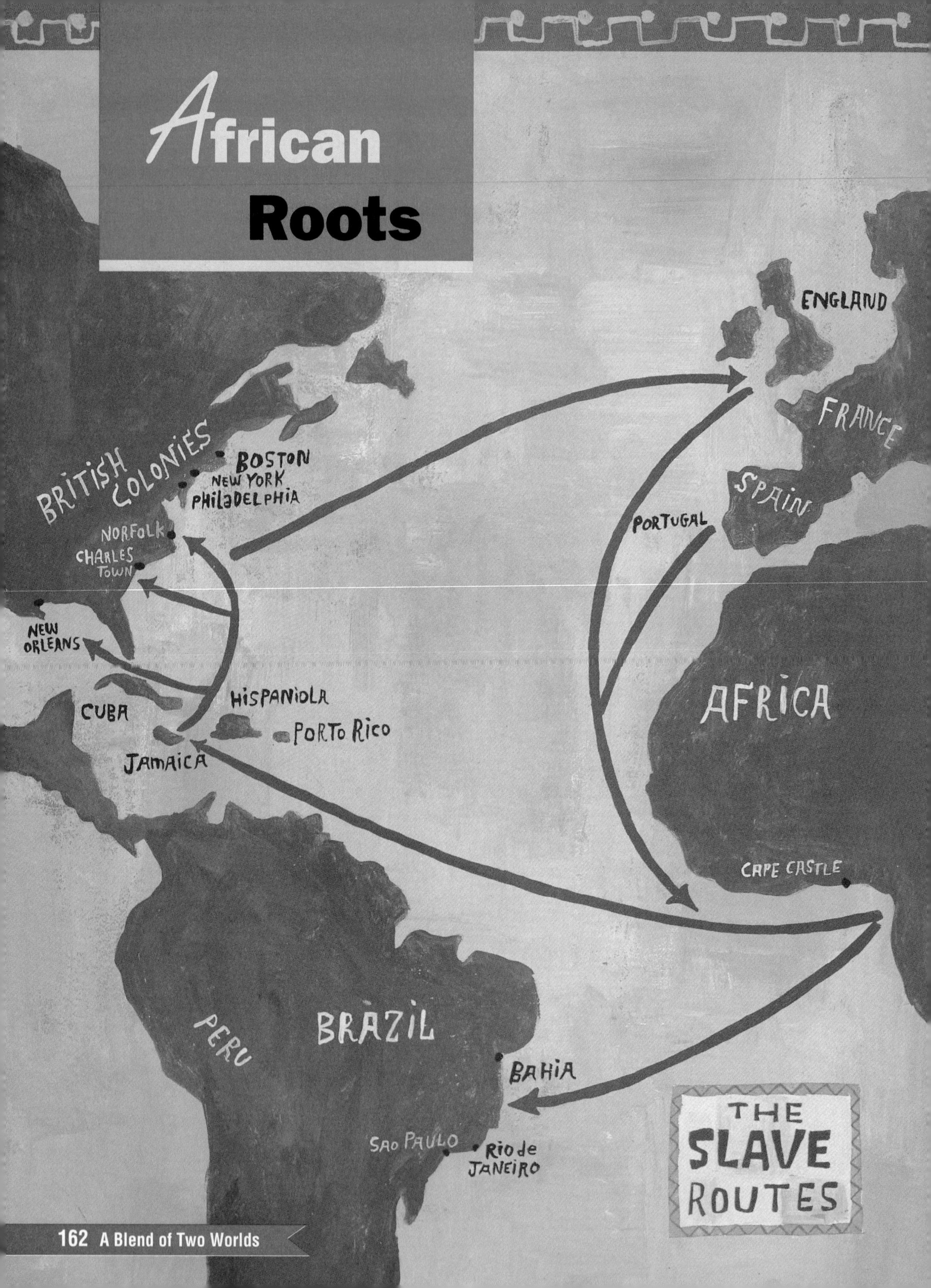

ENGLAND

FRANCE

SPAIN

PORTUGAL

BRITISH COLONIES

BOSTON
NEW YORK
PHILADELPHIA

NORFOLK
CHARLES TOWN

NEW ORLEANS

CUBA

HISPANIOLA

PORTO RICO

JAMAICA

AFRICA

CAPE CASTLE

PERU

BRAZIL

BAHIA

SAO PAULO

RIO DE JANEIRO

THE SLAVE ROUTES

Imagine that aliens from another planet came to your town, kidnapped you and others in your neighborhood, and took you to another galaxy to work there as slaves for the rest of your lives.

Something like that did happen to millions of people who lived in western and central Africa 300 years ago. The invaders, though, were not from outer space; they came from Europe. Over a period of 200 years, slave ships sailed to Africa to capture their human cargos and transport the captives to South America, the West Indies, and America to be sold into slavery. Often, rival African groups would capture weaker neighbors and sell them to the sea captains.

The impact of these events is still evident. This song, sung mostly in the Wolof language of Senegal, is by a modern African composer.

Africa Remembers (excerpt)
............Youssou N'Dour

Yesterday has passed but needs to be
          remembered
My ancestors suffered under slavery
A tree grows outward from its roots
And I just won't stop remembering

Follow me, if you like
Yes, I'm delving into the past
I'm remembering

Long ago they'd come for you in your home
Tie your hands and take you far away
You wouldn't see your family or your
          belongings
Ever, ever again

Now, Black people have had to try and try
Until finally we got back the most
important thing we own
Our culture
Don't trade away your culture for anything
          in the world.
(Translation by Boubacar N'Dour)

*M*eet the *M*usician

Youssou N'Dour   (1960-   )

Born in the west African country of Senegal, Youssou N'Dour (YOO SOO EN DOOR) comes from a family of storytellers and oral historians. He began singing as a child at traditional feasts and ceremonies, surrounded by the lively rhythms and sounds of his native culture. After performing with a number of rock bands, N'Dour formed his own band, the Super Étoile (ay twahl). He has since become the master of a unique musical style that mixes traditional Senegalese sounds with a variety of other styles, including jazz, flamenco, soul, and Arabic music.

Africa Remembers was produced at a new recording studio that N'Dour built in Dakar, the capital of Senegal.

Some countries and regions—such as Brazil, Latin America, and the Spanish and French islands in the Caribbean—allowed the slaves to hold on to their native languages, customs, and music. Other countries, however, forbade it. The slaves on the plantations of the southern United States, for example, were not allowed to retain their customs, for the slaveholders were afraid that the slaves would use their language to communicate secretly. But the slaves found a way. They developed a musical style, based on European traditions, that allowed them to continue to communicate with each other much as they had done in Africa—and right

Into Bondage   *Aaron Douglas*

under their masters' noses! Little did the owners realize that this music was the beginning of a fusion of African and European music that would one day be heard all over the world. Some of the musical features contributed by the African culture are named below.

SOME FEATURES OF AFRICAN MUSIC

1. Much use of percussion instruments and percussive sounds

2. Rhythm patterns repeated over and over (ostinatos)

3. Use of complicated and varied rhythm patterns

4. Several different rhythms performed at once

5. Call-and-response form in vocal music

African Beat

As you might have guessed by looking at the list on the preceding page, rhythm is an extremely important element in African music. All music may have rhythm, but African rhythm creates a unique and exciting sound. Listen to this example of African drumming.

  Manyanga Drum Rhythms...
Nyamwezi Drummers

Percussion group from Zambia

African Rhythm Complex

Many African societies have developed their own sets of rhythm patterns. Here is a simplified version of a **rhythm complex**. To perform it, first set a steady beat and continue to count from one to eight with it. Using percussion instruments that contrast well, play only on the indicated beats for each line, always feeling the underlying pulse. Start with one or two lines, then gradually work up to all five. When you're ready, try playing the rhythm complex in different tempos.

 # RHYTHM COMPLEX

	1	2	3	4	5	6	7	8
A	1				5			
B		2	3	4		6	7	8
C	1			4			7	8
D	1	2			5	6		
E	1		3			6		8

Make Your Own Rhythm Complex

It's easy to create a rhythm complex of your own. Using the chart above as a guide, fill in selected beats on the blank chart on the right. Remember that to make your rhythm complex interesting, there should be spaces between the sounds.

	1	2	3	4	5	6	7	8
A								
B								
C								
D								
E								

Once you've worked out your rhythm complex, use it to accompany this jazz classic performed by the Cuban musician Mongo Santamaria.

 Watermelon Man.................Mongo Santamaria

A Song of the Yoruba

In the west-central African country of Nigeria, the Yoruba (YAWR uh buh) people worship a god called Elegua. When the Yoruba crossed the ocean to Cuba, they brought their beliefs with them, so it was natural for a song to be written about Elegua. Although the words are Spanish and the harmonies Western, the song is rhythmically African.

Yoruba Hegun headdress.

African wood sculpture. Private Collection. Art Resource, NY.

Elegua

Words and Music by Eduardo Davidson   English Words by Samuel Maqui

E - le - gua,   E - le - gua, san - to bo - ni - to; —
eh - leh - gwah   eh - leh - gwah sahn - toh boh - nee - toh

E - le - gua,   E - le - gua, san - to chi - qui - to. †   E - le - gua, ca -
eh - leh - gwah   eh - leh - gwah sahn - toh chee - kee - toh   eh - leh - gwah kah -
E - le - gua, you

ba - llo ne - gro — con ban - de - ra co - lo - rao.   E - le - gua, ca -
bah - yoh neh - groh kohn bahn - deh - rah koh - loh - rau   eh - leh - gwah kah -
ride a black horse — and car - ry a scar - let flag.   *E - le - gua, you*

ba - llo ne - gro — con ban - de - ra co - lo - rao.
bah - yoh neh - groh kohn bahn - deh - rah koh - loh - rau
ride a black horse — and car - ry a scar - let flag.

°lovely saint   † little holy doll

The Influence GROWS

You will hear two male singers on this recording. One is an African American blues singer from Mississippi and the other, an African singer from Senegal. What similarities do you hear in the two performances?

Lousiana and *Field Song from Senegal*

Did you notice that the two melodies rise and fall in a similar fashion? There is also a similarity in the way the singers ornament the melodies.

The singers slide up and down on the pitches, sometimes not even singing exact pitches at all.

Max Roach

Back to the Beat

African rhythm has had a strong influence on almost all of our popular musical styles. Here are three examples, each played by a solo percussionist. Which rhythm do you think sounds the most "African"? Why?

 Drum solo—jazz style

 Drum solo—rock style

Debbie Peterson

Drum solo—Latin American samba

In this recording by an African rock musician, you'll hear a strong percussion track that uses modern rock instruments as well as traditional African instruments. You've heard examples of the influence of African music on American rock; the Nkosi selection shows that American rock returned the favor.

 Africa (What You Gonna Say)
..............Dan Nkosi (en KOH see)

Sheila e

Mino Cinelu

Inspired by Africa

Many of our modern percussion instruments owe much to Africa. The tom-tom, the maracas, the claves (KLAH vehs), the conga drum, and many others, are all derived from African influences.

While studying in sub-Saharan Africa, the composer Phil Faini (fah EE nee) was inspired to write a piece for percussion ensemble. Here is the main theme of *Afro-Amero*.

Try clapping the main rhythmic theme, written here in the rhythm-complex format.

1	2	3	4	5	6	7	8	9	10	11	12
1		**3**		**5**	**6**		**8**		**10**	**11**	

Now follow the call chart on the next page. It will show you what happens.

Harriet Tubman Series No. 4   *Jacob Lawrence*

Hampton University Museum

Call Chart 13

Afro-Amero .... Phil Faini

1. Main rhythmic theme; marimba; rhythmic theme again.

2. Main melodic theme; slow tempo.

3. Loud main rhythmic theme; *p*, followed by layering of rhythms (polyrhythms).

4. Timpani.

5. Tom-tom leading to (>) sudden stop; short, sharp patterns and silences.

6. Rhythmic theme and melodic theme at the same time; melody, in smaller note values, moves faster now; sudden stop; short, sharp patterns and silences.

7. Strong rhythm

   Timpani begin a layering of rhythms.

8. Melody, in still smaller note values, moves even faster; energetic rhythm of Call 7 reappears *ff*.

9. Polyrhythms *ff*.

10. Melody, in even smaller note values, is slightly syncopated; coda

The Jazz Connection

As the cultural traditions of the African slaves mixed with those of the New World, a remarkable musical transformation began to take place. The rhythmic, driving, exciting elements in African music were combined with the European-based harmonies prevalent in this country. That resulted in new kinds of music, including a purely American musical style called **jazz**.

An important element in jazz grew from the fact that African musicians rarely write down their music. They like to vary the music according to their feelings at the time they perform. (This is a tradition in many of the cultures of the world.) In jazz, although the performers follow a basic chord pattern or a set melody, they don't really know what is going to happen until the actual moment of performance. This kind of exciting music making is called **improvisation**.

The jazz piece *Seven Come Eleven* doesn't sound all that African. But the many layers of complex rhythms plus the players' improvisations are reflections of its African musical heritage. Follow the call chart as you listen.

Call Chart 14

 Seven Come Eleven.................Benny Goodman

1. Drum set.

2. String bass enters.

3. Saxophone and vibraphone play theme.

4. Clarinet improvisation with accompaniment.

5. Saxophone and vibraphone play theme.

6. Guitar improvisation with vibraphone.

7. Guitar with resonating vibraphone accompaniment.

8. Guitar with vibraphone.

9. Vibraphone improvisation with accompaniment.

10. Vibraphone improvisation with accompaniment.

11. Clarinet improvisation.

12. Saxophone and vibraphone play theme, ending in coda.

Improvise a Riff

You've already heard that African music repeats patterns again and again. Repeated patterns—or ostinatos—are known as **riffs** in the jazz and rock worlds. Here are some of the more noticeable riffs in *Seven Come Eleven*. If you follow the call chart on page 175 again as you listen, you will hear these riffs at the calls shown.

Here's your chance to improvise some of your own riffs to accompany *Seven Come Eleven*. You will need to become familiar with these five chords.

	A♭	C₇	F₇	B♭₇	E♭₇

(notes below staff: A♭ C E♭   C E G B♭   F A C E♭   B♭ D F A♭   E♭ G B♭ D♭)

This chart shows the form and the chord pattern for *Seven Come Eleven*. Each box represents one **measure** of two beats. Try to play the notes of these chords in any order as you listen to the recording. Wait for the drum and bass introduction and begin to improvise when the saxophone enters.

Section								
A	A♭	A♭	A♭	A♭	A♭	A♭	A♭	A♭
A	A♭	A♭	A♭	A♭	A♭	A♭	A♭	A♭
B	C₇	C₇	F₇	F₇	B♭₇	B♭₇	E♭₇	E♭₇
A	A♭	A♭	A♭	A♭	A♭	A♭	A♭	A♭

Seven Come Eleven (without call numbers)...............Goodman

You've probably sung or heard this song before. Try singing it now.

Jazz Ensembles

When the Saints Go Marching In

African American Spiritual

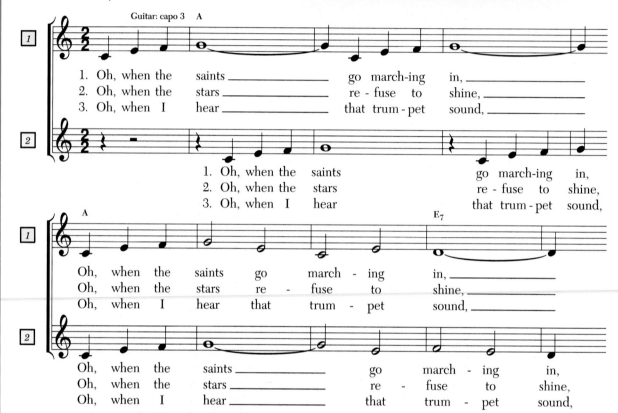

The people of New Orleans developed a very special kind of ensemble—the Dixieland band. In Dixieland jazz, the melody is played by everyone, and then each player in turn improvises on the melody while all the others provide a little harmonic support. (The audience is encouraged to applaud after each solo.) Dixieland bands usually have five to seven players. Listen to what this group does with "When the Saints Go Marching In."

Can you name the instruments that are playing?

When the Saints Go Marching In ....African American Spiritual (Preservation Hall Jazz Band)

1. Oh, Lord, I want to be in that num - ber, _____

2. Oh, Lord, I want to be in that num - ber,

1. When the saints go march - ing in. _____
   When the stars re - fuse to shine. _____
   When I hear that trum - pet sound. _____

2. When the saints go march - ing in. _____
   When the stars re - fuse to shine. _____
   When I hear that trum - pet sound. _____

New Orleans Ragging Home   *Romare Bearden*

Courtesy Estate of Romare Bearden

Quincy Jones and His Orchestra

Jazz ensembles may range in size from the small and intimate (piano, bass, and drums, for example) to a large group containing instruments from all four families (see pages 113-114). Quincy Jones has composed and conducted music involving many types of jazz ensembles. After you have read about this musician, locate and share some of his recordings with your classmates.

Meet the Musician

Quincy Jones   (1933-   )

Quincy Jones is a musical Renaissance man whose remarkable career has encompassed the roles of composer, arranger, conductor, performer, producer, and media executive. To date, his Grammy Awards number 25 (out of 74 nominations), second only to the great classical conductor George Solti (SHOL tee).

Jones was born in Chicago and grew up in Seattle. He wrote his first arrangements as a teenager while playing trumpet in dance bands. After a period of study in Paris, the young musician toured throughout Europe and the United States with his jazz band. He later distinguished himself as a record company executive (the first African American to hold such a position) and as a founding member of the Institute for Black American Music.

Jones has written the music for more than 30 films, including *In the Heat of the Night* and *The Color Purple*. His television credits include the music for *Roots* and *The Bill Cosby Show*. As a composer, this wide-ranging artist has created musical fusions of such diverse styles as big band, gospel, funk, rhythm-and-blues, jazz, classical, African and Brazilian music, and electronic music. In his capacity as producer/arranger, Jones made major contributions to the historic recording session for "We Are the World" and to many of Michael Jackson's most successful albums. In 1993, for the Presidential Inaugural celebration in Washington, D.C., Jones served as executive producer of the "Call for Reunion" concert at the Lincoln Memorial.

Country Music Ensembles

From the early days of our country, African Americans and white Americans "borrowed" from the music of the other. The mixtures made for some interesting instrumental combinations.

Listen to this performance of *Cripple Creek.* This traditional country "fiddle tune" is especially popular in the South and West. In addition to the fiddle (a folk name for a violin), the ensemble consists of banjo, guitar, harmonica, and string bass. Which one of these instruments do you think was borrowed from the African American tradition?

 Cripple Creek ....Traditional American

Turn the page to discover an activity that can be performed with the recording of *Cripple Creek.*

The Sources of Country Music   *Thomas Hart Benton*

"Texas Star" Square Dance

"Texas Star" is a popular square dance that can be performed with the recording of *Cripple Creek*. With your teacher's help, learn the movements while counting the beats for each pattern. Next, practice dancing to the music while still counting the beats out loud.

"Patter calls" are often used to direct square dancers. When your movements are secure, add a caller to chant the "Texas Star" patter call below. Keep a steady beat by accenting the underlined words. (The style is similar to that of rap.) Notice that the caller is often four beats ahead of the dancers.

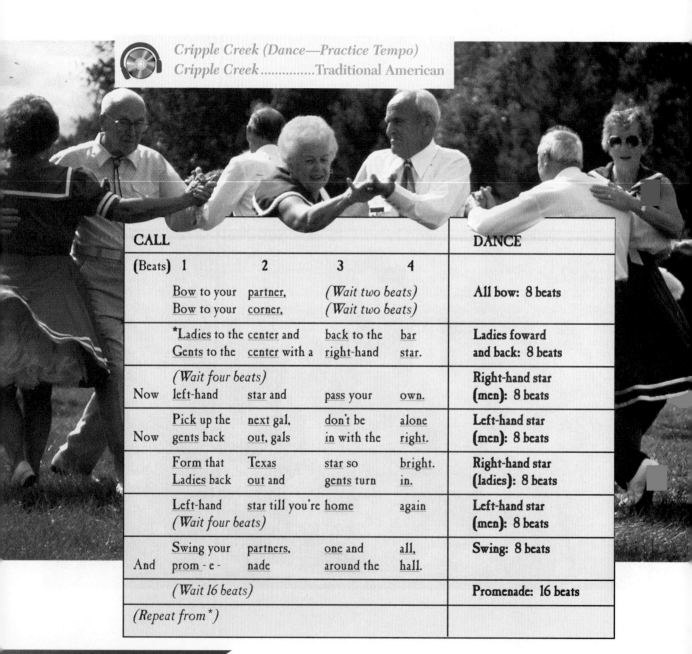

Cripple Creek (Dance—Practice Tempo)
Cripple Creek ....Traditional American

CALL				DANCE
(Beats) 1	2	3	4	
Bow to your partner,		(*Wait two beats*)		All bow: 8 beats
Bow to your corner,		(*Wait two beats*)		
*Ladies to the center and	back to the	bar		Ladies foward
Gents to the center with a	right-hand	star.		and back: 8 beats
(*Wait four beats*)				Right-hand star
Now left-hand star and	pass your	own.		(men): 8 beats
Pick up the next gal,	don't be	alone		Left-hand star
Now gents back out, gals	in with the	right.		(men): 8 beats
Form that Texas	star so	bright.		Right-hand star
Ladies back out and	gents turn	in.		(ladies): 8 beats
Left-hand star till you're home	again			Left-hand star
(*Wait four beats*)				(men): 8 beats
And Swing your partners,	one and	all,		Swing: 8 beats
prom - e - nade	around the	hall.		
(*Wait 16 beats*)				Promenade: 16 beats
(*Repeat from*)				

Country Pop

Country-music group Alabama

The sound and composition of country-music ensembles have certainly changed since the early days of the twentieth century. While some of the traditional folk instruments have been kept, new instruments from rhythm-and-blues and rock music have been added. Today, most country groups include electric guitars (lead, rhythm, bass), percussion, and keyboard.

In this example by the group Alabama, listen for the one melody instrument that you also heard in *Cripple Creek*. Country music may have changed over the years, but, as the title of this song suggests, it hasn't forgotten its roots.

 If You're Gonna Play in Texas (You Gotta Have a Fiddle in the Band)...............Kellum and Mitchell/Alabama

The group Banda R-15 specializes in a popular Mexican musical style called *banda*, which is simply Spanish for "band." Listen to this ensemble play *La chica contry* ("The Country Girl"), a recent composition inspired by the sound of traditional country music.

 La chica contry ....Rodríguez/Banda R-15

A Different Kind of
Rock Group

You're probably quite familiar with the instruments that make up a typical rock music ensemble— electric guitars, percussion, synthesizers. But since the sounds these instruments produce can also be re-created and manipulated with the use of electronics and computer technology, rock ensembles today are anything but typical. In fact, an "ensemble" may consist of one person in a studio, with perhaps other musicians adding **over-dubs** at a later time.

One innovative musician who has worked this way is British rock star Peter Gabriel. Once the lead singer with the group Genesis, Peter now creates most of his music in a recording studio complex built in a converted water mill in England. Listen to an interview with the rock artist that includes a discussion of elements in one of his most interesting songs, *The Rhythm of the Heat*.

Careers in Music—Peter Gabriel

Peter Gabriel

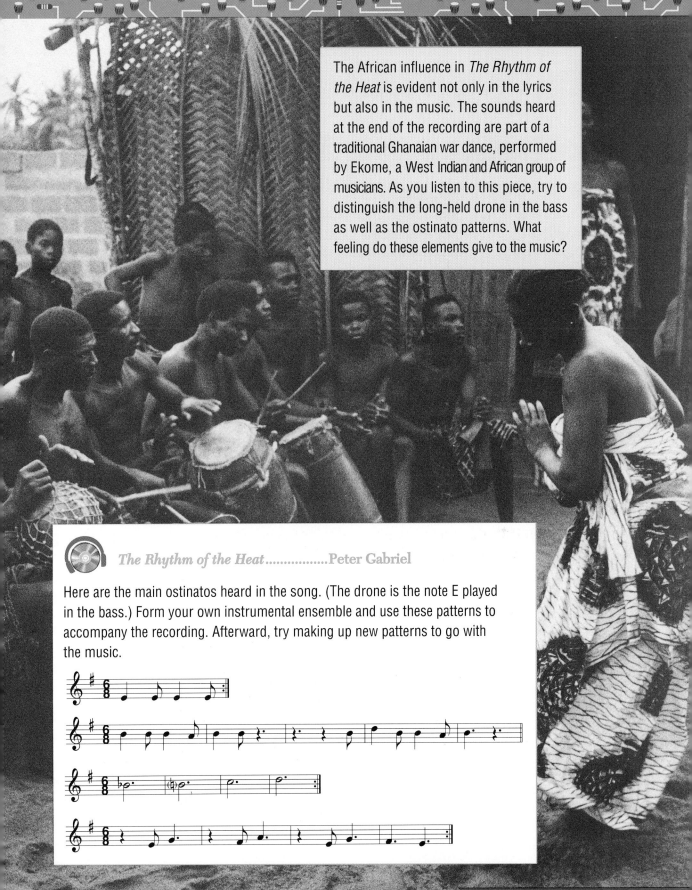

The African influence in *The Rhythm of the Heat* is evident not only in the lyrics but also in the music. The sounds heard at the end of the recording are part of a traditional Ghanaian war dance, performed by Ekome, a West Indian and African group of musicians. As you listen to this piece, try to distinguish the long-held drone in the bass as well as the ostinato patterns. What feeling do these elements give to the music?

The Rhythm of the Heat ....Peter Gabriel

Here are the main ostinatos heard in the song. (The drone is the note E played in the bass.) Form your own instrumental ensemble and use these patterns to accompany the recording. Afterward, try making up new patterns to go with the music.

Ewe celebration, Ghana

A "Small World" Ensemble

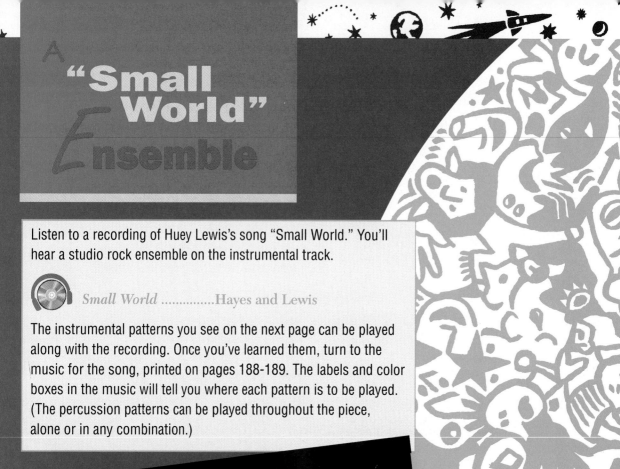

Listen to a recording of Huey Lewis's song "Small World." You'll hear a studio rock ensemble on the instrumental track.

Small World ....Hayes and Lewis

The instrumental patterns you see on the next page can be played along with the recording. Once you've learned them, turn to the music for the song, printed on pages 188-189. The labels and color boxes in the music will tell you where each pattern is to be played. (The percussion patterns can be played throughout the piece, alone or in any combination.)

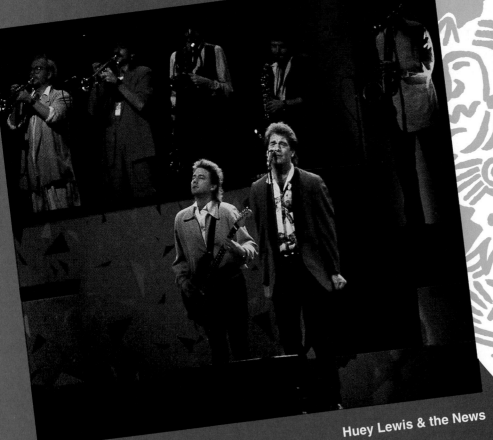

Huey Lewis & the News

Keyboard/Bass guitar

Using the same chord tones, try to work out variations on these patterns.

Small World

Words and Music by Chris Hayes and Huey Lewis

© 1988 Hulex Music (ASCAP) Used by permission of Bob-a-lew Music

Or we can help one an-oth-er, the way it's s'posed to be.

Pattern 2

If we all give a lit-tle,

it could real-ly mean a lot. It's a small, small

Pattern 1

world, but it's the on-ly one we got. Small world,

Pattern 3
4   7

Small, small world.

(ad lib.) **Pattern 1**

Small world, Small, small world.

Pattern 3
4

It's a small world, small world, small world.

(ad lib. and fade)

Ensembles from around the World

There doesn't seem to be a culture anywhere on earth that hasn't developed a rich musical tradition. These traditions are expressed through a great variety of musical ensembles.

Let's begin our short musical travelogue with this selection from the Yunnan province, in China. The music is played by an orchestra of traditional Chinese instruments, some of which are pictured here.

Dancing in the Moonlight
............Traditional Chinese

Gaohu

Sanxian

P'ipa

West Indian steel drum band

An Unusual Instrument

In the West Indies of the early twentieth century, ships delivered oil in large steel drums. The residents of the islands found many uses for the empty drums, including one use that has come to symbolize the West Indies—as instruments for steel drum bands. People found that hitting different areas of the steel drums produced different pitches and that smaller drums had higher sounds than larger ones did. By denting the tops of the drums, scales could be produced. It was also discovered that cutting a drum in half would increase its resonance. Listen to the tone color in this steel drum selection.

El merecumbe ....Steel Drum Band

The Sounds of Mexico

The most popular type of musical folk ensemble in Mexico is probably the mariachi (mah ree AH chee) band. You can find mariachi groups at all kinds of *fiestas* (celebrations), playing the popular melodies and rhythms of the Mexican culture. The **instrumentation** usually consists of violins, guitars, and trumpets. And as you will hear, members of the mariachis sing as well!

Cielito lindo ....Traditional Mexican

Jarocho ensemble

The port of Veracruz is the heart of the Jarocho (hah ROH choh) region of Mexico. This area has a special association with the cultures of the Caribbean, especially those of the coastal regions of Venezuela. Here is a recording of a typical Jarocho ensemble. The lead part is played by a small, guitarlike instrument called a requinto (reh KEEN toh). You'll also hear a harp and two jaranas (hah RAH nahs), which are similar to the requinto but larger.

La iguana ....
Traditional Mexican

A Musical Collaboration

In some ways this last selection is the most representative of today's world, in which different cultures can join forces and share their rich traditions.

The American musician Paul Winter and his ensemble got together with a group of singers from Russia. One result is this arrangement of a traditional song from the Kursk region in southern Russia.

Kurski Funk ....Halley, Castro-Neves, Winter/Traditional Russian

*F*ollowing *a* Score

"There are so many things going on! How can it all be kept together?"

Yes, it can be mystifying how a composer or a conductor deals with all those vocal and instrumental parts that make up a musical score. But in music there are several ways to keep track of what's happening. Let's start off with just the melody of a song.

Young Person's Guide to the Orchestra — Benjamin Britten.
© Copyright 1946 by Hawkes and Son (London) Ltd;
Renewed 1973. Reprinted by permission of Boosey & Hawkes, Inc.

Glee Reigns in Galilee   (*Gilu Hagalilim*)

English Words by Dav ben Shmuel   *Hebrew Folk Song*

Be joy - ful, Ga - li - le - ans, raise up your voic - es;
Gi - lu ha - ga - li - lim gi - bo - rei he - cha - yil;

Be glad, be joy - ful____ morn - ing and eve - ning.
Si - su v' - sim - chu____ yo - mam va - la - yil.

Be joy - ful, Ga - li - le - ans, raise up your voic - es;
Gi - lu ha - ga - li - lim gi - bo - rei he - cha - yil;

Be glad, be joy - ful____ morn - ing and eve - ning.
Si - su v' - sim - chu____ yo - mam va - la - yil.

Here's the same song with piano accompaniment. Remember, the voice part is always on the top line, so it's easy to keep your place.

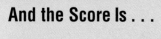

And the Score Is . . .

Musical scores can be written to serve many sizes, from a trio or quartet to a complete orchestra. In a full score, each different instrument is shown on its own staff.

Look at the score for this particular instrumental ensemble. We have flute, trumpet, trombone, percussion, and bass. You can see that, as on the preceding pages, the melody is highlighted in yellow, even as it skips from instrument to instrument.

Glee Reigns in Galilee (Gilu Hagalilim)

Hebrew Folk Song

The FULL Score

Look at the opening page of the full score for Benjamin Britten's *Young Person's Guide to the Orchestra*. The woodwinds are at the top, shown here in green. The brass are next, in red; then come the percussion instruments, in yellow. The strings are at the bottom, in blue.

Young Person's Guide to the Orchestra BENJAMIN BRITTEN

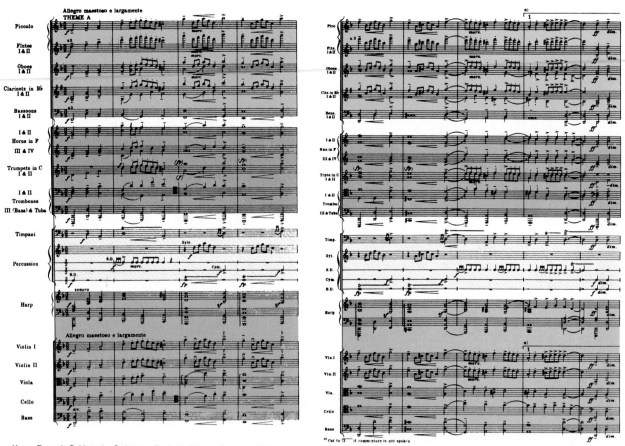

Young Person's Guide to the Orchestra—Benjamin Britten.© Copyright 1946 by Hawkes and Son (London) Ltd; Renewed 1973.
Reprinted by permission of Boosey & Hawkes, Inc.

Young Person's Guide to the Orchestra,
"Introduction" ....Benjamin Britten

1. Full orchestra
2. Woodwinds
3. Brass
4. Strings
5. Percussion
6. Full orchestra

As you listen to this selection, follow the call chart and find the appropriate instrument groups in the score and in the seating plan. Remember those colors. It will help you find them.

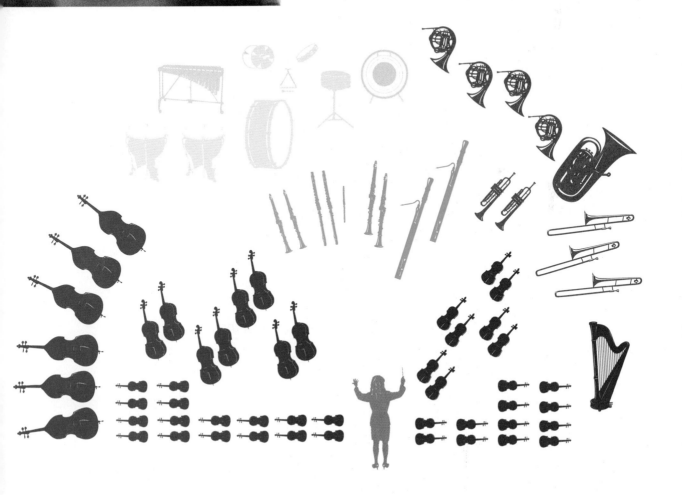

Singing in Parts

Here is part of the choral movement from Beethoven's *Ninth Symphony*. As you listen, try to focus on the voices.

 Symphony No. 9 in D Minor, Movement 4 (excerpt) ....Ludwig van Beethoven

You may have noticed that the chorus and soloists were singing different notes at the same time. In other words, they were singing in *parts*. This is what helped to create such a dramatic effect. Let's try an experiment. Here is a **unison** line from a song that could be sung by a soloist.

Now let's add another vocal part. The song is no longer a **solo**, it's a **duet**.

Add another part and the song becomes a **trio**—an ensemble of three performers.

We've been building up the parts in the song "Laredo." Try singing the song with your class, adding one part at a time.

Laredo

English Words by Margaret Marks   Folk Song from Mexico

1. I'm off for Laredo, farewell, my love, I'm sorry to
2. I've brought you a handsewn saddle, my love, A blanket and
1. *Ya me voy para el Laredo, mi bien, Te vengo a de-*
2. *Toma esa llavita de oro, mi bien, Abre mi pecho*

cause you pain; I promise to send a letter, my love, To
bridle fine; So when you go past the bunkhouse, my love, The
cir adiós, Ya me voy para el Laredo, mi bien, Te
y verás: Toma esa llavita de oro, mi bien, Abre

say when we'll meet again. Don't follow across the prairie, my
cowboys will know you're mine. I've brought you a key of silver, my
vengo a decir adiós. De allá te mando decir, mi
mi pecho y verás: Lo mucho que yo te quiero, mi

love, Don't follow me where I go, But wait till I send a
love, Attached to a golden chain, To lock up your heart for-
bien, Como se mancuernan dos. De allá te mando
bien, Y el mal pago que me das. Lo mucho que yo te

message, my love, Till then I will miss you so.
ever, my love, If never we meet again.
decir, mi bien, Como se mancuernan dos.
quiero, mi bien, Y el mal pago que me das.

The Andrews Sisters

Close Harmony

"Laredo" was arranged in *close harmony*. That just means harmony in which the chord notes are close together, producing a very rich sound. This type of vocal arrangement can be found in many different styles of music.

Listen to these two examples of female trios. The first is sung by The Andrews Sisters, a popular 1940s trio known for their movie appearances and for tirelessly entertaining military units during World War II. The group Wilson Phillips—Carnie, Wendy, and Chynna—represents a more recent style of close-harmony singing.

 Boogie-Woogie Bugle Boy ....Prince/Raye

I Hear You (Reprise) ....Carnie Wilson

Wilson Phillips

Priority Male

The Male Quartet

Men can certainly sing in close harmony, too. Barbershop, gospel, and country are just some of the types of male **quartets** that have been around for a while. A recent trend in pop music is the **a cappella** male quartet. This kind of performance requires excellent musicianship, since the voices must blend perfectly and stand on their own, without any instrumental accompaniment. Listen to one such performance.

 Straight from the Heart.............Priority Male

The Vocal Backups

Listen to this recording by the Mexican American group The Triplets. (Yes, they really are triplet sisters.) How would you describe the vocal arrangement?

Adonde quíera que vas ....The Triplets

The Triplets

Did you notice that the lead singer sometimes sang by herself and at other times was accompanied by the other singers? This type of arrangement makes use of a special element of harmony.

You, the Performer

You can add your own vocal parts behind an existing composition. First listen to this piece. There are only a few ideas repeated again and again.

The Photographer, "A Gentleman's Honor" ....Philip Glass

You probably heard slight variations as the piece went on. The one unchanging element was this eight-measure chord pattern.

Add a vocal backup to the piece by choosing a note from each chord in the progression. Adding words (or syllables) and rhythm will help to make the performance more effective. Try this combination.

do   wah _____   do   wah _____   do   wah _   do   wah _   do   wah _____

Think of some patterns of your own. There are many that will fit.

Meet the Composer

The grandchild of Russian immigrants, Philip Glass (1937-) began his musical "career" at age 12, working in his father's record store. After a period of formal musical training, Glass met the great Indian sitar player Ravi Shankar, who introduced the young composer to the mysterious world of Hindu music. Travels to such exotic places as India, North Africa, and the Himalayas further influenced Glass's music. Upon his return to the United States, he worked with painters and sculptors who wanted to create expressive works using a minimum of materials. Glass,too, used a minimal approach in his music, and the style became known as **minimalism** (a term the composer always disliked). With its mesmerizing use of lengthy repetition, strong rhythms, and frequent amplification, Glass's music resembles many rock styles.

The Photographer is a stage work based on the life and career of the nineteenth-century American photographer Eadweard Muybridge (ED wurd MĪ brij). (See the illustration on page 18.)

$\mathcal{S}$potlight on
Andrew Lloyd Webber

These program covers illustrate just some of the musical theatre sensations written by Andrew Lloyd Webber. On the next few pages, you'll have opportunities to listen to and sing selections from three of this brilliant English composer's shows.

$\mathcal{M}$eet the $\mathcal{C}$omposer

Andrew Lloyd Webber (1948-   ) was fortunate to grow up in a musical family. His father was director of the London College of Music as well as a church organist, and his brother Julian is a concert cellist. Andrew had his first piece of music published when he was only nine. His first hit show was *Joseph and the Amazing Technicolor Dreamcoat*, a popular-style retelling of the biblical story of Joseph. This "pop oratorio" was originally written for school performance and later expanded for the stage. The "rock opera" *Jesus Christ Superstar* soon followed, the first of Lloyd Webber's many successful Broadway shows. Lloyd Webber has the distinction of being the only composer to have three shows running simultaneously in London and on Broadway.

The Perons of Argentina

A poor but beautiful young girl from a small town in Argentina becomes an actress and then the wife of a ruthless general. When the general is elected president of Argentina, his wife becomes the most powerful woman in South America. Blinded by ambition, she does little to help her people; yet she is worshipped as a saint after she suffers an early death.

It's an unlikely story for a musical, but Lloyd Webber based *Evita* on actual events in the life of such a woman—the notorious Eva ("Evita") Peron (peh ROHN). In an early scene, Evita wins the hearts of the people with the song "Don't Cry for Me, Argentina."

Evita, "Don't Cry for Me, Argentina"
....................Andrew Lloyd Webber

Mr. Mistoffelees and Friends

Most of the lyrics in the show *Cats* are taken from a collection of poems by T.S. Eliot called *Old Possom's Book of Practical Cats.* And what great names these cats have— Old Deuteronomy, Jennyanydots, Rum Tum Tugger, Grizabella, Skimpleshanks, Rumpleteazer, Macavity, and others. And what about the mysterious Mr. Mistoffelees? Well, turn the page to find out.

Mr. Mistoffelees *from Cats*

Words by T.S. Eliot   Music by Andrew Lloyd Webber

2.

G   Bm   **4**   *rubato* A

- fe-lees.   And not long a-go — this phe-

A   A₇

nom-en-al cat — pro-duced sev-en kit-tens right out of a hat! —

A *(slower)*   D   A   Em₇   A₇

And we all say: Oh! Well I nev-er, Was — there ev - er a cat so clev-er as

D   G   A₇ *a tempo* D

Mag-i-cal Mis - ter Mis-tof - fe-lees.   Oh! Well I

A   Em₇   A₇   D

nev - er, Was — there ev - er a cat so clev-er as Mag-i-cal Mis -

1.,2.   3.

D   G   A₇   G   Bm

- ter Mis-tof - fe-lees.   - fe-lees.

Speaking for the author, the wise
Old Deuteronomy has the final word
on the subject of cats.

You've read of several kinds of Cat,
And my opinion now is that
You should need no interpreter
To understand their character.
You now have learned enough to see
That cats are much like you and me.

(From The Ad-dressing of Cats *by T.S.Eliot)*

Starlight Express

Imagine—"trains happening through roller skates"! That's how Andrew Lloyd Webber described the idea behind *Starlight Express*, a show that is performed by cast members whizzing around the huge set on roller skates. The plot centers around a competition to find the fastest locomotive in the world, with cast members portraying rival trains from various nations. One of the trains is a conceited, arrogant diesel named Greaseball. The biggest and strongest of all the rigs, Greaseball hasn't the slightest doubt that he will win the big race.

An unlikely rival to Greaseball is Rusty, an outdated, neglected steam engine. Rusty desperately wants to win the competition, but he is intimidated by the other trains and has lost all confidence in himself. Just before the race, he is visited by the mystical title character, Starlight Express. In this song, Starlight reveals an important secret to Rusty.

I Am the Starlight   from *Starlight Express*

Words by Richard Stilgoe   Music by Andrew Lloyd Webber

Starlight
On - ly you ___ have the pow - er ___ with - in ___ you. _

Just be - lieve _ in your-self; The sea will part be-fore you, stop the rain _

_ and turn the tide. _____ If on - ly you ___

use the pow - er ___ with - in ___ you, _ Need-n't beg the world _ to

turn a - round _ and help _ you, ___ if you draw on what you have with - in ___ you

poco rall. Rusty *a tempo*
some-where deep in - side. Star-light Ex - press, _ you must con - fess. _ Are you

real? Yes, or no? Star-light Ex - press, _ please an-swer me "yes." _

Starlight Rus- ty, you're blind. _
I don't want you _ to go. ___ Look in your mind, _ I'm

there; noth-ing's new. The Star-light Ex - press _ is no more nor less _

_ than you, Rus-ty. _ I am you; I'm you and on - ly

you. _____ Have the pow - er _ with-in _ you. _

Rusty
I am the Star - light. _ I can a -

Just be - lieve _ in your-self; The sea will part be-fore you, stop the rain _

chieve an - y - thing; _

and turn the tide. _____ If on - ly you __

All the things I did-n't be - lieve I could do.

__ use the pow-er __ with-in __ you, __

I am the Star-light. _ I can see it __ through. _

Both
__ Need-n't beg the world _ to turn a - round _ and help _ you, __

if you draw on what is deep in - side. _____

As in most fairy tales, there's a happy ending to this story. Greaseball, having fallen victim to his bloated ego, is defeated by the inspired and determined efforts of an old steam engine who finally learned to believe in himself.

Fiddler on the Roof

50 CENTS

Late Edition

"ONE OF THE GREATEST MUSICAL COMEDIES OF OUR ERA!"

"Richness of flavor marks Fiddler. And Tevye is one of the most glowing creations in the history of the musical theatre."

"One of the most unforgettable stage musical creations of modern Broadway history."

Green Violinist   Marc Chagall

Solomon R. Guggenheim Museum, New York, Gift, Solomon R. Guggenheim, 1937. Photo: David Heald
© The Solomon R. Guggenheim Foundation, New York.

Who would have thought that the critics would rave so about a musical dealing with such topics as persecution, poverty, and the loss of family and cultural traditions? But *Fiddler on the Roof* struck a universal chord. From its opening night on September 22, 1964, it went on to become one of the most successful Broadway productions of all time, winning Tony Awards for Best Musical, Best Score and Lyrics, and Best Book.

On the following pages, you'll have the opportunity to learn more about the story and music of *Fiddler on the Roof*. Through singing, listening, and narration, you can become an active participant in this tale filled with humor, sadness, and <u>tradition.</u>

Setting the Stage

The main characters

TEVYE (TEV yuh)
A poor dairyman

GOLDE (GOHL duh)
Tevye's wife

TZEITEL (TZĪT uhl)
HODEL (HUH duhl)
CHAVA (HKHAH vah)
Tevye and Golde's daughters

YENTE (YEN tuh)
The village matchmaker

MOTEL (MUH tuhl)
A tailor

PERCHIK (PUR chik)
A student

LAZAR (LAY zur) **WOLF**
A butcher

The place: Anatevka (ah nuh TEV kuh), a small village in Russia

The time: 1905, on the eve of the Russian revolutionary period

 Overture

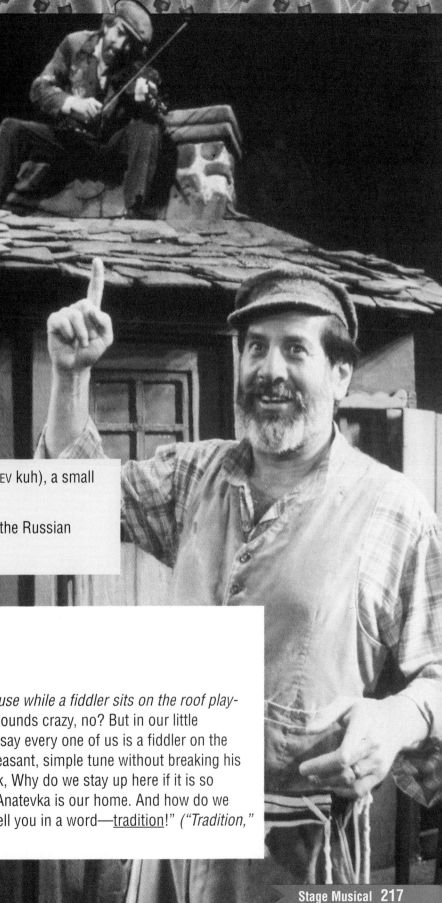

ACT I, PROLOGUE

TEVYE *(standing outside his house while a fiddler sits on the roof playing):* " 'A fiddler on the roof.' Sounds crazy, no? But in our little village of Anatevka, you might say every one of us is a fiddler on the roof, trying to scratch out a pleasant, simple tune without breaking his neck. It isn't easy. You may ask, Why do we stay up here if it is so dangerous? We stay because Anatevka is our home. And how do we keep our balance? That I can tell you in a word—tradition!" *("Tradition," page 218)*

Tradition from *Fiddler on the Roof*

Words by Sheldon Harnick   Music by Jerry Bock

Tevye and Papas

Who, day and night, must scram-ble for a liv - ing, feed a wife and chil - dren,

say his dai - ly prayers? And who has the right, as mas-ter of the house, to

All

have the fi-nal word at home? The pa-pa, _____ the pa-pa.

Tra-di-tion. The pa-pa, _____ the pa-pa. Tra-di-tion.

The daugh-ters, _____ the daugh-ters. Tra-di-tion.

Papas
Who, day and night, must scram-ble for a liv - ing, feed a wife and chil - dren,

Mamas
Who must know the way to make a prop - er home, a

Sons
At three I start - ed He - brew school, at

Daughters
And who does ma - ma teach to

say his dai - ly prayers? And who has the right, as mas - ter of the house, to

qui - et home, a ko - sher home? Who must raise a fam - i - ly and

ten I learned a trade. I hear they picked a

mend and tend and fix, Pre - par - ing me to

have the fi-nal word at home? The pa-pa. _____

run the home, so pa-pa's free to read the Ho-ly Book? The

bride for me, I hope she's pret-ty.

mar - ry who - ev - er pa - pa picks?

_____ Tra - di - tion. The

ma - ma. _____ Tra - di - tion. The

The sons. _____ Tra - di - tion. The

The daugh-ters. ____ Tra - di - tion. The

(All)

pa - pa, _____ the pa - pa.   Tra - di - tion!
ma - ma, _____ the ma - ma.   Tra - di - tion!
sons, _____ the sons. ____   Tra - di - tion!
daugh- ters, _____ the daugh-ters.   Tra - di - tion!

TEVYE: "Tradition—tradition. Without our traditions, our lives would be as shaky as—as a fiddler on the roof!"

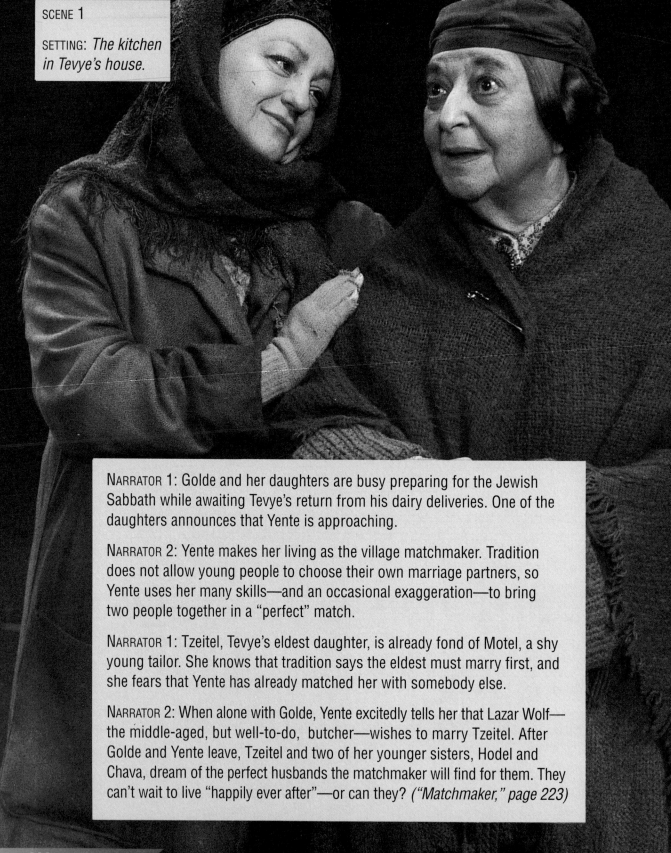

NARRATOR 1: Golde and her daughters are busy preparing for the Jewish Sabbath while awaiting Tevye's return from his dairy deliveries. One of the daughters announces that Yente is approaching.

NARRATOR 2: Yente makes her living as the village matchmaker. Tradition does not allow young people to choose their own marriage partners, so Yente uses her many skills—and an occasional exaggeration—to bring two people together in a "perfect" match.

NARRATOR 1: Tzeitel, Tevye's eldest daughter, is already fond of Motel, a shy young tailor. She knows that tradition says the eldest must marry first, and she fears that Yente has already matched her with somebody else.

NARRATOR 2: When alone with Golde, Yente excitedly tells her that Lazar Wolf—the middle-aged, but well-to-do, butcher—wishes to marry Tzeitel. After Golde and Yente leave, Tzeitel and two of her younger sisters, Hodel and Chava, dream of the perfect husbands the matchmaker will find for them. They can't wait to live "happily ever after"—or can they? *("Matchmaker," page 223)*

Matchmaker
from *Fiddler on the Roof*

Words by Sheldon Harnick   Music by Jerry Bock

(Hodel) Match-mak-er, match-mak-er, make me a match; Find me a find,
(Chava) Match-mak-er, match-mak-er, I'll bring the veil, You bring the groom —
(Both) Match-mak-er, match-mak-er, make me a match; Find me a find,

Last time to Coda

catch me a catch.   Match-mak-er, match-mak-er, look through your book and
slen-der and pale.   Bring me a ring, for I'm long-ing to be the
catch me a catch.   Night af-ter night in the dark I'm a-lone, So

1. | 2.

Hodel

make me a per-fect match.   see.____ For Pa - pa,
en - vy of all I

Chava   Both

make him a schol-ar; For Ma - ma, make him rich as a king; For me,

D.C. al Coda

well, I would-n't hol-ler if he were as hand-some as an - y - thing.

Coda   *poco rit.*   **Very fast**

find me a match of my own.____

(Tzeitel) Ho - del, oh Ho - del, have I made a match for you! He's
(Tzeitel) Cha - va, I found him! Will you be a luck-y bride! He's

hand-some! He's young! All right, he's six - ty two. But he's a nice man, a
hand-some! He's tall! That is, from side to side. But he's a nice man, a

good catch. True? True! I prom-ise you'll be hap-py and e - ven if you're
good catch. Right? Right!

not, There's more to life than that— Don't ask me what!

Tempo I

Chava

Match-mak - er, match-mak - er, you know that I'm

Hodel

still ver - y young. Please, take your time. Up to this min-ute I mis-un-der -

Chava and Hodel

stood that I could get stuck for good. ____ Dear Yen - te,

see that he's gen-tle; Re - mem - ber, you were al - so a bride. It's not

All

that I'm sen - ti - men-tal, It's just that I'm ter - ri - fied! _

Match-mak-er, match-mak-er, plan me no plans; I'm in no

rubato

rush, may-be I've learned: Play-ing with match-es a girl can get burned.

a tempo

Hodel Chava Tzeitel All

So bring me no ring, Groom me no groom, Find me no find, Catch me no catch,

Un-less he's a match-less match!

SCENE 2

SETTING: *Outside Tevye's house.*

NARRATOR 1: Tevye arrives, exhausted, pulling his milk cart. (It seems his horse has lost a shoe.) As he sits alone on the seat, he has one of his frequent conversations with God. This time, in a song filled with dreams and sprinkled with humor, Tevye asks why the Almighty didn't decide to make him rich, rather than poor. *("If I Were a Rich Man," page 227)*

If I Were a Rich Man
from *Fiddler on the Roof*

Words by Sheldon Harnick   *Music by Jerry Bock*

SCENE 3

SETTING: *Inside Tevye's house.*

NARRATOR 1: It is sundown, Friday, and preparations for the Sabbath are complete. Observing the tradition of generations past, Tevye and his family gather to light the Sabbath candles. As the small group repeats the ancient blessings and prayers, the scene gradually opens up to include the entire community. All join together in expressing the hopes and the desires of countless generations, past and future.

 Sabbath Prayer

SCENE 4

SETTING: *The village inn.*

NARRATOR 2: Golde, believing that Lazar Wolf is a good match for Tzeitel, has convinced Tevye to meet him at the inn. Tevye mistakenly believes that Lazar wants to discuss buying Tevye's new cow, while Lazar's plan is to ask for Tzeitel's hand in marriage. A mixed-up conversation ensues until, finally, the confusion is cleared. Tevye agrees to the marriage, and both men propose a toast: "To our agreement! To our prosperity! To good health and happiness! And, most important, to life!" *("To Life," page 230)*

To Life from *Fiddler on the Roof*

Words by Sheldon Harnick   Music by Jerry Bock

To life, to life, L'-chai-im! L'-chai-im, L'-
life, to life, L'-chai-im! (All) L'-chai-im, L'-

chai-im, to life! Here's to the fa-ther I've tried to be. Here's to my
chai-im, to life! May all your fu-tures be pleas-ant ones, Not like our

bride to be. Drink, L'-chai-im, To life, to life. L'-chai-im!
pres-ent ones. Drink, L'-chai-im, To life, to life, L'-chai-im!

L'-chai-im, L'-chai-im, to life! Life has a way of con-
L'-chai-im, L'-chai-im, to life! It takes a wed-ding to

fus-ing us, Bless-ing and bruis-ing us. Drink, L'-chai-im, to life! ____
make us say: "Let's live an-oth-er day." Drink, L'-chai-im, to life!

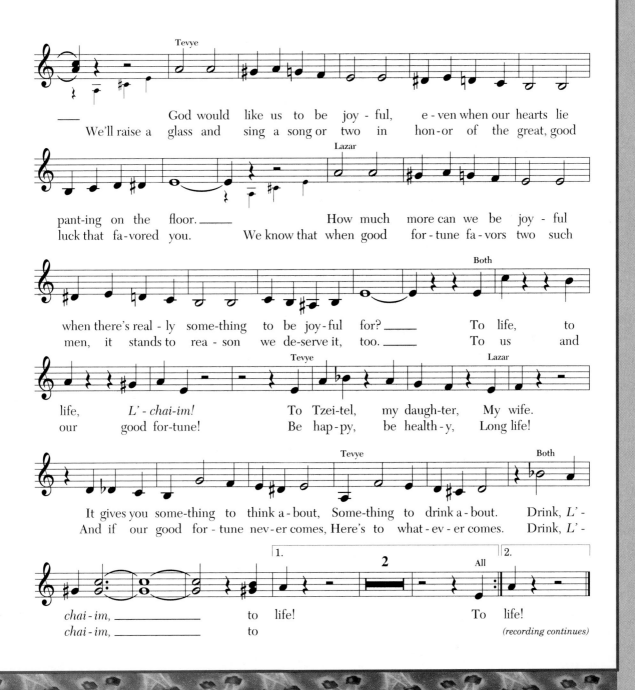

NARRATOR 1: Tevye's jubilant mood changes abruptly with the appearance of the village constable. The constable forewarns his friend Tevye that the authorities, in a demonstration of brutal persecution, have orders to damage the homes and property of all Jews in the district. But just when this will happen, he cannot say.

SCENE 5

SETTING: *Outside Tevye's house.*

NARRATOR 2: The following day, Tevye informs Tzeitel of her "arranged" marriage to Lazar Wolf. As she pleads with her father not to insist on the match, they are interrupted by the breathless entry of Motel.

NARRATOR 1: Together, the young couple confess their secret pledge to one another to marry. Tevye is at first shocked at this blatant disregard for tradition. But, impressed by Motel's uncharacteristic show of courage and the depth of Tzeitel's feelings, he eventually gives his consent. The ecstatic couple agree—this is a miracle!

 Miracle of Miracles

SCENE 6

SETTING: *Tevye and Golde's bedroom.*

NARRATOR 1: Now Tevye faces another dilemma: He must convince Golde that Tzeitel should marry Motel instead of Lazar. This time, his conversation with God is brief: "Help!"

NARRATOR 2: It is the middle of the night when Tevye puts his scheme into motion. Pretending to have awakened from a nightmare, he describes to Golde how the ghosts of Grandma Tzeitel and Lazar's first wife, Fruma Sarah, have appeared to him in a terrifying spectacle. It seems the two women have some news—and a warning!

Tevye's Dream

NARRATOR 1: Grateful that his elaborate effort was success-ful, Tevye silently mouths his next short conversation with God—"Thank you"—and peacefully falls asleep.

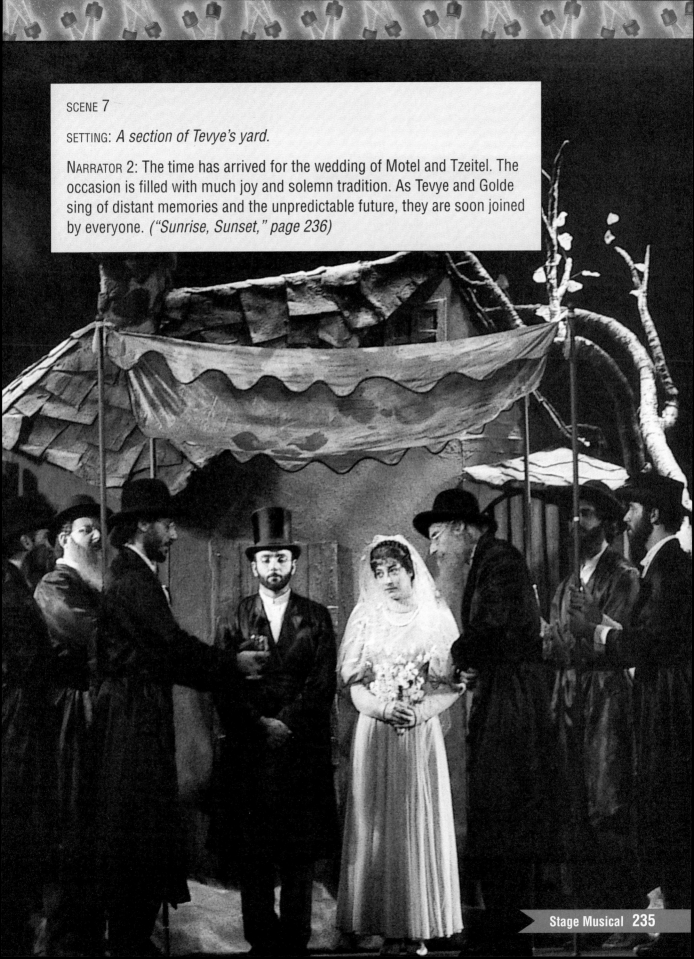

SCENE 7

SETTING: *A section of Tevye's yard.*

NARRATOR 2: The time has arrived for the wedding of Motel and Tzeitel. The occasion is filled with much joy and solemn tradition. As Tevye and Golde sing of distant memories and the unpredictable future, they are soon joined by everyone. *("Sunrise, Sunset," page 236)*

Sunrise, Sunset
from *Fiddler on the Roof*

Words by Sheldon Harnick   Music by Jerry Bock

Is this the lit-tle girl I car-ried? Is this the lit-tle boy at
When did she get to be a beau-ty? When did he grow to be so

play? I don't re-mem-ber grow-ing old-er. When did they?
tall? Was-n't it yes-ter-day when they

were small?

Boys Sun-rise, sun-set,
Girls Sun-rise, sun-set,

Sun-rise, sun-set, Swift-ly flow the days.
Sun-rise, sun-set, Swift-ly fly the years.

Seed-lings turn o-ver-night to sun-flow'rs, Blos-som-ing e-ven as we gaze.
One sea-son fol-low-ing an-oth-er, La-den with

2.
hap-pi-ness and tears. ___

Golde What words of wis-dom can I
Perchik They look so nat-u-ral to-

give them? How can I help to ease their way? Now they must
geth - er, Hodel Just like two new-ly-weds should be. Both Is there a

1.
learn from one an - oth - er, Day by day. ___
can - o - py in store

2.
rall. *a tempo* All
for me? _____ Sun - rise, ___ sun-set, Sun - rise, ___

___ sun - set, Swift - ly ___ fly the years. ___ One sea - son

rall.
fol-low-ing an - oth - er, La - den with hap-pi-ness and tears. ___

NARRATOR 1: With the traditional breaking of the drinking glass and a shout of "Mazeltov!" the formal part of the wedding ceremony is over. The celebration continues with festive music and dancing.

Wedding Dance

NARRATOR 2: At the height of the celebration, the constable and his men arrive to carry out the threatened pogrom. They overturn tables, smash dishes, and destroy wedding gifts. As Act One comes to an end, a stunned Tevye looks to God for an explanation.

Entr'acte

ACT II, PROLOGUE

TEVYE (*gesturing toward heaven*): "That was quite a dowry you gave my daughter Tzeitel at her wedding. Was that necessary?

Anyway, Tzeitel and Motel have been married almost two months now. They work very hard, they are as poor as squirrels in winter. But they are both so happy they don't know how miserable they are. Motel keeps talking about a sewing machine. I know you're very busy—wars and revolutions, floods, plagues, all those little things that bring people to you—couldn't you take a second away from your catastrophes and get it for him? How much trouble would it be? Oh, and while you're in the neighborhood, my horse's left leg—Am I bothering you too much? I'm sorry. As the Good Book says—Why should I tell you what the Good Book says?"

NARRATOR 1: Earlier in the story, Tevye had met Perchik, a poor student from Kiev with determined ideas of his own. Perchik agreed to teach Tevye's daughters in return for his keep.

SCENE 1

SETTING: *Outside Tevye's house.*

NARRATOR 2: As Act Two opens, news has reached Anatevka about the troubles that are spreading through Russia. Perchik decides to join the revolutionaries in their struggle against the czar. Before he leaves, he asks Hodel, Tevye's second daughter, to marry him. Her consent inspires Perchik to sing of his elation and love.

 *Now I Have Everything*

NARRATOR 1: Tevye is once again faced with a threat to tradition. And once again he is unable to resist a daughter's pleas. As he reluctantly gives Perchik and Hodel his blessing, he considers the fact that his daughters have married for love rather than by arrangement. This leads him to ponder his own marriage, and he approaches Golde with a very important question.

Do You Love Me?

SCENE 2

SETTING: *Outside the railroad station.*

NARRATOR 1: The village hears that Perchik has been arrested and sent to a settlement in Siberia. Hodel immediately decides to join him and marry him there. In her farewell to her father, she tries to explain why she must leave the home and family she so dearly loves.

 Far From the Home I Love

NARRATOR 2: Tearfully, Tevye bids his daughter farewell, knowing they may never see each other again. He asks God to take care of her.

NARRATOR 2: When Tevye learns that his third daughter, Chava, has secretly been married to a Russian by a priest, he finds that he can bend the laws of tradition no more. Heartbroken, he severs all communication with her and denies her existence.

SCENE 3

SETTING: *Outside Tevye's house.*

NARRATOR 1: Tevye's family and the world he has struggled so hard to build are about to experience the hardest blow of all.

NARRATOR 2: Even little Anatevka cannot escape the political turmoil that is sweeping the land. An edict decrees that all Jewish families must evacuate their homes and leave Russia within three days. As they gather their few belongings, the villagers reminisce about their lives together and mourn for their small, sad village.

 Anatevka

NARRATOR 1: Tevye, Golde, and their two remaining daughters have finished packing. They spend one last moment bidding a final farewell to their friends and neighbors. Slowly, Tevye begins to pull the loaded wagon—the first steps in the long journey to a new life in America. Hearing the familiar theme of the fiddler, Tevye turns and motions for him to join the family as the curtain closes on *Fiddler on the Roof.*

Sweet Land of Liberty

One early version of this American patriotic hymn began with the phrase *God save the Thirteen States*. Then, in 1832, Samuel Smith set down the words that have become a permanent part of our collective identity. Why, do you think, has this song remained so popular for over 160 years?

The Declaration of Independence   *John Trumbull*

Yale University Art Gallery

America

Words by Samuel Francis Smith   Traditional Melody

1. My coun-try! 'tis of thee, Sweet land of
2. My na-tive coun-try, thee, Land of the
3. Let mu-sic swell the breeze, And ring from
4. Our fa-ther's God, to thee, Au-thor of

lib-er-ty, Of thee I sing; Land where my
no-ble free, Thy name I love; I love thy
all the trees, Sweet free-dom's song; Let mor-tal
lib-er-ty, To thee we sing; Long may our

fa-thers died, Land of the Pil-grims' pride,
rocks and rills, Thy woods and tem-pled hills,
tongues a-wake, Let all that breathe par-take,
land be bright with free-dom's ho-ly light,

From ev-'ry mountain-side, Let free-dom ring!
My heart with rap-ture thrills Like that a-bove.
Let rocks their si-lence break, The sound pro-long.
Pro-tect us by thy might, Great God, our King!

National Anthem

The year is 1814 and America has been at war with Great Britain for more than two years. The British forces have attacked Washington, D.C., and have burned the Capitol, the President's House, and most of the other public buildings. During the raid, a friend of an American lawyer named Francis Scott Key has been captured and held aboard a British warship near Baltimore. Key and an American agent are allowed to board the ship to secure the friend's release.

During the negotiations, the British fleet launches an attack on Baltimore at Fort McHenry. Key and the two other Americans are told that they will not be allowed to depart until after the battle. In a proud display of patriotism, a special flag is flown by the defiant Americans at the nearly defenseless fort.

The bombardment rages on through the night. When dawn finally arrives, Key anxiously looks toward Baltimore. The American flag is still flying over the fort! Deeply moved, he pulls an envelope from his pocket and begins writing the words *Oh, say! can you see . . .*

The Star-Spangled Banner

Words by Francis Scott Key   Music by John Stafford Smith

1. Oh, __ say! can you see, by the dawn's ear - ly light,
2. On the shore, dim - ly seen through the mists of the deep,
3. Oh, __ thus be it ev - er when __ free men shall stand

What so proud - ly we hailed at the twi - light's last gleam - ing,
Where the foe's haught-y host in dread si - lence re - pos - es,
Be - tween their loved homes and the war's des - o - la - tion!

Whose broad stripes and bright stars, through the per - il - ous fight,
What is that which the breeze, o'er the tow - er - ing steep,
Blest with vict - 'ry and peace, may the heav'n - res - cued land

O'er the ram - parts we watched were so gal - lant - ly stream - ing?
As it fit - ful - ly blows, half con - ceals, half dis - clos - es?
Praise the Pow'r that hath made and pre - served us a na - tion!

The Bombardment of Fort McHenry, Baltimore, on 13-14 September 1814   *John Bowen*

And the rock-ets' red glare, the bombs burst-ing in air,
Now it catch-es the gleam of the morn-ing's first beam,
Then con-quer we must, for our cause it is just,

Gave proof through the night that our flag was still there.
In full glo-ry re-flect-ed now shines on the stream;
And this be our mot-to "In God is our trust!"

Oh, say, does that Star-Span-gled Ban-ner yet wave
'Tis the Star-Span-gled Ban-ner, oh, long may it wave
And the Star-Span-gled Ban-ner in tri-umph shall wave

O'er the land of the free and the home of the brave!

The "broad stripes and bright stars" of our nation's flag have inspired many works of art. (You saw one example on page 76.) The unusual depiction below is made up entirely of television monitors and measures over 6 feet by 11 feet. The accompanying poem, by a high school student, describes the writer's reaction to this dramatic art work.

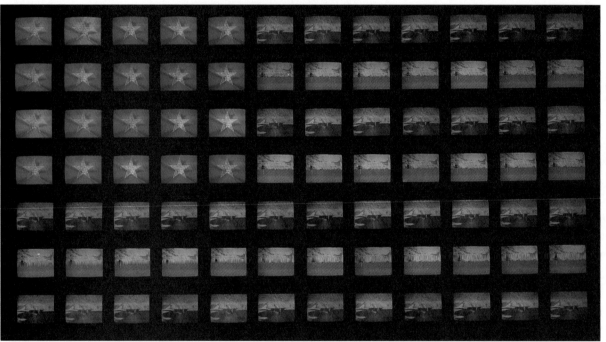

Video Flag x   *Nam June Paik*

Video Flag

A screen with many colors
all blending together with each other.
You can look close and see stars
shining bright
like the lasting glow of stars on an endless night.
This time flags are coming together

not in a war game
but to share pride and learn
each other's name—all in the
video flag.

Melchishaua Person

A Song of Pride

Fourth of July Night

The little boat at anchor
in black water sat murmuring
to the tall black sky.

A white sky bomb fizzed on a black line.
A rocket hissed its red signature into
   the west.
Now a shower of Chinese fire alphabets,
a cry of flower pots broken in flames,
a long curve to a purple spray,
three violet balloons —

Drips of seaweed tangled in gold,
shimmering symbols of mixed
   numbers,
tremulous arrangements of cream
   gold folds
of a bride's wedding gown —

A few sky bombs spoke their pieces,
then velvet dark.

The little boat at anchor
in black water sat murmuring
to the tall black sky.

Carl Sandburg

Gift of Elizabeth R. Vaughan, © The Art Institute of Chicago

Picnic Scene   *Susan Merritt*

An important ingredient in our nation's patriotic songs is the pride
of the American people in their country. This feeling is expressed in
"I Like It Here," on page 252.

I Like It Here

Words and Music by Clay Boland

I like the U - nit - ed States of A - mer - i - ca, _____
I am so luck - y to be in A - mer - i - ca, _____

I like the way we all live with - out fear; _____
And I am thank - ful each day of the year, _____

I like to vote for my choice, _ speak my mind, raise my voice,
For I can do as I please, _ 'cause I'm free as the breeze,

1.
Yes, I like it here. _____

2.
like it here. _____

I'd like to climb to the top of a moun - tain so high, ___

Lift my head to the sky ___ and say how grate - ful am I _____

For the way that I'm liv - ing, I'm work - ing and giv - ing

And help - ing the land I hold dear, _____ Yes,

I like it, I like it, I like it here. _____

Right Freedom

For Right and Freedom

"The Marines' Hymn" is the official song of the United States Marine Corps. Can you name the song of another branch of the military?

The Marines' Hymn

Traditional

From the halls of Mon-te-zu - ma To the shores of Trip-o - li; ___

___ We _ fight our coun-try's bat - tles In the air, on land, and sea. __

___ First to fight for right and free - dom And to keep our hon-or clean, _

___ We are proud to claim the ti - tle of U - nit-ed States Ma - rine. ___

Courtesy of the United States Marine Corps

Visitors at the Vietnam Veterans Memorial, Washington, D.C.

A State Song

Our people's sense of pride extends not only to our country but to our states and communities as well. Every state has something that its citizens can be proud of, whether it is bountiful crops, beautiful scenery, vital industrial centers, an important role in past historical events, or a particularly rich cultural tradition. Name some important features of <u>your</u> state.

Many states have their own official songs. "Texas, Our Texas" is one example. Does your state have its own song? If so, sing it with pride!

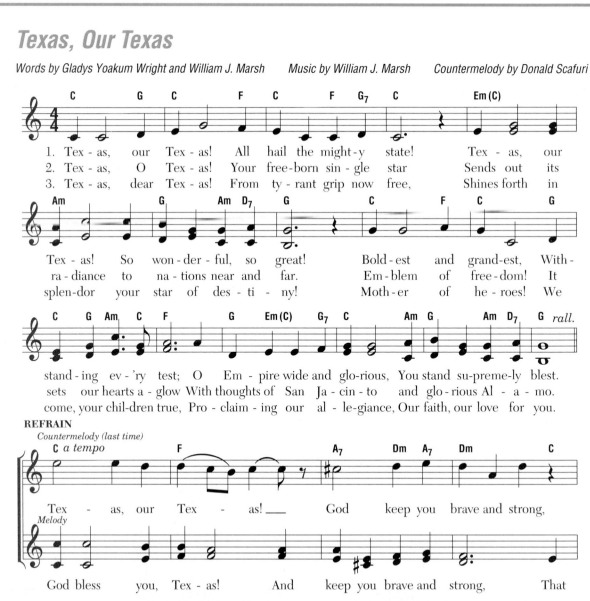

Texas, Our Texas

Words by Gladys Yoakum Wright and William J. Marsh   Music by William J. Marsh   Countermelody by Donald Scafuri

1. Tex - as, our Tex - as! All hail the might - y state! Tex - as, our
2. Tex - as, O Tex - as! Your free-born sin - gle star Sends out its
3. Tex - as, dear Tex - as! From ty - rant grip now free, Shines forth in

Tex - as! So won - der - ful, so great! Bold - est and grand - est, With -
ra - diance to na - tions near and far. Em - blem of free - dom! It
splen - dor your star of des - ti - ny! Moth - er of he - roes! We

stand - ing ev - 'ry test; O Em - pire wide and glo - ri - ous, You stand su - preme - ly blest.
sets our hearts a - glow With thoughts of San Ja - cin - to and glo - ri - ous Al - a - mo.
come, your chil - dren true, Pro - claim - ing our al - le - giance, Our faith, our love for you.

REFRAIN
Countermelody (last time)

Tex - as, our Tex - as! ___ God keep you brave and strong,

Melody

God bless you, Tex - as! And keep you brave and strong, That

The Alamo,
San Antonio, Texas

Grow in pow'r and worth, Through-out the a-ges long. God bless you,

you may grow in pow'r and worth, Through-out the a-ges long.

Tex - as, our Tex - as! God keep you brave and strong,

God bless you, Tex - as! And keep you brave and strong, That

rall. (last time)

Grow in pow'r and worth, Through-out the a-ges long.

you may grow in pow'r and worth, Through-out the a-ges long.

Songs of Freedom

Throughout history, from biblical days to the twentieth-century civil rights movement, the love of freedom has been expressed best by those who have been deprived of this sacred right. In music, the desire for physical and spiritual freedom is often expressed through imagery in the lyrics, as in the spiritual "Yonder Come Day."

Which phrases in the lyrics symbolize a longing for freedom?

Yonder Come Day

Spiritual from the Georgia Sea Islands   *Additional Words and Arrangement by Judith Cook Tucker*

(Begin with step-clap for two measures)

This map shows the Georgia Sea Islands, the area where "Yonder Come Day" originated. The islands were among the last strongholds of slavery on the American East Coast. The slaves lived on the islands and boated to the "big houses" on the mainland to work.

Hold On
to the
Dream

A Ride for Liberty—The Fugitive Slaves   *Eastman Johnson*

The Brooklyn Museum

During the struggle for African Americans' civil rights, many people were imprisoned unfairly and without justification. It must have been hard for these people to keep their "eyes on the prize." How do you think songs such as the following helped the prisoners to "hold on" in their ride for liberty?

Keep Your Eyes on the Prize

African American Freedom Song

Guitar: capo 3   Am

1. Paul and Si - las, bound in jail, ____ had no
2. Paul and Si - las be - gan to shout, ___ the jail door
3. We fought jail and vio - lence, too, ____ but God's
4. The on - ly chain that a man can stand ___ is the

Am   E₇   Am

mon - ey _____ to go their bail, _
o - pened _ and they walked on out, _
love _ has _ seen us through, _
chain _ of a hand in hand, _   Keep your eyes on _ the prize, _

REFRAIN
Part 1

Am   Dm₇   Am   G   Am   Am₇

_ Hold _ on, hold on. Hold _____

Em

Part 2

on, _ (Hold _ on,) _ Hold _ on, _ (Hold _ on,) _ Keep your _

Am   E₇   Am   G   Am

eyes on _ the prize, _____ Hold _ on, hold on.

Even while imprisoned for his commitment to human rights and equality,
Martin Luther King, Jr. was an inspiration to people of all races and creeds.
This song is a contemporary tribute to the man and his vision.

Dr. Martin Luther King

Words and Music by Joan Hillsman

1. Doc - tor Mar - tin Luth - er King was a pow - er - ful man,
marched for e - qual - i - ty and civ - il rights;
dream lives on in the hearts of all

he was a man with a mas - ter plan. He spoke out for peace and
he fought for jus - tice for hu - man - kind. He gave up his life for
and the dream will nev - er die. We'll keep march - ing on for

har - mo - ny, he want - ed free - dom for ev - 'ry - one;
lib - er - ty, and died for free - dom for ev - 'ry - one;
u - ni - ty, and strive for free - dom for ev - 'ry - one;

REFRAIN

Free - dom for ev - 'ry - one. Free - dom,

free - dom, free - dom for ev - 'ry - one. Free - dom,

(rit. last time)

free - dom, free - dom for ev - 'ry - one;

1,2. | 3. *rit.*

Free - dom for ev - 'ry - one. 2. He Free - dom for ev - 'ry - one.
3. His

Martin Luther King Jr.

A man went forth with gifts.

He was a prose poem.
He was a tragic grace.
He was a warm music.

He tried to heal the vivid volcanoes.
His ashes are
    reading the world.

His Dream still wishes to anoint
    the barricades of faith and of control.

His word still burns the center of the sun,
    above the thousands and the
        hundred thousands.

The word was Justice. It was spoken.

So it shall be spoken.
So it shall be done.

Gwendolyn Brooks

Much of the music of the civil rights movement
was drawn from the black gospel tradition and
performed in the style of congregational singing.
As you listen to the following example, notice the
use of call and response. This historic "field"
recording was made in 1963, the same year
Dr. King delivered his inspirational "I Have a
Dream" speech.

*Woke Up This Morning with My Mind
on Freedom* ....Traditional

The Sights and Sounds of Freedom

The composer of this song, a member of the folk trio Peter, Paul, and Mary, imagines what life would be like without the freedom to enjoy his favorite sights and sounds. What do you cherish most about freedom?

Don't Ever Take Away My Freedom

Words and Music by Peter Yarrow   *Arranged by Donald Scafuri*

Three hors-es graz-ing out_ my win-dow, _____ Brown, black_ and

white they stand. _____ Roll-ing pas-tures they can wan-der, _____

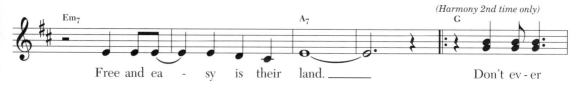

Free and ea - sy is their land. _____ Don't ev - er

take a-way my free-dom, _____ Don't ev - er take it a-

way. _____ Let me cher-ish_ and keep that one part of my life, _____

And the rest ___ I'm gon-na find one of these days, _____ One _ of these days.

Is that the sound of rain - drops _ I hear fall - ing? ____

How ___ I love, _____ I love to hear that sound. _____ It makes me think of all the peo-ple _ that I love, _____ and all the qui-et _ winds I've found. _____ ___ There is a time ___ for _ the sing-ing _ and the sun - shine, _____ There is a time ___ for _ the thun-der _ and the rain, _____ There is a time ___ for _ the chang - ing of

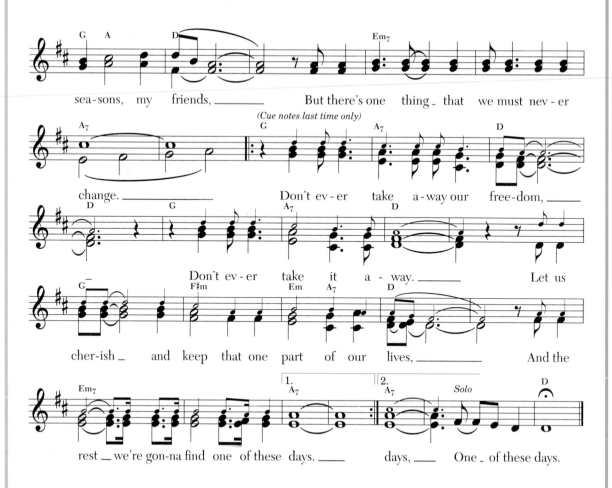

sea-sons, my friends, _____ But there's one thing _ that we must nev - er

(Cue notes last time only)

change. _____ Don't ev - er take a-way our free-dom, _____

Don't ev - er take it a - way. _____ Let us

cher-ish _ and keep that one part of our lives, _____ And the

rest _ we're gon-na find one of these days. ____ days, ___ One _ of these days.

Spread Your Wings and Fly

The Broadway musical *Big River* is based on Mark Twain's novel *Adventures of Huckleberry Finn*, set in the 1840s. Huck and the runaway slave Jim face many challenges and share many adventures as they travel down the Mississippi River from Hannibal, Missouri, to Hillsboro, Arkansas.

Jim, having suffered the cruel indignities of slavery, dreams of the day when he will truly be free. He expresses these feelings in this poignant song that recalls the traditional spiritual of the same name.

 Big River, "Free at Last"
......................Roger Miller

What imagery is used in the song to describe Jim's longing for freedom?

Jim and Huck Finn
in *Big River*

In this excerpt from Twain's book, Huck describes Jim's treatment at the hands of the runaway slave's captors.

> They cussed Jim considerable, though, and gave him a cuff or two side the head once in a while, but Jim never said nothing . . . and they took him to the same cabin, and put his own clothes on him, and chained him again, and not to no bed leg this time, but to a big staple drove into the bottom log, and chained his hands, too, and both legs, and said he warn't to have nothing but bread and water to eat after this till his owner come, or he was sold at auction . . . and said a couple farmers with guns must stand watch around about the cabin every night, and a bulldog tied to the door in the daytime . . .

(From Adventures of Huckleberry Finn *by Mark Twain)*

Thanksgiving with a *Beat*

Although Thanksgiving is observed as an official holiday only in the United States and Canada, the sentiment behind the occasion crosses many political and cultural boundaries. "Thanksgiving Calypso" celebrates this international spirit of the holiday.

Thanksgiving Calypso

Words and Music by David Eddleman

1. Once a year we set a-side a day for cel-e-brat-ing in a
2. Say a thank-you for the air we breathe, the rain-y days a-mak-ing

spe-cial way, To count our bless-ings, count 'em by the score: the
shin-y leaves; The sun a-beam-ing on the gar-den wall is say-ing,

things we have to be thank-ful for. Let's sing a song of grat-i-
"Hap-py Thanks-giv-ing" to one and all. Let's sing a song of grat-i-

tude, Let's sing a song of hap-py days; We'll sing a thank-you song to

you, We'll sing a song of joy and praise.

2. *Chorus*

Say, "Thank you" for the fields of grain, Say, "Thank you" for the fall - ing rain,

Say, "Thank you" for the chance to live in peace and har - mo - ny. ___

Solo

For - ests grow - ing on the moun - tain - side, ___ might - y hills ___ that near - ly touch the sky, ___

Chorus

Say, "Thank you" for the fields of grain, Say, "Thank you" for the fall - ing rain,

Flow - ing riv - ers with their wa - ters blue, ___ for our home and coun - try we are

Say, "Thank you" for the chance to live in peace and har - mo - ny. ___

thank - ful, too. — Let's sing a song of grat - i - tude, Let's sing a

Unison

song of hap - py days; We'll sing a thank-you song to you, We'll sing a

song of joy and praise! _____

div.

How is the idea of different people joining together represented musically in "Thanksgiving Calypso"?

The Festival of Lights

The origins of Chanukah (also called the festival of lights) go back over 2,000 years in history. People of the Jewish faith celebrate this holiday for eight days during the month of December.

Look for references to the familiar symbols of the holiday in "Here We Come A-Singing," on page 272. What rhythmic element helps to give this song its energy?

Here We Come A-Singing

Words and Music by David Eddleman

Here we come a-sing-ing the fes-ti-val of lights, sing-ing of a lamp that
Hap-py times are here for the peo-ple ev'-ry-where; laugh-ing voi-ces sing-ing

1.

burned eight nights;
here and there; Spin the drey-dl, light the me-nor-ah, sing of the he-ro's fight.

2.

gifts from the ones who care. Cel-e-brate the vic-to-ry time, __ cel-e-brate with

sing-ing and rhyme; Cel-e-brate the sto-ry they told __ of the eight-day

sub. mf

mir-a-cle of old. _____ Fes-ti-val of sing-ing and fes-ti-val of joy,

cheer-ing ev-'ry hap-py girl and boy; Spin the drey-dl,

2

light the me-nor-ah, time that we all en-joy.

A Poet's Song

For centuries, the image of a shepherd guarding his flock has been a popular source of inspiration for artists, poets, and composers. The song on page 276 uses this setting in describing the first Christmas.

The Good Shepherd   *Henry Ossawa Tanner*

Hampton University Museum

Henry Ossawa (AHS uh wuh) Tanner was born in Pittsburgh, Pennsylvania, the son of a bishop in the African Methodist Episcopal Church. As a young man, Tanner studied in Philadelphia under the famous artist Thomas Eakins. He first gained recognition for his depictions of black life on the Southern plantations.

In 1891, Tanner moved to Europe and eventually settled in Paris. Reflecting his religious upbringing, he began to paint pictures with biblical themes. *The Good Shepherd*, on page 275, is one of his many paintings on this subject. The devastating events of World War I horrified Tanner. But they only served to deepen the artist's concern for human suffering and injustice—themes that found expression in many of his later paintings.

Meet the Artist

Henry Ossawa Tanner   (1859-1937)

Self Portrait   *H. O. Tanner*

Photo M. Baldwin

So My Sheep May Safely Graze

Words and Music by Rod McKuen

Guitar: capo 5

1. So my sheep may safe-ly graze _ I'd climb the high-est hill, _ And
2. All good shep-herds watch their flocks _ to the low-est lamb _
3. Last night there were sol-diers on _ the road _ be-low the town _ And

keep a watch _ out for the hawk _ and for the howl-ing wolf. _ I
So that they _ may safe-ly graze _ and nev-er come to harm. _
crea-tures _ in the heav-ens with _ wings _ of shin-y gold. _

made a friend out of the wind _ and got to know the snow. So
Guard-ed from the hunt-er's horn, _ shield-ed from the sun.
One of them came close to me, _ say-ing, "Do not be a-fraid. A

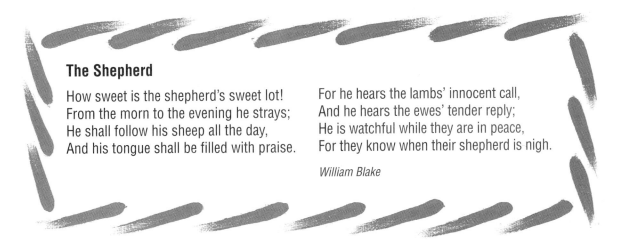

The Shepherd

How sweet is the shepherd's sweet lot!
From the morn to the evening he strays;
He shall follow his sheep all the day,
And his tongue shall be filled with praise.

For he hears the lambs' innocent call,
And he hears the ewes' tender reply;
He is watchful while they are in peace,
For they know when their shepherd is nigh.

William Blake

A Holiday Greeting

Feliz Navidad

Try adding the instrumental parts on page 279 to this lively holiday song.

Christmas celebration in San Juan, Puerto Rico

Merry Christmas

Feliz Navidad

Words and Music by José Feliciano

Fe-liz Na-vi-dad, Fe-liz Na-vi-dad, Fe-liz Na-vi-dad, Prós-pe-ro a-ño y fe-li-ci-dad. ___

I want to wish you a Mer-ry Christ-mas, ___ I want to wish you a Mer-ry Christ-mas, ___ I want to wish you a Mer-ry Christ-mas from the bot-tom of my heart. ___ a-ño y fe-li-ci-dad. ___

Fröhliche Weihnachten

Maracas

Claves

Woodblock

Bongos

Cowbell or
Guiro

Here is the chord progression for "Feliz Navidad," written in a simple rhythm for keyboard. Experiment with playing the progression in different rhythms along with the recording of the song.

Keyboard

READING

Have you ever wanted to learn to play
the guitar or a keyboard instrument? Now's
your chance. How about getting a group together to
perform for your friends? This section of your book
will help you get started. You'll also have the
opportunity to learn a variety of songs
from around the world.

The key to experiencing these
activities is knowing how to read music notation, and
learning it is easier than you think.

Before long, you'll find that understanding
the written language of music will open up new
worlds for you to explore.

section

3

Choral *Sight Singing*

Sing a Spiritual

Look at the chorus response at the ends of lines 1 through 3 in "He's Got the Whole World in His Hands." You'll notice that this response is arranged in two-part harmony. More specifically, the harmony is in intervals of a third. (See page 57.)

The exercises below will help prepare you to sing this arrangement of the song. Use syllables such as *ah* or *oo*.

F   G   A   A   B♭   C
             F   A

G   A   B♭   B♭   C   D
             G   B♭

He's Got the Whole World in His Hands

African American Spiritual

1. He's got the whole world __ in his hands,
2. He's got the wind and rain __ in his hands,
3. He's got - a you and me broth - er in his hands, __

He's got the whole world __ in his hands,
He's got the wind and rain __ in his hands,
He's got - a you and me sis - ter in his hands, __

He's got the whole world __ in his hands, __
He's got the wind and rain __ in his hands, __
He's got - a you and me broth - er in his hands, __

He's got the whole world in his hands. _____
He's got the whole world in his hands. _____
He's got the whole world in his hands. _____

On the following pages you'll find two versions of a ballad about a servant girl named Emily, better known as the "yellow rose" of Texas. The first version is in the key of A♭. Here is the A♭ chord, which uses notes 1, 3, and 5 of the scale.

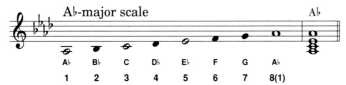

The following excerpts, from the melody of "The Yellow Rose of Texas," outline the A♭ chord. Can you find the excerpts in the song?

Now look at the harmony in the song. What interval is used, other than the third?

The interval of a sixth is just a third "turned upside down." You can do this by taking the lower note of a third and *raising* it an octave or by taking the upper note of a third and *lowering* it an octave.

Practice the following sixths before you sing "The Yellow Rose of Texas."

The Yellow Rose of Texas

Traditional

1. There's a yel - low rose in Tex - as that I am goin' to see.
2. Oh, I'm go - in' back to find her, my heart is full of woe.

No oth - er fel - low knows her; no - bod - y else but me.
We'll sing the songs to - geth - er we sang so long a - go.

She cried so when I left her, it al - most broke my heart,
I'll pick the ban - jo gai - ly and sing the songs of yore.

And if I ev - er find __ her, we nev - er more shall part.
The Yel - low Rose of Tex - as, she'll be mine for - ev - er - more.

REFRAIN

She's the sweet - est lit - tle rose - bud that Tex - as ev - er knew.

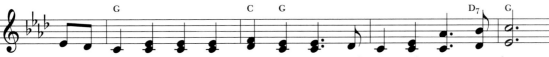

Her eyes are bright as dia - monds, they spar - kle like the dew.

You may talk a - bout your Clem - en - tine and sing of Ros - a - lee,

But the Yel - low Rose of Tex - as is the on - ly girl for me.

There's a Yellow Rose in Texas

Traditional   Arranged by David W. Guion

1. There's a yel-low rose in Tex - as I'm go - in' there to see.
2. Where the Ri - o Grande is flow - ing and the stars are shin - ing bright,
3. O, I'm go - in' back to see her, my heart is full of woe.

No oth - er cow - boy knows her; no - bod - y, on - ly me.
We walked a - long to - geth - er on a qui - et sum - mer night.
We'll sing the songs to - geth - er we sang so long a - go.

She cried so when I left her, it liked to broke her heart,
She said, "If you re - mem - ber, we part - ed long a - go.
I'll pick the ban - jo gai - ly and sing the songs of yore,

And if we ev - er meet a - gain, we nev - er - more shall part.
You prom - ised to come back a - gain and nev - er leave me so."
And the Yel - low Rose of Tex - as will be mine for - ev - er - more.

REFRAIN

(melody)

She's the sweet - est rose of col - or this cow - boy ev - er knew.

Her eyes are bright as dia - monds, They spar - kle like the dew.

You may talk a - bout your dear - est maids and sing of Ro - sy Lee,

But the Yel - low Rose of Tex - as beats the belles of Ten - nes - see.

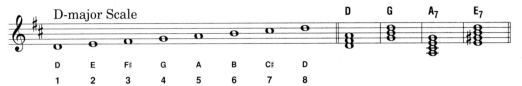

This second version of the song is in the key of D. Both the melody and harmony of "There's a Yellow Rose in Texas" make use of the notes from the
D-major scale and the chords shown below.

As you can see, the verses of the song are arranged in unison. How does
the harmony in the refrain differ from that of the preceding song?

Practice the new intervals before you sing the song.

An American *Folk Song*

In the alto part of "Goin' Down the Road," the notes of the F-major scale are altered by the use of **accidentals**.

♯ = Sharp (raises a note by a half step)

♭ = Flat (lowers a note by a half step)

♮ = Natural (cancels a sharp or flat)

Practice reading this **chromatic** passage before you sing the song.

Goin' Down the Road

Folk Song from the United States   *Arranged by Donald Scafuri*

1. I'm goin' down the road feel - in' bad (feel - in' bad), I'm
2. I'm goin' where the cold winds don't blow (winds don't blow), I'm
3. I'm goin' where the climate suits my clothes (suits my clothes), I'm

goin' down the road___ feel - in' bad (feel - in' bad), I'm
goin' where the cold___ winds don't blow (winds don't blow), I'm
goin' where the cli - mate suits my clothes (suits my clothes), I'm

goin' down the road feel - in' bad, feel - in' bad,
goin' where the cold winds don't blow, winds don't blow, And I
goin' where the climate suits my clothes, suits my clothes,

ain't gon - na be treat - ed this - a - way.___

A Song of
Hope

"From a Distance," on page 290, contains many syncopated rhythm patterns. Clap and count the following exercises in preparation for singing the song.

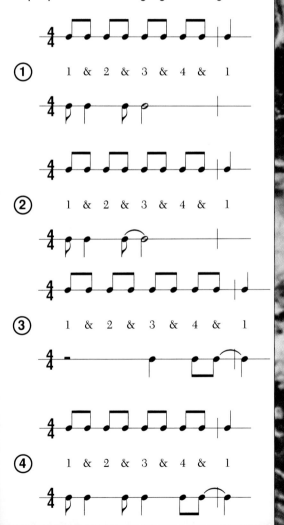

①   1   &   2   &   3   &   4   &   1

②   1   &   2   &   3   &   4   &   1

③   1   &   2   &   3   &   4   &   1

④   1   &   2   &   3   &   4   &   1

About the Song

"From a Distance" is one of those rare songs that appeals to people everywhere. The first recorded version, by the pop-country singer Nanci Griffin in 1986, became a big hit in Ireland. Although it is not specifically a religious song, its inspirational message quickly won it a place in hymn books in Ireland for both Catholics and Protestants. The song has since been recorded by 15 performers, including Bette Midler, Judy Collins, and The Byrds. In 1991, "From a Distance" was the most requested song on Saudi Arabian radio during the Persian Gulf War. That same year, it was honored with the Grammy Award for best song. When asked about the song, Julie Gold, the composer of "From a Distance," had this to say: "The song is really about the difference between appearance and reality, about the fact that the way things look is not always the way they are. It is questioning more than answering."

From a Distance

Words and Music by Julie Gold   *Arranged by Donald Scafuri*

1. From a dis-tance, the world looks blue and green,
   dis-tance, we all have e-nough,
   dis-tance, you look like my friend

and the snow-capped moun-tains white. From a dis-tance,
and no one is in need. There are no guns,
e-ven though we are at war. From a dis-tance,

the o-cean meets the stream, and the
no bombs, no dis-ease, no
I just can-not com-pre-hend what

ea-gle takes to flight. From a dis-tance, there
hun-gry mouths to feed. From a dis-tance, we
all this fight-ing is for. From a dis-tance, there

is har-mo-ny, and it ech-oes through the land.
are in-stru-ments march-ing in a com-mon band;
is har-mo-ny, and it ech-oes through the land.

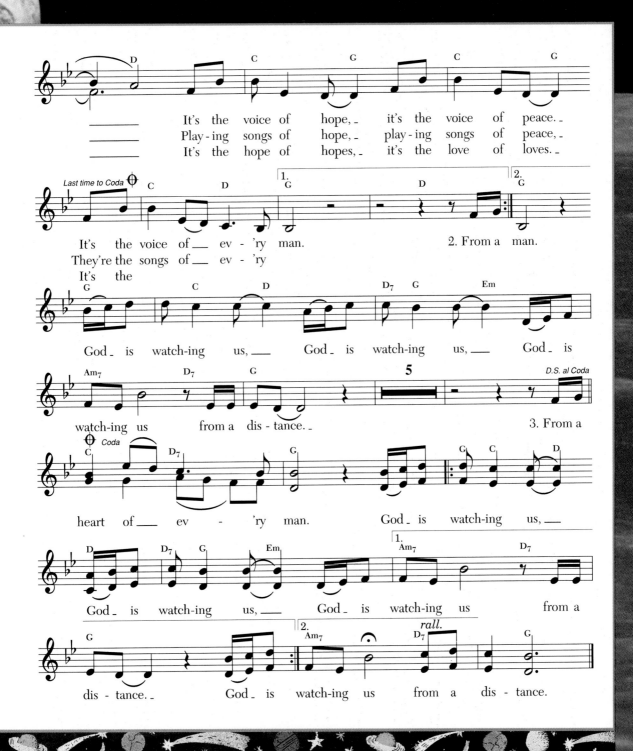

A Zulu Song

"Mangwani Mpulele" uses a **cross-rhythm** pattern of three beats against two beats—a common element in the music of Africa south of the Sahara. Practice the rhythms on pages 294 and 295 before performing the song with the percussion accompaniment.

Mangwani Mpulele

Zulu Song   *Adapted by Theodore Bikel*

With strong rhythm

Mang - wa - ni   mpu - le - le   ki - nel - wa ki - tu - la. (a mang - wa - ni)
mahng - wah-nee mpoo - lay-lay kee-nehl-wah kee-too - lah (ah mahng-wah-nee)

In this exercise for the bongo part, notice the shifting accents. Measures 1, 2, and 4 could actually be written in $\frac{6}{8}$ meter. As you pat your thighs, keep the tempo of the eighth note constant.

Practice the following rhythms by first patting and clapping one line at a time. Then, with your classmates, pat the lines in various combinations.

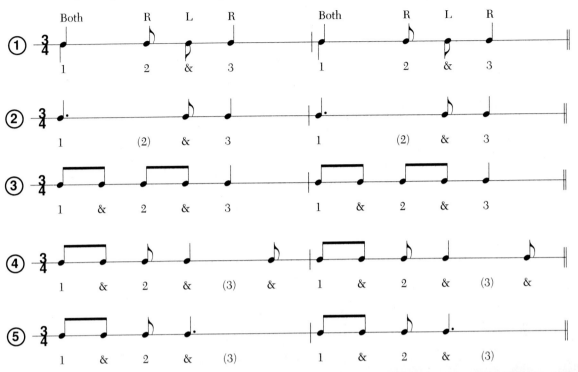

Zulu dancers, Natal

A Native American Song

"Wi Yo He Yo" is a social dance song and a favorite of Native American young people, particularly in the Southwest. Look at the meter in the song. Can you see where the time signature changes from ¾ to ²⁄₄, and from ²⁄₄ to ¾? As you clap and count the following exercise, keep the quarter-note beat the same throughout.

Wi Yo He Yo

Native American Song

Transcribed from the Library of Congress recording AFSL36.

Think Twice

The rock musician Phil Collins sometimes finds inspiration in unexpected places. While playing in Washington, D.C., as part of a United States tour with the group Genesis, Phil couldn't help but notice the large number of homeless people sleeping on the streets. Deeply moved, he wrote the song "Another Day in Paradise" to express his feelings and also to help bring attention to the plight of these people.

Before you sing "Another Day in Paradise," on page 300, practice the following syncopated patterns that appear in the song. Begin by patting the eighth-note subdivision of the beat, as shown in line A. Then, as you continue to pat the eighth-note pattern, speak the rhythms of lines B, C, and D.

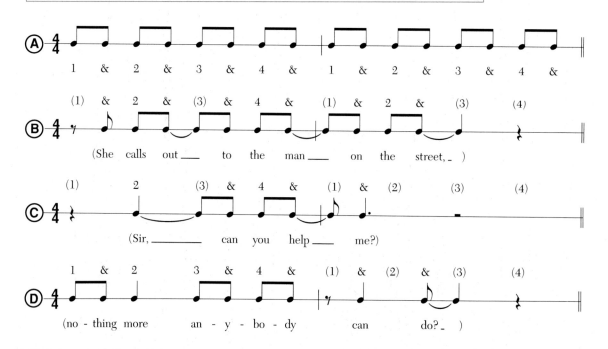

"Another Day in Paradise" is based on the C-minor scale. Sing the following pattern, using syllables or the indicated scale steps.

C minor

1 2 3 4 5 5 6 5 4 3 2 2 1 7 6 7 1

**Phil Collins
(1951-   )**

Phil Collins—singer, composer, drummer, keyboard player, and record producer—was born in London, England, and began playing drums when he was just five years old. Music quickly became an important part of his life and he developed a passion for British rock and American rhythm and blues.

Meet the Composer

(Among his favorite American groups were the Supremes and the Temptations.) In 1970 he became the drummer for the group Genesis, led by Peter Gabriel. (See page 184.) Five years later, Gabriel left the group for a solo career, and Phil took over as lead singer.

"Another Day in Paradise" isn't the only Phil Collins song to address a difficult, sensitive topic. Some of his other titles and topics are "That's Just the Way It Is" (about Northern Ireland), "Colours" (about South Africa), and "Heat On the Street" (about urban tension). Concerning such songs, Phil has said that he writes them "as a man on the street who says, 'listen, this is enough.' ...I've got a short fuse nowadays, and maybe I can draw someone's attention to something they might otherwise just pass by."

Another Day in Paradise

Words and Music by Phil Collins

A **Blues** *Folk Song*

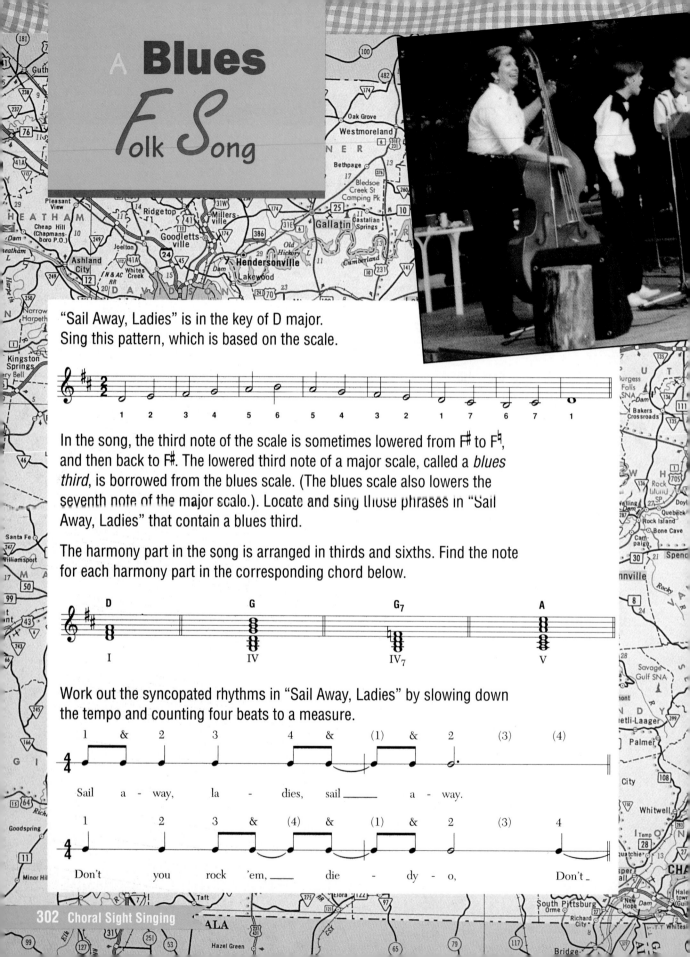

"Sail Away, Ladies" is in the key of D major.
Sing this pattern, which is based on the scale.

1 2 3 4 5 6 5 4 3 2 1 7 6 7 1

In the song, the third note of the scale is sometimes lowered from F♯ to F♮,
and then back to F♯. The lowered third note of a major scale, called a *blues
third*, is borrowed from the blues scale. (The blues scale also lowers the
seventh note of the major scale.). Locate and sing those phrases in "Sail
Away, Ladies" that contain a blues third.

The harmony part in the song is arranged in thirds and sixths. Find the note
for each harmony part in the corresponding chord below.

D   G   G₇   A
I   IV   IV₇   V

Work out the syncopated rhythms in "Sail Away, Ladies" by slowing down
the tempo and counting four beats to a measure.

1 & 2 3 4 & (1) & 2 (3) (4)

Sail a - way, la - dies, sail _____ a - way.

1 2 3 & (4) & (1) & 2 (3) 4

Don't you rock 'em, _____ die - dy - o, Don't _

Sail Away, Ladies

Folk Song from the Southern United States   *Arranged by Lawrence Eisman*

1. Ain't no use to sit an' cry,
2. I've gotta home in Ten - nes - see,   Sail a - way, la - dies, sail a - way.
3. Close your eyes an' go to sleep,

You'll be an an - gel by an' by,
That's the place I wan - na be,
Four - teen an - gels watch do keep,

Sail a - way, la - dies, sail a - way. Don't you rock 'em, die - dy - o,

Don't you rock 'em, die - dy - o,

Don't you rock 'em, die - dy - o, Don't you rock 'em,

1., 2. die - dy - o.

3. - dy - o.

A Silly Story

Work out the challenging rhythms on page 306 for "The Alligator" before singing the song.

The Alligator   (Se va el caimán)

English Words by Aura Kontra   *Dance Song from Colombia*

1. Let me tell a sil - ly sto - ry _____ on a
2. What this ga - tor has for din - ner _____ is a
1. *Voy a em - pe - zar mi re - la - to _____ con a -*
2. *Lo que co - me es - te cai - mán _____ yo le*

light and hap - py note, ___   Let me tell a sil - ly sto -
won - der to be - hold, ___   What this ga - tor has for din -
le - grí a y con a - fán. ___   *Voy a em - pe - zar mi re - la -*
ten - go ad - mi - ra - ción, ___   *Lo que co - me es - te cai - mán _*

3. On the far side of the river,
   fishermen reeled in a perch, *(2 times)*
   It had swallowed the guitarist,
   now they've called off the search. *(2 times)*
   Refrain

3. *Al otro lado del río*
   pescaron a una mojarra, (2 times)
   Y del buche le sacaron
   él que toca la guitarra. (2 times)
   Refrain

Begin the rhythm exercises for "The Alligator" by establishing the sixteenth-note subdivision of each beat.

1 e & a 2 e & a   1 e & a 2 e & a   1 e & a 2 e & a

Now count and speak the rhythm patterns of the following lines as you continue to tap the sixteenth-note subdivision.

(1)   (2)   & a   1 & 2   & a   (1)   &   (2)

Let me tell a sil - ly sto - ry _____

(1)   (2)   & a   1 & 2   a 1   &   (2)

On the riv - er Mag - da - le - na, _____

(1)   (2)   &   tri- pl- et 2 e   a   (1) e   a 2   &

He's leav - ing for Ba - rran - qui - lla; Oh, there he

(1)   (2)   &   tri- pl- et 2 e   a   (1) e   (2)

He's leav - ing for Ba - rran - qui - lla.

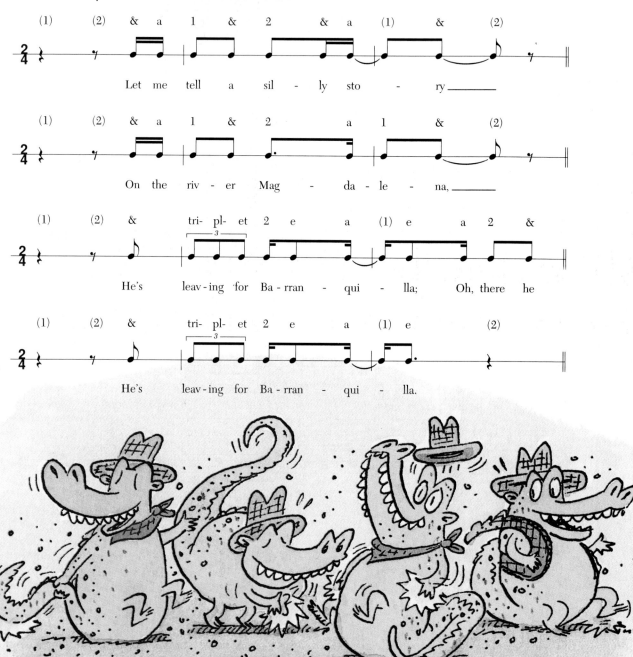

Sharps, flats, and naturals are used throughout the show tune "Step to the Rear" to alter the melody. Practice singing the resulting half steps and whole steps in these examples.

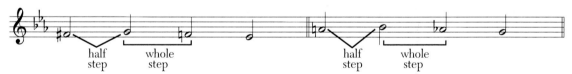

Sequences are also frequently used in this song, which begins on page 308. Here is one example. After you've sung it, look for others.

Step to the Rear
from *How Now, Dow Jones*

Words by Carolyn Leigh   *Music by Elmer Bernstein*

Will ev - 'ry one here ___ kind - ly step to the rear ___

___ And let a win - ner lead the way; _____

Here's where we sep - a - rate the notes from the noise, ___ The

men from the boys, ___ the rose from the poi - son i - vy.

Back in the bunch, ___ I came up with a hunch, ___ This was an

up and at 'em day; _____ It's one of those spells ___

___ when you hear the right bells ___ And your hor - o-scope tells ___

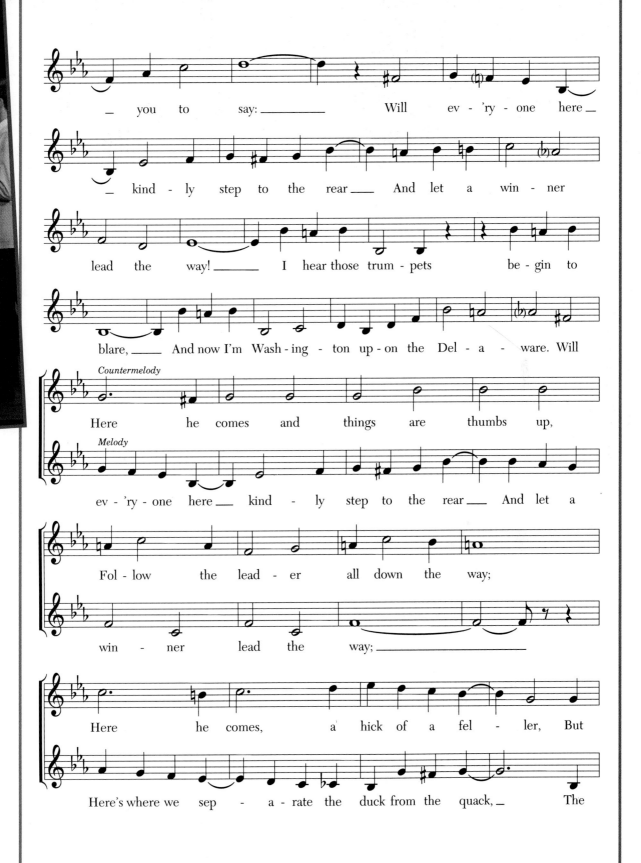

_ you to say: _____ Will ev - 'ry - one here _

_ kind - ly step to the rear ___ And let a win - ner

lead the way! _____ I hear those trum - pets be - gin to

blare, ___ And now I'm Wash - ing - ton up - on the Del - a - ware. Will

Countermelody

Here he comes and things are thumbs up,

Melody

ev - 'ry - one here __ kind - ly step to the rear ___ And let a

Fol - low the lead - er all down the way;

win - ner lead the way; _____

Here he comes, a' hick of a fel - ler, But

Here's where we sep - a - rate the duck from the quack, _ The

ar   and pheas-ant for din - ner,   A win - ner will

_ kind - ly step to the rear__ And let a win - ner

lead the _ way,   Just let a win - ner, let a win - ner, let a

lead the way,   Just let a win - ner

cool and crow-ing win - ner lead the way._____

lead the way._____

A **Sad** *Goodbye*

If you look carefully, you will discover a *skeleton melody* hidden within most songs. The skeleton melody is like an outline of a sentence, without all the adjectives and adverbs. Learning to look for the skeleton melody will help you recognize patterns and make you a better music reader.

Below are the first two lines of the Mexican song "Adiós en el puerto." The full melody is written on the upper staff, with the skeleton melody on the lower staff. Sing and compare the two melodies.

Since the form of this song falls nicely into four eight-measure phrases (A A´ B B´), can you find the skeleton melody for the B and B´ phrases?

Adiós en el puerto (Farewell by the Shore)

Words and Music by Ernesto Dominguez   English Words by Sandra Longoria Glover

Jun - to al mar, _____ da - me el úl - ti - mo a - diós, _____
Pe - ro yo, _____ ¡ay! qué tris - te me voy, _____
By the sea we stand, ____ as you tell me good - bye,
But, for me, ____ oh, how sad - ly I leave,

por - que le - jos yo me voy, _____ le - jos de a - quí. _____
por - que só - lo sa - be Dios ____
For I'm go - ing a - way, _____ so far from here.
For ___ on - ly God ___ knows

1.

2. ___ si vol - ve - ré. _____ Ya tu pa - ñue - lo ____
___ if I'll re - turn. _____ co - mo ga - vio - tas ____
Your scarf is wav - ing, _____ like a lone - ly
And ___ the sea - gulls

___ se es - tá a - gi - tan - do en - tre la in - men - si - dad ____ co - mo ban - de - ra de la
___ que a - bren sus a - las ba - jo el cie - lo a - zul, ____ so - bre la pla - ya don - de
___ wav - ing in ____ the dis - tance ____ like a lone - ly
___ op - en their wings ___ to the blue ___ sky, ____ o - ver the shore ___ where I

1.   2.

so - le - dad ____ que di - ce a - diós, ____ ___ to - do mi a - mor. _____
que - da - rá ___ ___ with all my love. _____
flag that waves ___ its sad good - bye, ____
leave ___ you ___

© 1941 by Promotora Hispano Americana de Música, S.A.

A Song for Spring

The pentatonic (five-note) scale that is most familiar to us derives from steps 1, 2, 3, 5, and 6 of the major scale. This scale is widely used throughout the Western world, and it is the scale used in most Chinese music.

The pentatonic scale can begin on any one of the five steps. Each version of the scale, called a *mode*, takes on a whole different flavor. Several of these modes sound quite "minor," while others sound "major."

Play and sing through each of the five pentatonic modes. Do any of them remind you of other melodies that you know? (The last mode, on *la*, is used extensively in blues and rock.)

Do	Re	Mi	Sol	La
1	2	3	5	6

Re	Mi	Sol	La	Do	Mi	Sol	La	Do	Re
2	3	5	6	1	3	5	6	1	2

Sol	La	Do	Re	Mi	La	Do	Re	Mi	Sol
5	6	1	2	3	6	1	2	3	5

Although it sometimes uses the Chinese pentatonic scale, Japanese music more often employs a distinctive pentatonic scale that contains half steps between notes. The well-known Japanese folk song "Sakura" is based on this scale.

La	Ti	Do	Mi	Fa	La	Ti	Do	Mi	Fa
6	7	1	3	4	6	7	1	3	4

Sakura *(Cherry Blossoms)*

Folk Song from Japan   *Arranged by Bruce Saylor*

Sa - ku - ra, Sa - ku - ra, ya yo i no

so ra - wa, mi - wa - ta - su ka - gi - ri,

ka su mi ka ku mo - ka, ni o i zo ___

pp
I za ya i za ya

p
i zu - ru. ___ I za ya ___

© 1985 Bruce Saylor

A Spanish Folk Song

"Con el vito," like many Spanish folk songs, uses the melodic minor scale to achieve its characteristic style. The sixth and seventh notes of the melodic minor scale are raised when this scale ascends. Sing the following pattern based on this scale, using *ah* or *oo*.

E melodic minor

1 2 3 4 5 4 3 2 1 7 6 5 #6 #7 1

In the $\frac{3}{8}$ meter of "Con el vito," the eighth note gets the beat. But the tempo is so fast that you should feel the meter as one beat per measure. Practice clapping these patterns from the song.

① $\frac{3}{8}$ 1 2 3 | 1 2 3

② $\frac{3}{8}$ 1 (2) 3 | 1 (2) 3

③ $\frac{3}{8}$ 1 2 (3) | 1 2 (3)

④ $\frac{3}{8}$ rest 2 3 | rest 2 3

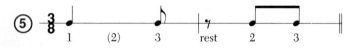

⑤ $\frac{3}{8}$ 1 (2) 3 | rest 2 3

Con el vito

English Words by Aura Kontra   *Folk Song from Spain*   *Arranged by Darrell Peter*

Con el vi - to, vi - to, vi - to, Con el
vi - to, vi - to, va.____ Con el vi - to, vi - to,
vi - to, Con el vi - to, vi - to, va.____ To the
U - na
bull - fights in Se - vi - lla, Went the Span - ish la - dy
ma - la - gue - ña fue a Se - vi - lla a ver los
rid - ing; She was cap - tured on the high - way
to - ros; Y en la mi - tad del ca - mi - no
By some Moor - ish ban - dits hid - ing.
La cau - ti - va - ron los mo - ros.

Playing
the Guitar

Introduction

Guitars and keyboards are two of the most popular instruments used in America for making music. The pages that follow will help you get started playing chords on the guitar as an accompanying instrument for singing.

Also included are opportunities to play melodies as solos or in ensembles. You will find that playing in an ensemble is a satisfying musical experience.

1966. Dallas Museum of Art, Gift of Mrs. James H. Clark 1968.14

Rock-Rock   *Richard Lindner*

The Guitar

There are three basic types of guitars—nylon-string classical, acoustic steel-string, and electric. Learn the names of the parts of the guitar.

Acoustic steel-string guitar

Electric guitar

HEAD

Tuning keys

Nut

NECK AND FINGERBOARD

Fret

Sound hole

Bridge

Nylon-string classical guitar

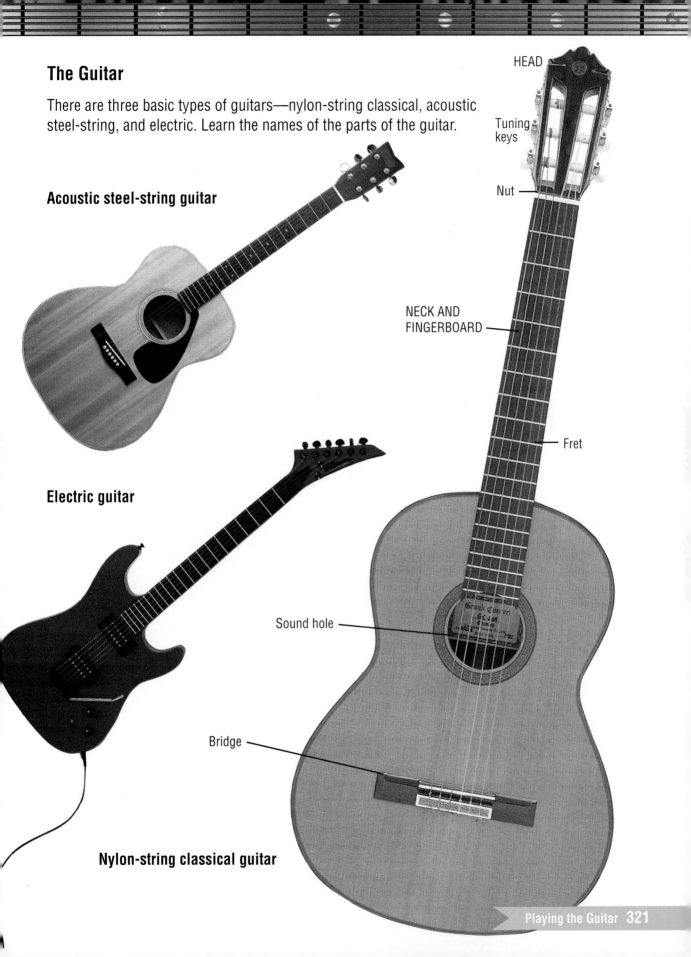

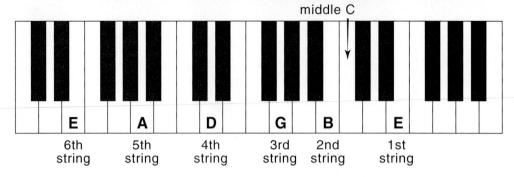

middle C

E | A | D | G | B | E

| 6th string | 5th string | 4th string | 3rd string | 2nd string | 1st string |

Tuning

In the first stages of playing, your teacher may tune your guitar for you.

You can tune your guitar to the appropriate keys of a keyboard. The diagram above shows the pitch for tuning each guitar string. Another possibility is tuning to one of the inexpensive electronic guitar tuners. Still another way to tune is called *relative* tuning. When you are ready to tune your own guitar, follow the steps on page 323 and then have your teacher or an experienced guitar player check your accuracy.

Electronic guitar tuner

How to Tune

- Tune the sixth, or lowest, string to E on the piano or pitch pipe.

- Press the sixth string at fret 5. This is the pitch A to which you tune your open fifth string. Pluck the depressed sixth string and the fifth string with your right thumb. When the two sounds match, you are in tune.

- Press the fifth string at fret 5 and tune the open fourth string to it. Follow the same procedure you used on the fifth and sixth strings.

- Press the fourth string at fret 5 and tune the open third string to it.

- Press the third string at fret 4 and tune the open second string to it.

- Press the second string at fret 5 and tune the open first string to it. Check the low E and the high E. They should be in tune with each other.

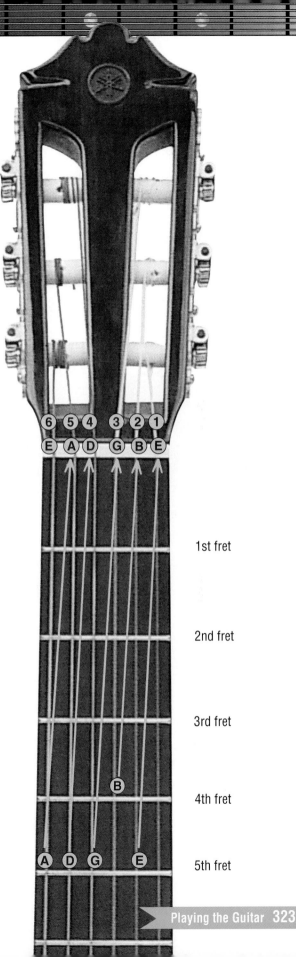

1st fret

2nd fret

3rd fret

4th fret

5th fret

Playing Position

There are several ways to hold your guitar comfortably. The following guidelines will help you to be a better player.

- Relax your muscles and avoid tension.

- The guitar neck should be either horizontal (see left photograph) or tilted upward (see right photograph). The neck should never be tilted downward.

- Keep the body of the guitar as vertical as possible. Try not to slant the top of the guitar so that you can see better. This puts your left hand in a bad position.

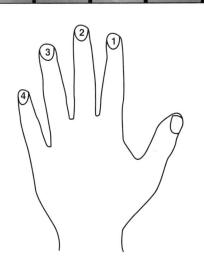

Left-hand fingers are numbered 1 through 4. (Pianists: The thumb is not number 1.) Place the thumb in back of the neck and arch your fingers. Never hold the neck like a baseball bat, with the palm against the back.

Your **right-hand thumb** will strum the strings by brushing across them in a downward motion.

The right hand can also use a **flat pick** to strum or pick the strings.

The Capo

A **capo** (KAY poh) makes it easy for you to play in different keys on the guitar. When you see, for example, *Guitar: capo 3* on a song with guitar chords, place the capo at the third fret and play the chords as indicated above the music. You will finger the chords in a key that is easier to play on the guitar, but the resulting sound will match the key in which the song is notated.

Elastic capo

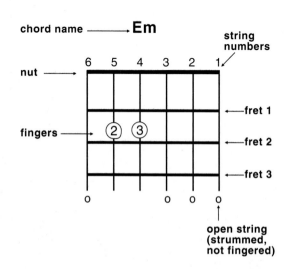

Capo in place at the third fret

How to Read Guitar Chord Diagrams

A guitar chord diagram shows you

- the **chord name** (The example is E minor.)
- **strings 6** (bass) through **1** (treble)
- the **nut**
- the **frets**
- **left-hand fingers**
- **open** (0) **strings**

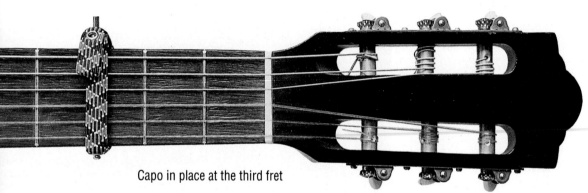

The Em and Partial G Chords

These chord diagrams show you how to play the E-minor (Em) and partial G chords.

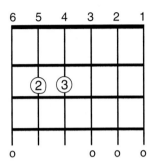

Em

Strum the Em chord from strings 6 through 1. Be sure that your second finger is on string 5 and your third finger is on string 4. Remember to arch your fingers so that they do not touch any other strings.

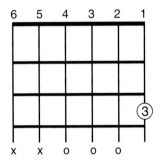

Partial G

This is an easy way to play the G chord without having to use all three fingers required to play the full chord. Strum only from strings 4 through 1. (An X in the diagram tells you not to play that string. Watch for the X in other chord diagrams to follow.) You will learn to play the full G chord later in this unit.

The song "Glee Reigns in Galilee," on page 194, uses just the Em and G chords. The strum pattern for the song is shown below. The strong beat (beat 1) is indicated by the chord symbol, and the repeated strum on beat 2 is shown by the slash (/). Practice playing the pattern with all down strums, using either your thumb or a pick. Then sing and play the song, following the chord symbols above the music.

$\frac{2}{4}$ Em / | Em / | Em / | Em / | Em / | Em / | Em / | Em / |

G / | G / | G / | G / | G / | G / | G / | G / :‖

The E₇ and A Chords

These chord diagrams show you how to play the E_7 and A chords.

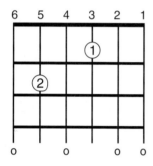

E_7

Strum the E_7 chord from strings 6 through 1.

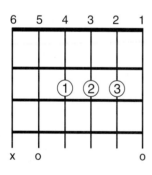

A

Strum strings 5 through 1. Arch your fingers and listen to be sure that string 1 is sounding, not dampened by the third finger.

With the capo at the third fret, you can play the E_7 and A chords with the song "De colores," on page 22. The song is in triple meter. Practice the strum pattern first by playing only on beat 1, then work up to three strums per measure. When you're ready, sing and play the song, following the chord symbols above the music. (Leave out the D chord for now.)

$\frac{3}{4}$ A / / | A / / | E_7 / / | E_7 / / :‖

Playing Notes on Strings 1 and 2

The diagram to the right shows individual notes on strings 1 and 2 in the first three frets. The circled notes are used in the practice melody at the bottom of the page. Memorize the fingerings, the letter names of the notes, and how the notes appear on the treble clef staff.

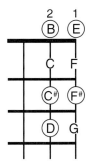

Finger numbers are given to the left of each note.

First play the notes of the practice melody below. Next strum the A and E₇ chords. Finally combine the two parts in a duet. Notice the key signature (key of A major); it tells you that the F and C (and G) notes are sharped throughout.

The A₇ and D Chords

These chord diagrams show you how to play the A₇ and D chords.

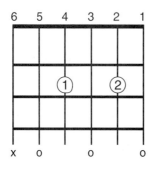

A₇

Strum the A₇ chord in a downward motion from strings 5 through 1. Do not play the bass string 6. Fingers 1 and 2 move as a unit from the A₇ chord to the D chord. Practice moving those fingers back and forth; then add the third finger on string 2 at the third fret to play the D chord.

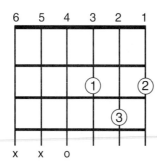

D

Strum the D chord in a downward motion from strings 4 through 1. Do not play the bass strings 5 and 6. Remember to arch your left-hand fingers and press the strings with the tips of your fingers.

Strum this pattern with your right-hand thumb or pick. Move your left-hand fingers quickly as a unit to the new chord. Strum once for each chord name and slash.

$$\frac{4}{4} \; D \; / \; / \; \mathcal{?} \; \left| \; A_7 \; / \; / \; \mathcal{?} \; \right| \; D \; / \; / \; / \; \left| \; A_7 \; / \; / \; / \; :\right\|$$

You can use the A₇ and D chords to accompany these songs in your book: "Elegua," page 168; "He's Got the Whole World in His Hands," page 283; "Panamam tombé," page 31; "Yonder Come Day," page 257.

If you add the G chord, you can accompany these songs: "¡Ay, Jalisco no te rajes!" page 86; "Laredo," page 201; "Oh, Susanna," page 47; "On My Journey," page 78; "Rock Around the Clock," page 66; "Sail Away, Ladies," page 303; "This Land Is Your Land," page 94.

If you add the G and E₇ chords, you can accompany the song "There's a Yellow Rose in Texas," page 286.

Playing Notes and Chords in the Key of A Major

Do you know what key the songs "When the Saints Go Marching In" and "De colores" (on page 332) are in? The three sharps (F♯, C♯, G♯) and the chord symbols tell you the key is A major. Here are the notes needed to play these songs. Locate the notes on the fingerboard at the right; then study the notes as they appear on the staff. The fingering is given to the left of each note.

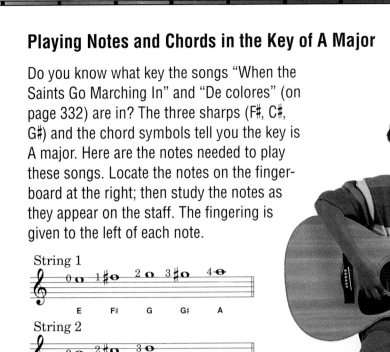

String 1

E   F♯   G   G♯   A

String 2

B   C♯   D

String 3

G♯   A

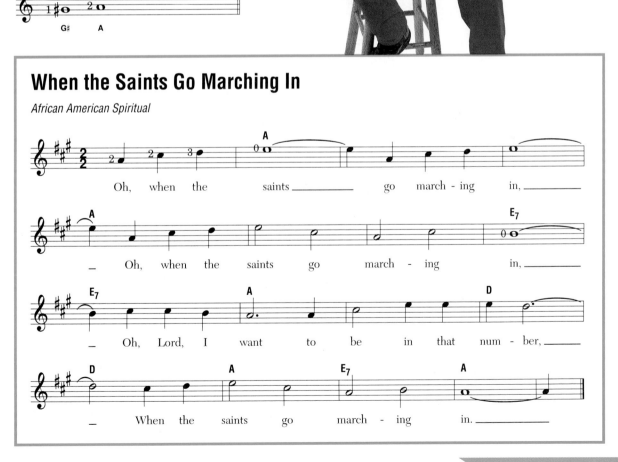

When the Saints Go Marching In

African American Spiritual

Oh, when the saints _____ go march - ing in, _____

_ Oh, when the saints go march - ing in, _____

_ Oh, Lord, I want to be in that num - ber, _____

_ When the saints go march - ing in. _____

De colores

Folk Song from Mexico

De colores, traditional, arranged, and adapted by Joan Baez © 1974, Chandos Music. (ASCAP)

The G Chord

The G chord can be played several different ways. The upper diagram shows the preferred fingering. The lower diagram shows a fingering for smaller hands.

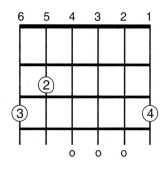

G (Preferred Fingering)

Strum strings 4 through 1 for the partial G chord. Strum strings 6 through 1 for the full G chord. As always, arch your left-hand fingers and press the strings with the tips of your fingers.

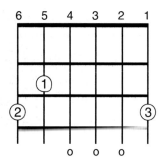

G (Fingering for smaller hands)

Strum strings 4 through 1 for the partial G chord. Strum strings 6 through 1 for the full chord. For another alternate fingering, substitute the fourth finger for the third.

Keep a steady beat as you strum this chord pattern.

$\frac{4}{4}$ D / / ≀ |G / / ≀ |D / / ≀ |A₇ / / ≀ :‖

You can use the D, A₇, and G chords to accompany these songs in your book: "¡Ay, Jalisco no te rajes!" page 86; "Laredo," page 201; "Oh, Susanna," page 47; "On My Journey," page 78; "Rock Around the Clock," page 66; "Sail Away, Ladies," page 303; "This Land Is Your Land," page 94. If you add the E₇ chord, you can accompany the song "There's a Yellow Rose in Texas," page 286. Use the full G chord and the Em chord to accompany the song "Glee Reigns in Galilee," page 194.

Playing Notes and Chords in the Key of D Major

The key signature for the songs "Amazing Grace" and "Yonder Come Day" (on page 336) contains two sharps: F♯ and C♯. That and the chords tell you that both songs are in the key of D major. Here are the notes needed to play these songs. Locate the notes on the fingerboard at the right; then study the notes as they appear on the staff. The fingering is given to the left of each note.

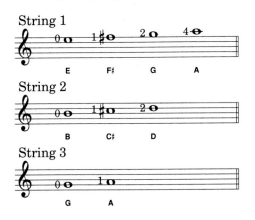

Amazing Grace

Words by John Newton   Early American Melody

Yonder Come Day

Spiritual from the Georgia Sea Islands

PART 1

Yon-der come day, Day is a-break-in', Yon-der come day,

Oh my soul;_____ Yon-der come day, Day is a-break-in', _____

Sun is a-ris-in' _____ in my _____ soul. _____

PART 2

Sun rise, Sun rise, Oh yon-der,

Sun rise, Sun is a-ris-in' _____ in my ___ soul. ___

PART 3

Yon - der, _____ Yon - der, _____ Yon - der, _____

Yon - der. ___ Yon - der, _____ Yon - der, _____

Sun is a-ris-in' _____ in my _____ soul. ___

The Dm and Am Chords

These chord diagrams show you how to play the Dm and Am chords.

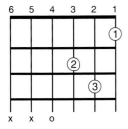

Dm

Strum strings 4 through 1. Do not play strings 5 and 6. Arch your fingers and listen to be sure that strings 2 and 1 are sounding. Remember to press the strings firmly.

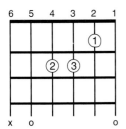

Am

Strum strings 5 through 1. Practice moving from the Dm chord to the Am chord and back again until you can make the changes smoothly.

Keep a steady beat as you strum the following chord patterns.

$\frac{4}{4}$ Dm / / / | Dm / / / | Am / / / | Am / / / :‖

$\frac{4}{4}$ Am / / / | Dm / / / | Am / / / | E_7 / / / :‖

Use the Dm, Am, and E_7 chords to accompany these songs in your book: "This Old Hammer," page 338; "Tumbalalaika," page 44.

Playing Notes and Chords in the Key of A Minor

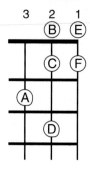

The key signature (no sharps or flats) and the chords indicate that the song "This Old Hammer" is in the key of A minor. Here are the notes needed to play this arrangement for two guitars.

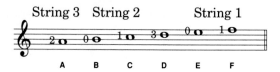

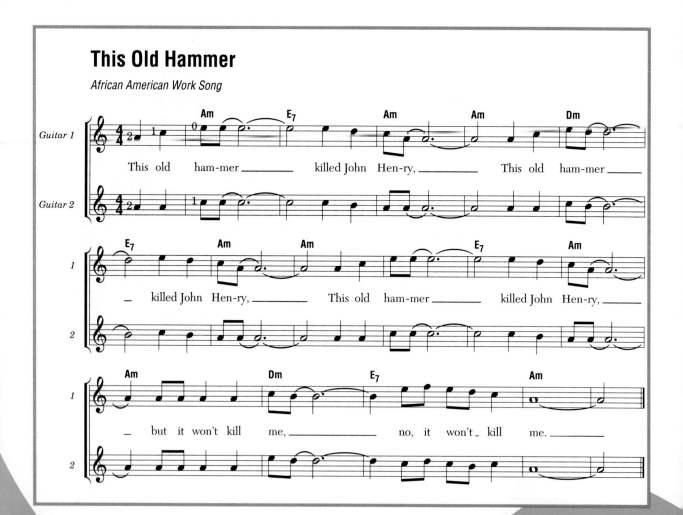

This Old Hammer

African American Work Song

Guitar 1

Am   E7   Am   Am   Dm

This old   ham-mer _____   killed John Hen-ry, _____   This old   ham-mer _____

Guitar 2

E7   Am   Am   E7   Am

_ killed John Hen-ry, _____   This old   ham-mer _____   killed John   Hen-ry, _____

Am   Dm   E7   Am

_ but   it   won't   kill   me, _____   no,   it   won't _ kill   me. _____

The G7 and D7 Chords

G$_7$

Start playing the G$_7$ chord as a partial chord, using only the first finger and strumming strings 4 through 1. Add the second and third fingers on strings 5 and 6 when you are ready. Notice how easy it is to change from the G chord.

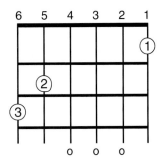

D$_7$

Strum the D$_7$ chord from strings 4 through 1. Do not play bass strings 5 and 6. Notice the triangular shape of this chord.

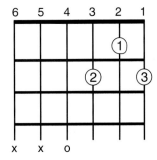

Go back and play "Rock Around the Clock," on page 66, using the G$_7$ and D$_7$ chords.

Strum Variations

Try subdividing the beat by strumming both down and up. The symbol for a down strum is ⌐ and the symbol for an up strum is ∨ .

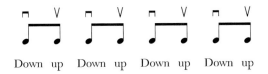

Down up   Down up   Down up   Down up

The C and F Chords

C

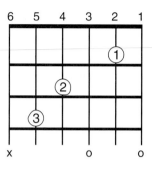

Strum strings 5 through 1. Do not play string 6. Arch your fingers and listen to be sure that strings 4, 3, and 1 are sounding. When you move from C to Am or D_7, hold down any fingers that the chords have in common.

F

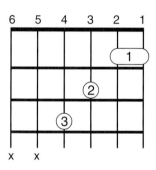

Strum strings 4 through 1. This chord uses a partial first-finger bar that depresses strings 1 and 2. The F chord will be easier if you pull your left elbow in and roll the first finger slightly. Don't expect this chord to sound good right away. Lifting up your third finger will give you a Dm_7 chord.

Strum the following chord patterns.

$\frac{4}{4}$ G / / / | Em / / / | C / / / | D_7 / / / :||

$\frac{4}{4}$ C / / / | Am / / / | Dm / / / | G_7 / / / :||
(or F)

Use the C chord with other chords you know to accompany these songs in your book: "Row, Row, Row Your Boat," page 93 (C); "The Alligator," page 304 (C, G, G_7); "One of Those Songs," page 88 (capo 5: C, A_7, Dm, G_7, Am, D_7); "Feliz Navidad," page 278 (G, C, Am, D_7); "Those Magic Changes," page 70 (capo 5: G, Em, C, D_7); "From a Distance," page 290 (capo 3: G, C, D, Em, D_7, Am); "America, the Beautiful," page 77 (capo 3: G, D, D_7, A_7, C); "(Ghost) Riders in the Sky," page 26 (Em, G, C, Am).

Use the F chord with other chords you know to accompany these songs: "De colores," page 22 (C, G_7, F); "Adiós en el puerto," page 313 (C, G_7, F); "The Swallow," page 16 (C, G, G_7, F); "Merry Minstrels," page 51 (C, G, G_7, Am, F, Em); "The Rose," page 40 (capo 5: C, F, G, G_7, Em, Am); "Hatikvah," page 53 (capo 5: Am, Dm, E_7, G_7, C, F); "One Tin Soldier," page 120 (capo 2: C, G, Am, Em, F, Dm).

Playing Notes and Chords in the Key of C Major

What do the key signature (no sharps or flats) and chord pattern tell you about the song "I Love the Mountains"? That's right, the song is in the key of C major. Here are the notes needed to play this familiar round.

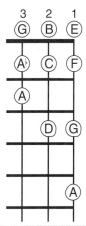

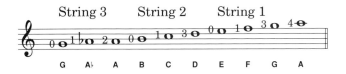

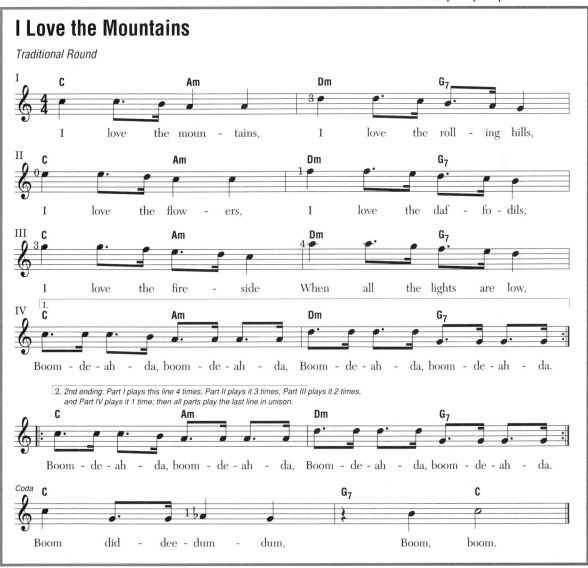

A short practice each day is better than a long practice once or twice a week. Patience and playing often will lead to a lifetime of enjoyment with the guitar.

Playing the Keyboard

Introduction

Have you ever taken lessons on piano or another keyboard instrument? If so, the first part of this unit will be basic review. Even if you haven't had any keyboard instruction, you will find that many of the concepts you have learned in music class will transfer easily to the keyboard.

Courtesy Estate of Romare Bearden

The Piano Lesson
Romare Bearden

Sitting Position

For maximum support at the keyboard, sit slightly forward on the bench, with feet resting on the floor at all times. Knees should be just under the front edge of the keyboard. Sitting too close pushes the elbows back and can cause unnecessary tension.

Hand Position

The most natural hand position is the shape of your hand as it hangs at your side. When you bring your hand up to the keyboard, the fingers are slightly curved at the middle joint, and the wrist is parallel to the keyboard.

Finger Numbers

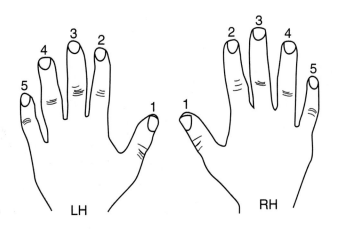

Fingering for Steps and Skips

On pages 15–19 you learned that melodies move by step, by leap (skip), and by repeated tones. How a melody moves determines the fingering to be used to play that melody on the keyboard.

By translating the keyboard examples to one- and two-line staves, it is easy to see the relationship between right and left movement on the keyboard and up and down movement of the **notation** on the staff.

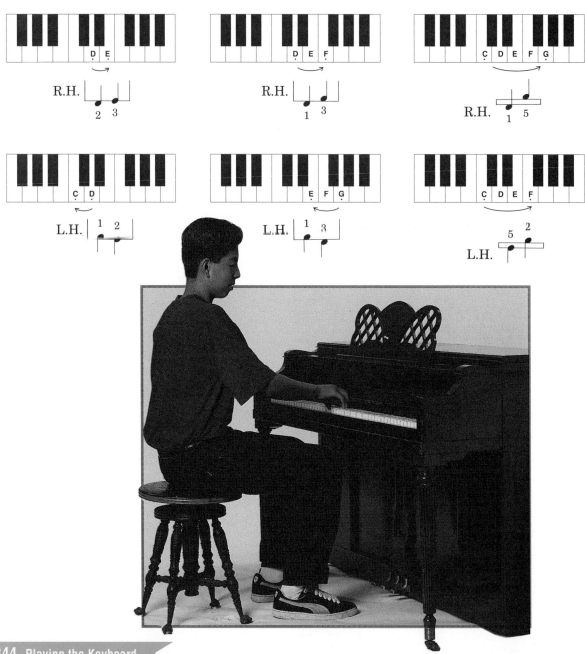

One- and Two-Line Reading

Before you play the following exercises, determine a logical fingering.
Experiment by starting on different pitches.

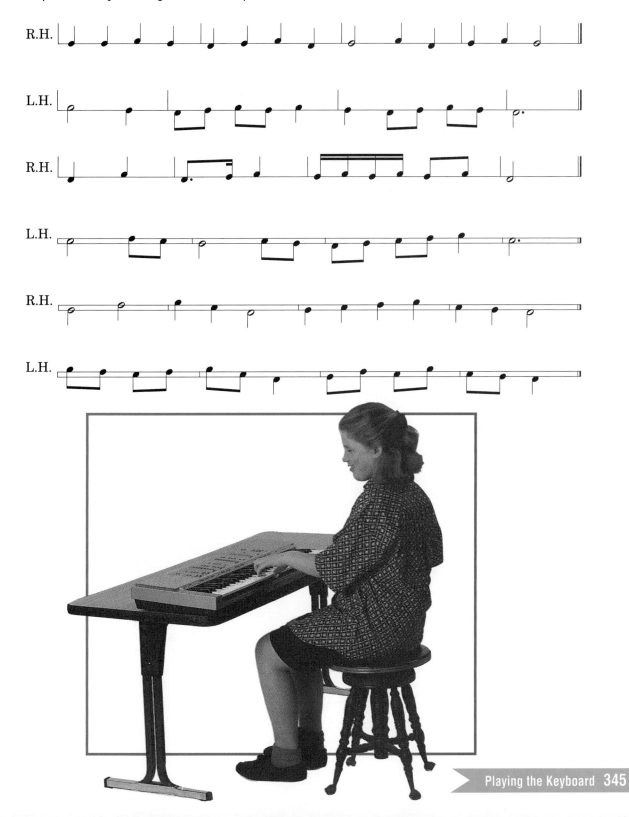

Playing from Treble and Bass Clefs

When singing music, you have learned to follow the upward and downward directions of a melody and to determine if it moves by step or by leap or if it stays on repeated tones. When playing, you must read music in the same way, as well as determine where to play the notes on the keyboard. Refer to the illustrations of the keyboard and **grand staff** in the front of your book. Each note in printed music indicates *one place and only one place* where it can be played on the keyboard.

Play the following melody fragments. The first two are written in the treble clef, and the last two are written in the bass clef.

Playing Pentascales

A **pentascale** is a five-note scale. The five notes are played in consecutive letter-name order and in a particular pattern of white and black keys. Refer to the graphic patterns below to determine which keys on the keyboard you will use to play pentascales that start on C, D, G, and A. The vertical rectangles represent white keys. The horizontal rectangle represents a black key. The first pattern is for a major pentascale that starts on the note C or G. The second pattern is for a major pentascale that starts on the note D or A.

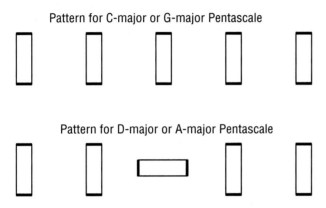

Pattern for C-major or G-major Pentascale

Pattern for D-major or A-major Pentascale

Here is the notation for the C-major and D-major pentascales. After you've played them, try to notate and play the G-major and A-major pentascales.

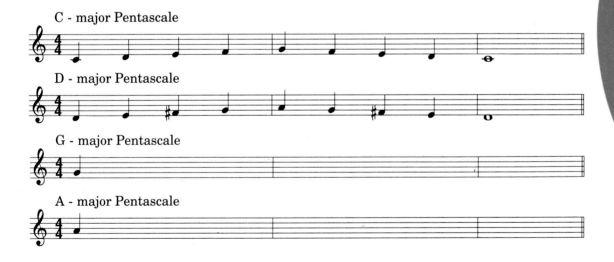

C - major Pentascale

D - major Pentascale

G - major Pentascale

A - major Pentascale

Reading Flashes—D Pentascale

The following examples use the D-pentascale range. Your teacher will determine the order in which the flashes are to be played. There will be a one-measure rest between examples.

Expansion of Five-Finger Range

The previous exercises used a maximum range of five notes and five fingers. We all know that music uses a much wider range. Play the following exercise, which expands the range of five fingers. Pay careful attention to suggested fingerings.

Playing Ostinato Patterns

Use the following ostinato patterns to play along with the recording of *River*.
Follow the pattern letter indications printed with the lyrics on page 35.

Accompanying with Harmonic Intervals

You studied melodic intervals on page 57 in this book. When the two notes
that form an interval are played simultaneously, the notes form a *harmonic*
interval. Play this example.

Use harmonic intervals to accompany "The Rose," on page 40.

"The Rose" Accompaniment

Performing an Original Multimeter Piece

"Four Three Five & Two" uses harmonic intervals throughout. Look for patterns that will make this multimeter composition easier to perform. Determine fingering before you begin to play.

FOUR THREE FIVE & TWO

Martha F. Hilley

© 1992 Martha F. Hilley

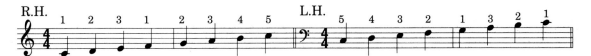

Using Traditional Scale Fingerings

To expand fingering to cover the octave range of a major scale, the following pattern is used for the major scales of C, D, E, G, and A.

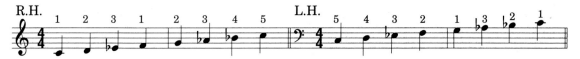

The same fingering is also used for the minor scales of C, D, E, G, and A.

Notate and play the following major and minor scales.

D major

E major

G major

A major

D minor

E minor

G minor

A minor

A Two-Handed Accompaniment

The following accompaniment for the song "I Love the Mountains,"
(page 341) uses harmonic intervals. Play the repeated pattern, using
alternating hands.

Playing Closest-Position Chords

On pages 60 and 61 in this book, you learned to build a triad on each note
of a major scale. Look at these chords, which are built on the first, fourth,
and fifth notes of the C-major scale.

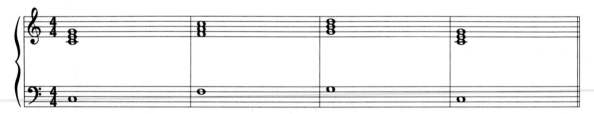

To make it easier to move from one chord to another, the chords may be
rearranged into closest position.

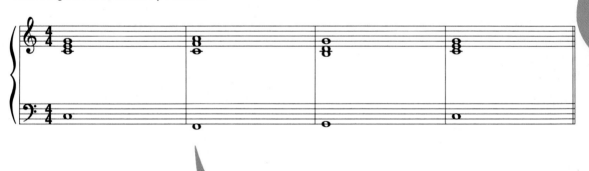

A Rock-'n'-Roll Accompaniment

You learned about a typical rock-'n'-roll chord progression on page 69 in this book. Practice playing the chords in closest position.

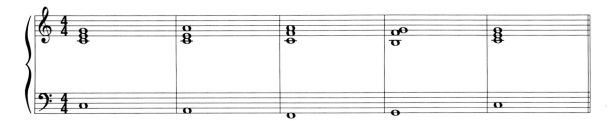

Now you're ready to learn this arrangement to accompany the song "Those Magic Changes," on page 70.

"Those Magic Changes" Accompaniment

An Arrangement of a Familiar Song

The keyboard arrangement of "America, the Beautiful"(page 356) uses
melodic intervals, harmonic intervals, and closest-position chords. It also
uses the pedal (called the *damper pedal* on acoustic pianos) that sustains
the sound. In the arrangement, the graphic below the bass-clef staff
indicates foot action on the pedal. Using your right foot, with the heel
on the floor, lower and raise the pedal with the ball of the foot.

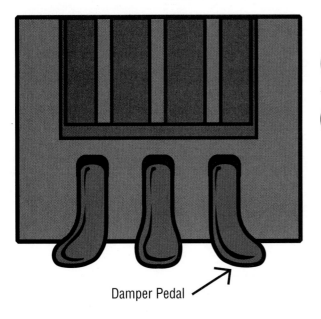

Damper Pedal

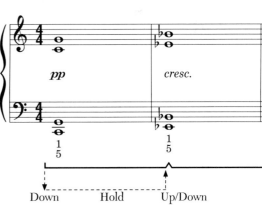

America, the Beautiful

Samuel A. Ward   Arranged by Lynn Freeman Olson

An Arrangement for Keyboard Ensemble

On pages 102 and 103 in this book, you studied and listened to selections from Brahms's *Variations on a Theme by Haydn*. Here is a multikeyboard arrangement of the theme. Determine fingering before you begin to play.

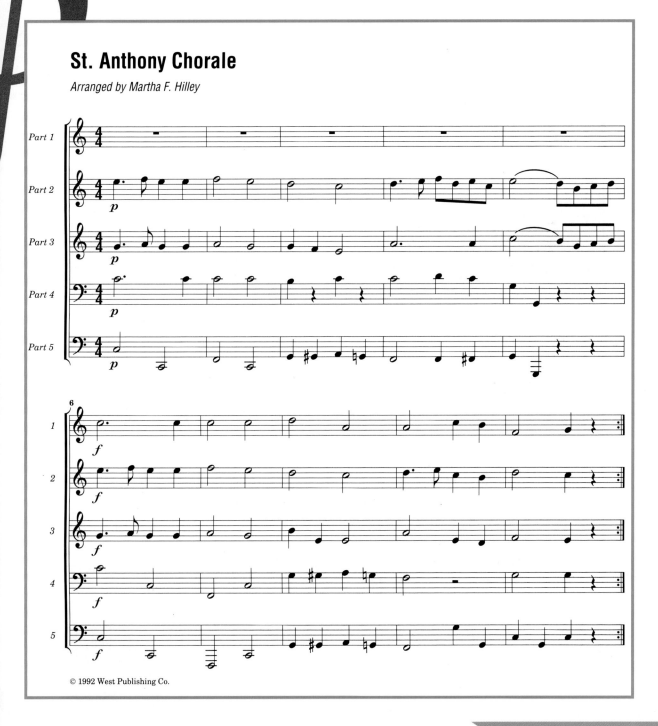

St. Anthony Chorale

Arranged by Martha F. Hilley

© 1992 West Publishing Co.

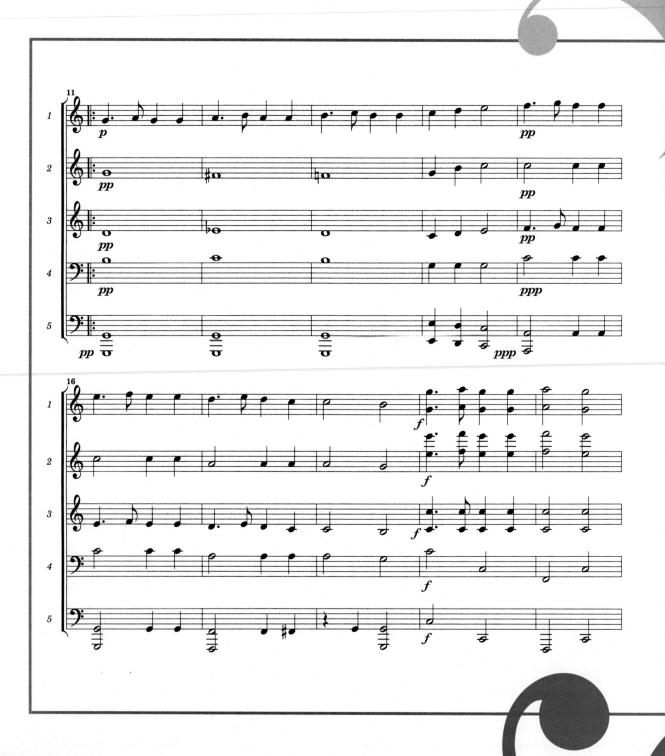

A Countermelody Accompaniment

This accompaniment for the song "One Tin Soldier" (page 120) consists of a harmonizing countermelody. Listen carefully to the recording of the song in order to match the singer's rhythms on the keyboard.

"One Tin Soldier" Accompaniment

A Syncopated Accompaniment

Create scat syllables to match the right-hand rhythm in this accompaniment for the song "Sentimental Journey" (page 122). Notice how the right-hand and left-hand parts change style for the B section.

"Sentimental Journey" Accompaniment

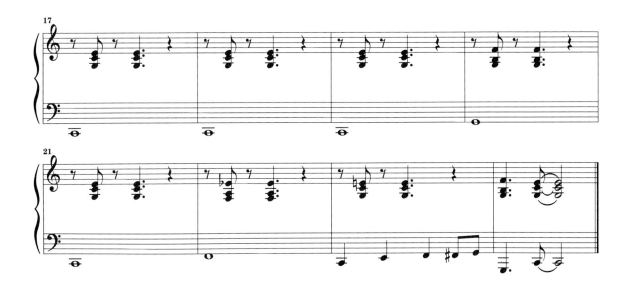

Sound Bank

ACORDEÓN DE BOTONES (ah kohr DYOHN deh boh TOH-nehs) (Button accordion) A small accordion with three rows of buttons in the keys of G, C, and F. After a button is depressed, pulling out the bellows produces one pitch; pushing the bellows in produces a different pitch.

The acordeón de botones, with its distinctive high-reed sound, is frequently used in the Mexican *norteña* (nor TAY nyah) style of music.   (p. 86)

AFRICAN DRUMS

DONNO (doh noh) A laced, double-headed, variable-tension drum that is played with curved beaters. The donno has an hourglass shape and is classified into types according to size. It is used by the Ashanti people of Ghana for ceremonial occasions and to accompany singing and dancing.   (p. 166)

DUNDUN (doon DOON) A West African double-headed drum. Most of the dundun drums have an hourglass shape. The ends are covered with goatskin drumheads that are fastened together with leather cords stretched down the length of the drum. Pressing the cordo tightens the drumheads, producing sharp and high sounds. Relaxing the pressure on the cords lowers the pitch of the sound produced.

Dundun drums are known as talking or singing drums. They are used to send messages and are played at many social events and dances.   (p. 166)

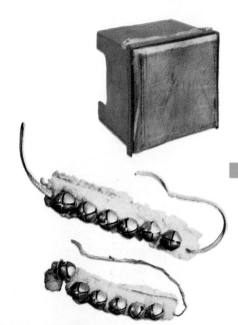

GOME (GOH meh) A large wooden drum with a cowhide drumhead. The drummer sits on the instrument and plays with the hands and the feet.

Used mainly in Ghana, the gome drum produces a low, loud resonant sound. When used in an ensemble, it usually assumes the position of lead drum.   (p. 166)

ANKLE BELLS A small hollow percussion instrument, usually made of metal. Ankle bells may be single objects containing jingling pellets, or they may be several rattling objects joined together. Bells are worn in many parts of the world. The Pueblo Indians of New Mexico wear them on their waists and ankles when performing ceremonial dances.

If the bells are of different sizes, they produce a combination of pitches.   (p. 297)

AXATSE (ahks AHT see) An African rattle made from a gourd. The gourd is cut, emptied of its seeds, dried in the sun, and covered with a loose-fitting net. Small beads or shells woven into the net create loud sounds as they hit the hollow gourd.

With its rhythmic, percussive sound, the axatse is popular with the Anlo-Ewe people of Ghana and is frequently included as part of a drum ensemble.   (p. 166)

BANJO A string instrument with a long fretted neck, five strings and a calfskin or plastic soundbox stretched over a hoop, or rim. The banjo is an African American instrument first made by slaves in the New World in the seventeenth century. A similar instrument, called a bania (BAHN yah), exists in West Africa .

The banjo has steel strings that are picked with the fingers or brushed with the nails. Its sound is bright and metallic and can be easily heard over other instruments.   (p. 181)

BASS DRUM A large cylinder-shaped metal drum with two heads made of stretched calfskin or plastic. The drum rests on its side, and the player stands behind it, beating either head with a large padded mallet.

The bass drum is often used for dramatic effect in the orchestra. It can produce a deep booming roar or a soft, thudding heartbeat.   (p. 116)

BASSOON A large tube-shaped wooden wind instrument with a double reed. The player blows into the reed to make the sound and changes the pitch by pressing keys on the body of the instrument.

In the low register, the bassoon can sound gruff or comical. The higher notes can be sweet and soft.   (p. 37)

BUTTON ACCORDION *See* ACORDEÓN DE BOTONES.

CASTANETS A small hand-held percussion instrument made of hollowed-out pieces of hardwood or ivory. These pear- or spoon-shaped clappers are tied together in pairs and looped around the player's thumb. Pairs usually differ in pitch. In traditional Spanish form, a dancer carries a pair in each hand and strikes the clappers together with the fingers.

The resonant clicking sound of the castanets adds a rhythmic element to music.   (p. 11)

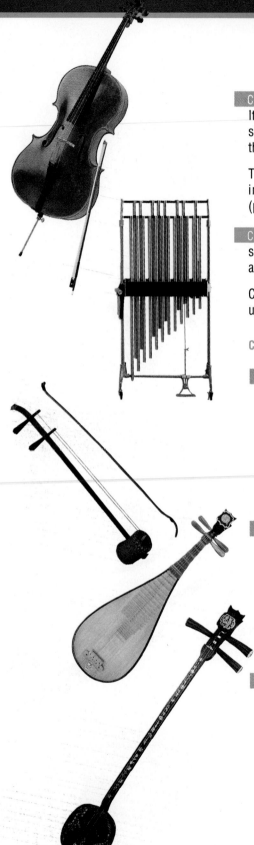

CELLO (CHEH loh)   A large string instrument made of wood. It is played with a bow or plucked with the fingers. The player sits with the cello between his or her knees and reaches around the front to play.

The sound of the cello is rich and warm, but it can sound gruff in the lower register and intense in the higher register. (p. 114)

CHIMES   A set of 20 long metal tubes (usually brass), suspended from a tall frame. The player stands beside them and strikes the tops of the tubes with a wooden hammer.

Chimes ring with a hollow, metallic tone and are frequently used to imitate church bells.   (p. 114)

CHINESE FOLK ENSEMBLE

GAOHU (h ī hoo)   A string instrument with a long round hardwood neck and two steel strings of varying thickness. The player holds the instrument in a vertical position with the resonator supported between the knees. In traditional Chinese fashion, the horsehair bow is inserted between the two steel strings.

The performer can vary the sound of the gaohu from harsh to mellow.   (p. 190)

P'IPA (PEE pah)   A pear-shaped fretted lute made of wood. The head of the p'ipa is slightly slanted and is usually in the form of a symbolic object, such as a dragon's head. Traditional p'ipas had four twisted silk strings, but the strings are now often made of nylon.

The light, delicate sound of the p'ipa is produced by strumming or plucking the strings with the fingernails. (p. 190)

SANXIAN (sahn hsyahn)   A string instrument with a long round hardwood neck and three silk strings of varying thickness. A skin membrane is stretched over the resonator. The strings are plucked with the fingernails or a small plectrum held in the right hand.

With its rich strong tone and wide range, the sanxian is a popular instrument used for vocal accompaniment and as a low-pitched ensemble instrument.   (p. 190)

SHENG (shehng) A mouth organ with a bowl-shaped wind chamber made of wood or metal. The sheng has 17 or 19 graduated bamboo pipes. Rhythmic breathing is an important part of the style.

The sound of the sheng can be shrill or pleasantly lyrical. (p. 190)

XIAO (hsyou) An end-blown notched flute made of bamboo wood. The xiao is long and slender, with five front finger holes, one thumb hole, and two or more holes at the lower end.

The xiao has a breathy, lyrical tone. (p. 190)

CLARINET A cylinder-shaped wind instrument, usually wooden but sometimes metal or plastic, with a single reed in the mouthpiece. The player blows into the mouthpiece to make the sound and changes the pitch by pressing keys on the body of the instrument.

The clarinet has three voices. The sounds in the lower register are soft and hollow sounding. In the middle register they are clear and bright, and the highest notes are more intense and can be very piercing. (p. 177)

CYMBALS Two shallow metal plates, usually made of brass, fitted with leather hand straps. One plate is held in each hand, and they are clapped together to produce the sound.

Cymbals vary in size. While large ones make an earth-shattering crash, small cymbals may be played for a light, delicate, rhythmic accompaniment. (pp. 114, 196)

DAN TRANH (dahn trahn[yuh]) (Vietnamese zither) A 16- or 17-string wooden instrument. The strings, usually made of silk or metal, are stretched over a thin, flat box. The player produces a melody by plucking the strings with the right hand. The left hand plucks the lower portion of the strings to ornament and accompany the melody.

The light delicate sound of the dan tranh can be heard in much Vietnamese folk music. (p. 54)

DONNO *See* AFRICAN DRUMS.

DRUM, NATIVE AMERICAN Hollow Native American drums are traditionally made of wood (frame) and animal skins (head) and may be single-headed or double-headed. The nonpitched, resonant sound is produced when the membrane, or skin, is

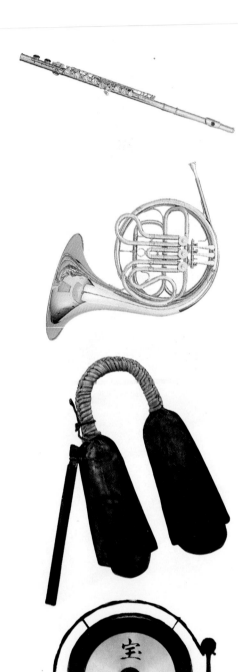

struck by a beater. Another kind of Native American drum is the vessel type, such as the water drum. When filled with water, the drum is so resonant that the sound can be heard for great distances.   (p. 297)

DUNDUN   *See* AFRICAN DRUMS.

FLUTE   A small metal instrument resembling a round piece of pipe. The player blows across an open mouthpiece in the side of the flute near one end and presses buttonlike keys to change pitches. Originally, flutes were made of wood, but most are now made of metal, some even of gold or silver.

The sound of the flute is pure, clear, and sweet. The lower notes are very soft and gentle; those in the higher register are brighter and louder.   (p. 155)

FRENCH HORN   A medium-sized brass instrument made of coiled tubing, with a large bell at one end. The player sits with the horn held down near his or her lap and keeps one hand in the bell to control the pitch and tone. The player buzzes the lips against the mouthpiece to make the sound. The pitch is changed by pressing valves on the side of the horn.

The sound of the French horn is mellow and warm and not as loud or assertive as the other brass instruments.   (p. 113)

GANKOGUI   (gahn KOH gwee)   A double clapperless metal bell that is struck with a stick. It is used by the Ewe people of southern Ghana and Togo to accompany dancing. The gankogui is also used in the Anlo-Ewe drum ensemble of Ghana.

The gankogui produces a hollow, metallic sound, similar to that of a cowbell.   (p. 166)

GAOHU   *See* CHINESE FOLK ENSEMBLE.

GOME   *See* AFRICAN DRUMS.

GONG   A broad concave metal disc usually made of brass and hung vertically in a frame. The player strikes the gong slightly off-center with a soft-headed mallet.

A sensitive player can evoke loud or soft, short or long tones from the gong, which reverberates with a rich, shimmering sound.   (p. 114)

GUITAR: ACOUSTIC, CLASSICAL   A flat-bodied, hollow wooden string instrument with a long fretted neck and six strings. The classical, or Spanish, guitar has nylon strings. Melodies or chords are played by plucking or strumming the strings with the fingers.

When played softly, this guitar is gentle and sweet. When played more loudly, it sounds lush and full.   (p. 192)

GUITAR: ELECTRIC   Flatter than the acoustic guitar, the electric guitar is one part of an electronic system that includes pickups, an amplifier, and loudspeakers. The body is solid and is usually made of wood.

Electric guitars are much louder than acoustic guitars and can also make many special sounds.   (pp. 33, 84)

GUITARRÓN   (gee tahr ROHN)   A large, round-backed, non-fretted guitar that was invented around the beginning of the twentieth century. It is strung with six harp strings and, because of its portability, has replaced the folk harp in roving mariachi groups in Mexico.

The guitarrón is either strummed or plucked, and has a rich, deep sound.   (p. 201)

HARMONICA   A small mouth organ consisting of a series of reeds. The reeds vibrate and produce sound when the player inhales and exhales across the reeds.

The harmonica has a breathy tone quality that is popular around the world. It is used for light entertainment and in folk music. (p. 181)

HARP   A large instrument with strings stretched vertically in an open, triangular frame. The player plucks the strings and operates foot pedals to play chromatic tones.

Present-day harps can play 6 1/2 octaves. Rippling chords are characteristic sounds of the instrument.   (p. 124)

HARPSICHORD   A small keyboard instrument, shaped something like a piano. When the keys are pressed, the strings inside the instrument are plucked by small points of quill, leather, or plastic. The harpsichord was popular from about 1550 until 1750, and it has again become widely heard in the 1900s, even occasionally in popular music.

Because the strings are plucked, not hammered like piano strings, the sound of the harpsichord is light and percussive, with a tinkling, airy quality. It is never very loud, unless it is amplified electronically.   (p. 79)

JARANA (hah RAH nah) An eight-string guitar used in various folk-music ensembles in the central Gulf Coast area of Mexico. It is always played with the fingers.

Harmonies are strummed rhythmically on the jarana to accompany *sones* (SOH nehs), the typical music of Veracruz, Mexico. This style is known as *jarocho* (hah ROH choh). *See also* REQUINTO. (p. 193)

MARACAS A pair of gourds with handles that are partially filled with seeds, beans, or pebbles. Maracas are used in the Caribbean area and are also characteristic of Venezuelan music.

The maracas, one held in each hand, produce a high, rattling sound when they are thrust forward and the seeds hit the inside walls of the gourds. (p. 114)

MARIMBA A percussion instrument similar to the xylophone but larger and with a deeper, richer tone. The marimba consists of rosewood or plastic bars of different lengths mounted in a frame. A player hits the bars with mallets of hard or soft playing heads made of rubber or yarn. The sound is amplified by a tuned resonator mounted beneath each bar.

The marimba is popular in Mexico and in Central and South America. The instrument produces a rich, mellow sound. (p. 168)

MBIRA (m BEE rah) An African finger xylophone made of 5 to 30 or more thin metal or cane tongues attached to a sounding board or box. The tongues are plucked with the thumbs and/or the forefingers. The length of each tongue determines its pitch. The sound may be amplified with a gourd. The mbira is especially popular in Nigeria, but it can also be found in Latin America. Other names for it are *kalimba, sansa,* and *thumb piano.*

When struck, each tongue of an mbira produces a soft sound similar to that of a xylophone but with more of a plucked tone quality. Rattles are sometimes attached to the tongues to add different sounds. (p. 105)

OBOE A small, wooden, cylinder-shaped wind instrument. The player blows into a double reed to make the sound and changes pitch by pressing keys on the body of the instrument.

The sound of the oboe is thin and sweet, often sounding exotic or melancholy. Unlike many other woodwind instruments, the sound gets sweeter and softer as it goes higher. (p. 113)

ORGAN, PIPE A wind instrument with a keyboard similar to that of a piano. It is the largest and most powerful of all instruments and may have as many as six keyboards. Large organs will have more than 5,000 pipes, while a smaller instrument will have only a few hundred. The sound is created by forcing air through these pipes.

The sound of a pipe organ can range from light and breathy to majestic and overpowering.   (p. 110)

P'IPA *See* CHINESE FOLK ENSEMBLE.

REQUINTO (reh KEEN toh)   A small Mexican guitar that is used to play fast, highly improvisational melodies. The strings are plucked with a long thin plastic pick.

The requinto has a high, guitarlike sound. Like the jarana, it is used in playing *jarocho* songs in the Veracruz style. It is the lead instrument in the *jarocho* ensemble. *See also* JARANA. (p. 193)

SANXIAN *See* CHINESE FOLK ENSEMBLE.

SAXOPHONE A woodwind instrument invented by Adolphe Sax in the nineteenth century by placing a clarinet-type reed mouthpiece on a piece of brass tubing.

The saxophone has a warm, brassy-but-mellow sound that makes it ideal in jazz ensembles.   (p. 177)

SHENG *See* CHINESE FOLK ENSEMBLE.

SNARE DRUM A small cylinder-shaped drum. Two heads made of calfskin or plastic are stretched over the metal shell and strings wrapped in wire (snares) are fixed to the bottom. When the player strikes the top with sticks, the snares vibrate in response.

A sharp, steady, rhythmic accompaniment is often played on the snare drum. It can also produce a long, raspy, rolling sound.   (p. 114)

STEEL DRUMS Tuned percussion instruments made from oil drums. They were developed in Trinidad and are used for Caribbean-style music. Rubber-headed pan sticks are used to strike dented areas on the tops of the drums.

Steel drums produce a hollow, metallic sound, and are usually played in steel band ensembles.   (p. 191)

STRING BASS   A large wooden string instrument that is either bowed or plucked. The string bass is taller than most players, who must stand up or sit on a tall stool to play it.

The sound of the string bass is very dark and resonant, particularly in the lower notes. The plucked notes are very useful for establishing a strong beat, both in classical music and popular music.   (pp. 37, 177)

SYNTHESIZER   A keyboard instrument, with keys like a piano's, that produces sound by means of electronic oscillators. Synthesizers come in all shapes and sizes. Each kind is capable of making a different combination of sounds, though many of the "standard" sounds are similar on all the synthesizers.

The synthesizer can sound like an electronic version of almost any of the standard orchestral instruments. It also has a wide range of unusual tone qualities and sound effects, such as the whistling of wind or the popping of popcorn.   (p. 159)

TAMBOURINE   A small shallow drum with one head and a wooden rim. Circular metal disks ("jingles") hang loosely in pairs around the rim. The player holds the tambourine in one hand and shakes it or strikes it with the other hand or on the hip.

A shimmery, metallic sound rattles from the tambourine. (p. 114)

TIMPANI   A set of two or more large basin-shaped drums made of copper or brass, with calfskin or plastic stretched over the tops. Each drum has a different pitch, which can be adjusted by means of a pedal at the base. Usually only one player is in charge of the timpani and plays them by striking the tops with one or two mallets.

The timpani (also called kettle drums) are the most important percussion instruments, for they provide strong rhythmic and tonal support for the orchestra. They usually produce a deep, insistent rumbling but can also punch out sharp, loud notes. (p. 173)

TROMBONE   A fairly large brass instrument with a large bell at the end of the tubing. The sound is made by buzzing the lips against the mouthpiece. The pitches are changed by pushing and pulling a metal slide, which lengthens and shortens the tubing.

The trombone can sound very aggressive and noisy but in its softer voice it can be warm and mellow.   (p. 196)

TRUMPET   A small brass instrument with a bell at the end of its coiled tubing. The player buzzes the lips against the mouthpiece to make the sound and changes pitch by pushing button-shaped valves on the top of the instrument.

The sound of the trumpet is bold and bright, but it can sound sweet, even melancholy, when playing a lyrical melody.   (p. 113)

VIBRAPHONE   A xylophone-like instrument with metal bars. An electronic device creates a slow or fast vibrato, giving the instrument its name.

The vibraphone has a mellow, sweet sound, especially when the vibrato device is engaged.   (p. 177)

VIOLIN   A small wooden string instrument. The violin is held under the player's chin. The strings are plucked or bowed with the player's right hand, and the pitches are changed by pressing the strings with the fingers of the left hand.

The violin has a number of very different voices. It also has a wide range of notes, from medium low to very high, and the tone quality can vary from a liquid "singing" sound to a harsh, angry, raspy sound, with many others in between.   (p. 32)

XIAO   *See* CHINESE FOLK ENSEMBLE.

XYLOPHONE   A pitched percussion instrument that has a keyboard of wooden bars and is played with mallets.

The xylophone has a bright, brittle sound that makes it effective in percussive or humorous passages.   (p. 115)

ZITHER, VIETNAMESE   *See* DAN TRANH.

Glossary

a cappella (p. 203) (ah kuh PEHL uh) A term used to indicate unaccompanied choral singing; "in chapel style."

accent (p. 38) A single tone or chord louder than those around it (>).

accidental (p. 288) A sign in music notation used to designate a chromatically altered note. The most common accidentals are ♯, ♭, ♮.

aria (p. 111) (AH ree uh) An extended song for solo voice in an opera, an oratorio, or a cantata; often a showpiece for the singer's vocal ability.

ballad (p. 284) A popular song that usually tells a story.

ballet (p. 153) (ba LAY) A theatrical production centered on dance, generally with costumes, scenery, and accompanying music; or the music written for such a production.

bar line (p. 38) The vertical line on the staff, used to mark off groupings of beats.

beat (p. 10) A repeating pulse that can be felt in some music.

cadence (p. 149) A group of chords or notes at the end of a phrase or piece that gives a feeling of pausing or finishing.

chord (p. 22) Three or more different tones played or sung together.

chorus (p. 111) (KOR uhs) A large group of singers.

chromatic (p. 288) (kroh MAT ik) A musical passage in which notes have been altered by the use of accidentals.

Classic period (p. 136) The period encompassing the latter half of the eighteenth century and the early nineteenth century, when the style of composition was generally marked by simplicity, balance, and restraint.

coda (p. 116) (KOH duh) A short closing section added at the end of a composition.

compound meter (p. 80) A grouping of beats in which three beats are felt as one (such as $\frac{6}{8}$, $\frac{9}{8}$).

concerto (p. 129) (kuhn CHER toh) A piece for a solo instrument with orchestra, usually in three movements.

countermelody (p. 78) A melody that is played or sung at the same time as the main melody.

cross-rhythm (p. 292) A rhythm in which the regular pattern of accents is altered to form a new pattern.

dissonance (dissonant) (p. 134) An interval or a chord that sounds unstable and pulls toward a consonance (an inactive, or "restful," combination of sounds).

downbeat (p. 38) The first, usually accented, beat of the measure.

duet (p. 200) Any two-part composition written for two performers; also the performers.

dynamics (p. 37) Degrees of loudness and softness.

ensemble (p. 118) A group of players or singers.

finale (p. 103) The last movement of a composition, such as a symphony or concerto.

flat (p. 51) *See* accidental.

folk song (p. 44) A song of unknown authorship that has for generations been current among the people of a nation or region.

form (p. 120) The structure of a composition; the way its musical materials are organized.

fret (p. 321) A strip of metal across the fingerboard of a guitar or similar instrument. The player raises or lowers the pitch by pressing a string into contact with a fret.

fugue (p. 107) A musical form based on imitation, in which the main melody (subject) and related melodies (countersubjects) are varied in different ways. The texture is polyphonic. *See* polyphonic texture.

grand staff (p. 346) A two-staff system with the soprano and alto parts shown in the treble clef and the tenor and baritone parts shown in the bass clef.

graphic notation (p. 160) Notation that uses pictures to represent sounds (rather than traditional notation for exact pitches).

harmony (p. 20) The sounding of two or more different notes at the same time.

homophonic texture (homophony) (p. 104) A melodic line supported by a harmonic accompaniment.

improvisation (p. 174) The art of making up the music as the performer goes along.

instrumentation (p. 192) The use of individual instruments and groups of instruments in writing or arranging a composition for an ensemble.

interval (p. 57) The distance from one tone to another.

The smallest interval in traditional Western music is the half step (f-f#, f#-g, and so on). Contemporary music often uses smaller intervals, as does music of other cultures.

inversion (p. 100)   Reversing the pitch direction of the tones of a melody.

jazz (p. 174)   A style that grew out of the music of African Americans, then took many different substyles, such as ragtime, blues, cool jazz, swing, bebop, rock. It features solo improvisations over a set harmonic progression.

key (p. 140)   The particular scale on which a piece of music or a section of it is based, named for its tonic or key-tone or "home-base" tone. (For example, the key of D major indicates that the major scale starting and ending on the tone D is being used.)

key signature (p. 51)   An indication of key, consisting of sharps or flats placed on the staff at the beginning of a composition.

major (p. 50)   Tonally, a key that is based on a major scale— a scale that contains this step pattern: whole, whole, half, whole, whole, whole, half.

measure (p. 177)   A grouping of beats set off by bar lines.

melody (p. 15)   A succession of single tones with rhythm, forming a recognizable musical idea.

meter (p. 38)   The way beats of music are grouped, often in sets of two (duple meter) or in sets of three (triple meter). The time signature (such as $\frac{3}{4}$, $\frac{2}{4}$) tells how many beats are in the group, or measure (top number), and the kind of note that gets one beat (bottom number).

minimalism (p. 205)   A twentieth-century style of composition that emphasizes extended repetition of a motive or group of motives.

minor (p. 52)   Tonally, a key that is based on a minor scale— a scale that contains this step pattern: whole, half, whole, whole, half, whole, whole.

modulation (p. 141)   A change of the tonal center, or key, within a composition.

monophonic texture (monophony) (p. 104)   A single unaccompanied melody line.

motive (p. 79)   A short musical fragment.

movement (p. 11)   Each of the smaller, self-contained sections (usually three or four) that together make up a symphony, concerto, string quartet, and so on.

multimeter (p. 44)   Changing from one meter to another in successive measures.

nationalism (p. 151)   An artistic movement dedicated to the promotion of certain national cultures through the use of folk elements and traditions.

natural (p. 288)   *See* accidental.

notation (p. 344)   Symbols that represent specific pitches and durations in music.

opera (p. 111)   A theatrical production combining drama, vocal and orchestral music, costumes, scenery, and sometimes dance.

oratorio (p. 111)   (or uh TOR ee oh) A musical drama for voices and orchestra, often based on a religious narrative; usually performed without scenery or action.

orchestra (p. 133)   A balanced group of instruments. The Western symphony orchestra usually consists of strings, woodwinds, brass, and percussion.

ostinato (p. 32)   A musical idea that repeats throughout a piece or a section of a piece.

overdub (p. 184)   Musical parts that are added to or superimposed on an existing recording.

pentascale (p. 347)   A five-tone scale in which the notes occur in consecutive letter-name order.

pentatonic (p. 54)   Music based on a five-tone scale. A common pentatonic scale corresponds to tones 1, 2, 3, 5, and 6 of the major scale.

phrase (p. 64)   A melodic idea that acts as a complete thought, something like a sentence.

pitch (p. 15)   The highness or lowness of a tone.

plainsong (p. 104)   Monophonic chant sung usually with even rhythm on Latin texts. Plainsong is one of the earliest examples of notated music. *See* monophonic texture.

polyphonic texture (polyphony) (p. 106)   Two or more independent melody lines sounding together.

polyrhythm (p. 173)   Several different rhythm patterns sounding at the same time, often resulting in conflicts of meter.

program music (p. 151)   Music that is inspired by an extramusical idea, such as a person, place, or story.

quartet (p. 203)   Any four-part composition written for four performers; also the performers.

retrograde (p. 100)   A melody, or motive, read backward.

rhythm (p. 43)   The combination of sounds and silences in the same or differing lengths.

rhythm complex (p. 166)   A percussion composition consisting of layers of contrasting rhythm patterns. *See* polyrhythm.

riff (p. 176)   A term used in jazz for a repeated, short, strongly rhythmic phrase. *See* ostinato.

Romantic period (p. 150)   That period in the nineteenth century, following the Classic period, when the style of composition was generally marked by lyricism, fantasy, and emotional expression.

rondo (p. 124)   A form in which the A section alternates with two contrasting sections, creating a plan of ABACA.

round (p. 106)   A form in which a melody begins in one part and then is continually and exactly repeated by other parts in an overlapping fashion.

scale (p. 50)   An arrangement of pitches from lower to higher according to a specific pattern of intervals. Major, minor, pentatonic, whole-tone, and chromatic are five kinds of scales. Each one has its own arrangement of pitches.

score (p. 157)   The musical notation of a composition, showing all vocal and instrumental parts.

sequence (p. 91)   The repetition of a melody pattern at a higher or lower pitch level.

sharp (p. 51)   *See* accidental.

solo (p. 200)   Music for a single performer, often with an accompaniment.

staff (p. 140)   A set of five equally spaced horizontal lines on which musical notes are written.

style (p. 128)   In music, *style* refers to the way in which melody, rhythm, and harmony create a special sound.

suite (p. 43)   (sweet) Any instrumental work of several short movements, often programmatic or descriptive.

symphony (p. 15)   A large orchestral composition, generally in three or four contrasting movements.

syncopation (p. 83)   An arrangement of rhythm in which prominent or important tones begin on weak beats or weak parts of beats, giving a catchy, off-balance movement to the music.

tempo (p. 12)   The speed of the beat.

texture (p. 104)   *See* homophonic texture; monophonic texture; polyphonic texture. (*Texture* may also refer to aspects of tone color and orchestration.)

theme (p. 102)   An important melody that occurs several times in a piece of music.

time signature (p. 39)   *See* meter.

tone cluster (p. 157)   A group of tones lying no more than a step apart and produced, often on the piano, by pressing down on a section of the keyboard with the fist, the forearm, or a board.

tone color (p. 24)   The special sound of an instrument or voice.

transpose (p. 100)   To write or perform music at a pitch other than the original one.

triad (p. 60)   A chord of three tones, usually built in thirds— an interval of a third on top of another interval of a third.

trio (p. 200)   Any three-part composition written for three performers; also the performers.

unison (p. 200)   The simultaneous playing or singing of the same notes by two or more performers, either at the same pitch or in octaves.

variation (p. 102)   Music that changes a theme in some important ways.

vibrato (p. 160)   A slight, rapid variation of pitch, used to heighten the expressiveness of a tone.

vocal (p. 82)   Any music or sound that is produced by the voice.

wave forms (p. 158)   Basic electronic tone colors produced by an oscillator. Each waveform has a name that describes the way it looks when seen on an oscilloscope.

Classified Index

HOLIDAY, SEASONAL, AND SPECIAL OCCASION

Small World (Huey Lewis)   188

Valentine's Day
Harnick/Bock: *Do You Love Me?*   242
How Sad Is True Love   20
Matchmaker   223
Priority Male: *Straight from the Heart*   203
Rose, The   40
There's a Yellow Rose in Texas   286
Triplets, The: *Adonde quíera que vas*   204
Yellow Rose of Texas, The   284

LISTENING SELECTIONS

Alabama: *If You're Gonna Play in Texas (You Gotta Have a Fiddle in the Band)*   183
Alford: *Colonel Bogey March*   124
Almeida/Modern Jazz Quartet: *One-Note Samba*   11
Bach, J.S.: *Fugue in G Minor*, "The Little"   110
Bach, J.S.: *Minuet*   79
Bach, P.D.Q. (Peter Schickele): *1712 Overture*   91
Banda R-15: *La chica contry*   183
Bartók: *Mikrokosmos*, "Wrestling"   156
Beck: *Led Boots*   33
Beethoven: *Egmont Overture* (Call Chart 11)   148
Beethoven: *Minuet in G*   156
Beethoven: *Symphony No. 7 in A*, Movement 2   90
Beethoven: *Symphony No. 9 in D Minor*, Movement 4   15, 200
Bolling: *Suite for Flute and Jazz Piano*, "Irlandaise"   155
Boyoyo Boys, The: *Alex Jive*   33
Brahms: *Variations on a Theme by Haydn*   102
Britten: *Young Person's Guide to the Orchestra*, "Introduction" (Call Chart 15)   199
Brubeck: *Unsquare Dance*   74
Chávez: *Toccata for Percussion*, Movement 3   11
Ciani: *Composition for Synthesizer*   99
Corelli/Pinelli: *Suite for String Orchestra*, Movement 3, "Badinerie"   114
Creed/Masser: *The Greatest Love of All*   5
DeFalla: *El amor brujo*, "Ritual Fire Dance"   38
Deodato: *Also Sprach Zarathustra (2001)*   11
Dick: *Or*   155
Dvorák: *Slavonic Dance in G Minor*   151
Eddleman: *Brass Quartet* "In Honorem Paul Hindemith," Movement 1   113
Eddleman: *Opus Vetrinus*   155
Eddleman: *Tales from the Latin Woods*   115
Ellington: *Dooji-Wooji*   81
Faini: *Afro-Amero* (Call Chart 13)   173
Faltermeyer: *Axel F*   72
Gabriel, Peter: *The Rhythm of the Heat*   185
Glass: *The Olympian*, "Lighting the Torch"   90
Glass: *The Photographer*, "A Gentleman's Honor"   40, 204
Goodman: *Seven Come Eleven*   177
Glière: *The Red Poppy*, "Russian Sailor's Dance" (Call Chart 8)   116

Gottschalk: *Pasquinade*, "Caprice"   85
Grieg: *Norwegian Dance No. 2 in A* (Call Chart 9)   123
Grieg: *Peer Gynt*, "In the Hall of the Mountain King" (Call Chart 2)   37
Handel: *Judas Maccabaeus*, "Hallelujah, Amen" (Call Chart 7)   112
Harnick/Bock: *Fiddler on the Roof* selections   216
Haubenstock-Ramati: *Interpolations for Flute*   155
Hindemith: *Sonata for Flute and Piano*, Movement 2   155
Joel, Billy: *I Go to Extremes*   10
Joplin: *The Entertainer*   85
LeCaine: *Dripsody*   25
Ledbetter: *Shorty George* (Call Chart 3)   65
Liszt: *Hungarian Rhapsody No. 2*   49
Liszt: *Transcendental Etude No. 8 in C Minor*   150
Lloyd Webber: *Evita*, "Don't Cry for Me, Argentina"   207
Mann, Aimee: *Voices Carry*   84
Marais: *The Bells of St. Geneviève*   32
McDaniels: *River*   35
Mexican Mariachi: *Cielito lindo*   192
Milhaud: *La cheminée du Roi René*, Movement 1   113
Miller: *Big River*, "Free at Last"   267
Mozart: *Concerto No. 21 in C Major for Piano and Orchestra*, Movement 2   129
Mozart: *Symphony No. 40 in G Minor*, Movement 3   133
N'Dour: *Africa Remembers*   163
Nkosi: *Africa (What You Gonna Say)*   171
Nyamwezi Drummers: *Manyanga Drum Rhythms*   165
Orff: *Carmina Burana*, "O Fortuna"   90
Penderecki: *Threnody for the Victims of Hiroshima*   157
Penniman/Ten Years After: *Going Back to Birmingham*   65
Preservation Hall Jazz Band: *When the Saints Go Marching In*   178
Prince/Raye: *Boogie-Woogie Bugle Boy*   202
Priority Male: *Straight from the Heart*   203
Prokofiev: *Classical Symphony*, Movement 3, "Gavotte"   19
Raaijmakers: *Contrasts* (Part 2) (Call Chart 12)   159
Ravel: *Le tombeau de Couperin*, "Minuet"   42
Read: *The Aztec Gods*, Movement 1   114
Santamaria: *Watermelon Man*   167
Schoenberg: *Concerto for Piano and Orchestra*, Movement 1   129
Shostakovich: *Symphony No. 5 in D Minor*, Movement 2, "Allegretto"   133
Sondheim: *Comedy Tonight*   83
Speech/Arrested Development: *Mr. Wendal*   34
Steel Drum Band: *El merecumbe*   191
Stravinsky: *Firebird Suite*, "Finale" (Call Chart 5)   97
Stravinsky: *The Rite of Spring*, "Finale"   153
Tailleferre: *Concertino for Harp and Orchestra*, Movement 3, "Rondo" (Call Chart 10)   124
Traditional: *Cripple Creek*   181
Traditional: *Lousiana* and *Field Song from Senegal*   169
Traditional: *Woke Up This Morning with My Mind On Freedom*   263
Traditional Chinese: *Dancing in the Moonlight*   190
Traditional Mexican: *La iguana*   193

Song Index — CD-Track Number

Photograph and Illustration Credits

Acknowledgments

Credit and appreciation are due publishers and copyright owners for use of the following materials.

"Get Up, Blues" by James A. Emanuel, from WHOLE GRAIN: COLLECTED POEMS, 1958–1989. Lotus Press, 1991. "Noise" by J. Pope, © PUNCH London. "Fourth of July Night," from WIND SONG © 1960 Carl Sandburg (renewed) 1988 by Margaret Sandburg, Janet Sandburg and Helga Sandburg Crile. Reprinted by permission of Harcourt Brace Jovanovich, Inc. "How Not to Have to Dry the Dishes" by Shel Silverstein, from A LIGHT IN THE ATTIC by Shel Silverstein. Copyright © 1981 by Evil Eye Music, Inc. "The Generals" by Shel Silverstein, from WHERE THE SIDEWALK ENDS by Shel Silverstein. Copyright © 1974 by Evil Eye Music, Inc.

"Martin Luther King, Jr" by Gwendolyn Brooks. © 1970 Gwendolyn Brooks Blakely. Reprinted by permission of Broadside Press. "Slowly" by James Reeves, from THE WANDERING MOON AND OTHER POEMS by James Reeves. Reprinted by permission of the Estate of James Reeves. "The Ad-dressing of Cats" by T. S. Eliot, from OLD POSSUM'S BOOK OF PRACTICAL CATS by T. S. Eliot. Used by permission of Faber & Faber Ltd. "Video Flag" by Melchishaua Person, from SUMMER IN MY BACKYARD. © 1992 Founders Society Detroit Institute of Arts. Julia Henshaw, Director of Publications, Detroit Institute of Arts, 5200 Woodward Avenue, Detroit, MI 48202. "Africa Remembers" by Y. N'Dour, translation by Boubacar N'Dour. © 1992 Editions Virgin Musique. All Rights Reserved. Used by Permission.

Every effort has been made to locate all copyright holders of material used in this book. If any errors or omissions have occurred, corrections will be made.

Illustration Credits

4–5: Maj-Britt Hagsted; Robert Roper, bdr. 6–7: Susan Greenstein. 8–9: Rita Lascaro. 10–11: Bill Mayer. 12–13: Janice Edelman-Lee. 14: Troy Thomas. 15–17: Cindy Lindgren. 18–19: Steve Moscowitz. 20–21: Bernard Adnet. 22–23: Oscar Hernandez. 24–25: Diane Bigda; Janice Edelman-Lee, chart. 26–29: Michelle Barnes. 32–33: Neil Shigley. 34–35: Calef Brown. 36–37: Bernard Adnet. 38–39: Sara Anderson. 40–41: Sara Schwartz. 42–43: Ron Broda. 44–45: Kat Thacker. 46–47: Juliette Borda. 50–53: Amanda Schaffer. 54–56: Michael McLaughlin. 57–59: Campbell Laird. 60–61: Janice Edelman-Lee. 62–63: Juliette Borda. 64–65: Paul Rogers; Oscar Hernandez, bdr. 66–68: Steve Moscowitz. 69–71: David Coulson. 72–73 Sergio Baradat. 74–75: Bernard Adnet. 76–77: Gil Adams. 78–79: Michael McLaughlin. 80–82: Jeff Nishinaka; Valerie Johnson, bdr. 83: Beata Szpura. 85–87: Jennie Oppenheimer; Bernard Adnet. 88–91: Kat Tacker. 94–95: Robert Pizzo. 96–97: Lin Wilson. 98–99: Dan Picasso. 100–101: Fran O'Neill. 102–103: Gwendolyn Wong. 106–110: Yan Nascimbene. 111–112: Alex Bloch. 113–114: Bernard Adnet; Peggy Tagel, bdr. 117: Greg Voth. 118–119: Dan Yaccarino. 120–123: Bernard Adnet. 124–125: Amanda Schatter. 126: Lisa Pomerantz. 128–129: Sally Jo Vitsky. 130–132: James Kaczman. 135: Albert Lemant. 136–143: Mark McConnell. 150–151: Kat Thacker. 155: Cathy Norris. 156–157: Andy Levine. 158–159: Jane Caminos. 160–161: Jane Sanders. 162–167: Calef Brown. 168–171: Bernard Adnet. 172–173: Lu Mathews, Eileen Hine, bdr. 174–177: Tracy Zungola. 178–180: Bob Shein. 181–183: Cathy Norris. 184–185: Lin Wilson. 186–189: Evan Polenghi. 190–193: Eileen Hine. 198–199: Bernard Adnet; Michael Sloan, bdr. 200–203: Lori Lohsteoter. 204–205: Elizabeth Brady. 206–215: Robert Levy. 216: Janice Edelman-Lee. 216–245: Joann Adinolfi. 246–247: Rita Lascaro. 248–250: Erni Cabat. 251–252: Janice Edelman-Lee. 253: Julie Schaut. 254–255: Mark McConnell. 256–259: Jennifer Hewitson. 260–263: David McLimans. 264–266: Michelle Manning; Robert Levy, bdr. 267: Robert Levy. 268–270: Jennifer Hewitson. 271–274: Robert Levy. 275–277: Amanda Schaffer. 278–279: Maj-Britt Hagsted. 282–283: David McLimans. 284–287: Lauren Scheuer. 288–291: Mark McConnell. 292–295: Janice Edelman-Lee. 298–301: Diane Bigda. 304–306: John Margeson. 307–311: Susan Swan. 312–313: Charles Shaw. 318–319: Erni Cabat.

Photograph Credits

All photographs are by Silver Burdett Ginn (SBG) unless otherwise noted. 4: t. Neal Preston, Courtesy of Nippy, Inc.; b.l. Fotex/H. Kuehn/Shooting Star; b.r. ©Tim Mosenfelder/LGI. 5: t.© 1993 Picture Perfect USA; b.l. Oliver Berin/Tony Stone Images; b.r.© Michael James/Sygma. 6: © 1993 Martha Swope. 10: Teit Hombak/Liaison International. 11: Orozco, Jose Clemente. Zapatistas, 1931. Oil on canvas, 45 x 55". The Museum of Modern Art, New York. Given anonymously. 12–13: bkgd. Mike Medici for SBG. 12: l. ©Zig Leszczynski/Animals Animals; m. Thomas Zimmermann/Tony Stone Images; r. ©David Weintraub/Photo Researchers, Inc. 13: l. ©Ben Osborne/Oxford Scientific Films/Animals Animals; r. Jim Tuten/Animals Animals. 14: Culver Pictures. 15: COMSTOCK. 28–29: Lawrence Migdale for SBG. 30–31: © 1992 Jack Vartoogian. 32: Culver Pictures, Inc. 33: Courtesy of Clive Risko, Reamusic. 34–35: © William McCoy/Rainbow. 36–37: Arnulf Husmo/Tony Stone Images. 38: Hale Observatories/SCIENCE SOURCE/Photo Researchers, Inc. 39: The Bettmann Archive. 40–41: © 1992 B.F. Peterson/West Stock. 43: c. Museo Teatrale alla Scala, Milan. Scala/Art Resource, NY; Ron Broda. 44: The Horniman Museum, London. 48: COMSTOCK. 50: ©90 Michael Liventson/The Stock Market. 52–53: The Granger Collection, New York. 55: Ngo Quoc Trung. Landscape Near My Home. Indochina Arts Project, Newton Centre, MA. 56: © 1990 Jack Vartoogian. 57: t. ©1978 Jack Vartoogian; b. John Terence Turner/FPG International. 58: Photofest. 60: Lawrence Migdale for SBG. 63: Hayden, Palmer C. The John Henry Series: John Henry on His Right. Oil on canvas, 30 x 40". Collection of The Museum of African American Art, Los Angeles, CA. Palmer C. Hayden Collection, Gift of Miriam A. Hayden. Photograph: Armando Solis. 68: Michael Ochs Archives. 69: Movie Still Archives. 70: COMSTOCK. 72: Movie Still Archives. 76–77: bkgd. Movie Stone Images; insert Johns, Jasper. Three Flags. Photograph by Geoffrey Clements, NY. 80–81: Jeff Nishinaka. 82: bkgd. Jeff Nishinaka; insert The Bettmann Archive. 84: Raj Rama/LGI. 85: Michael Ochs Archives. 89: Cezanne, Paul. Chestnut Trees at Jas de Bouffan, © 1885–87. Oil on canvas, 27 3/4 x 35 5/16". The William Hood Dunwoody Fund. The Minneapolis Institute of Arts. 91: Albers, Josef. Homage to the Square: Apparition, 1959. Solomon R. Guggenheim Museum, New York. Photograph: David Heald copyright The Solomon R. Guggenheim Foundation, New York. FN 61.1590. 92: Kandinsky, Vasily. Several Circles, January–February 1926. Solomon R. Guggenheim, New York, Gift, Solomon R. Guggenheim, 1941.© 1993 ARS, New York/ADAGP, Paris. Photograph: David Heald copyright The Solomon R. Guggenheim Foundation, New York. FN 41.283. 93: FPG International. 102–103: Gwendolyn Wong. 104–105: COMSTOCK. 106: Escher, M.C. Swans ©1956 M.C. Escher Foundation—Baarn—Holland. 107: Foto Marburg/Art Resource, NY. 110: © Hackett Collection/Archive Photos. 115: border © Raymond G. Barnes/Tony Stone Images. 117: border ©Raymond G. Barnes/Tony Stone Images; insert The Granger Collection, New York. 124: ©Dallas and John Heaton/WestLight. 128: t. Udaltsova, Nadezhda Andreevina. At the Piano. Photograph by Joseph Szaszfai; b. Grand Piano, ca. 1840. Erard & Co., London. The Metropolitan Museum of Art, Gift of Mrs. Henry McSweeny, 1959. (59.76). 129: t. ©Clive Barda/Performing Arts Library. 130–131: The Granger Collection, New York. 133: Auguste de Saint Aubin/engr. Duclos/Mary Evans Picture Library. 134: ©1987 by Blair Seitz/Photo Researchers, Inc. 135: Scala/Art Resource, NY. 136: SuperStock; bkgd. ©M. Angelo/WestLight. 138–139: ©1993 Picture Perfect USA. 140: bkgd. Letraset Phototone. 142–143: bkgd.©M. Angelo/WestLight. 143: bkgd. ©Adam Smith/WestLight; US Press/Shooting Star. 144: The Bettmann Archive. 146–147: The Granger Collection, New York; insert Culver Pictures, Inc. 151: The Bettmann Archive. 152: Courtesy US Postal Service. 153: Kandinsky, Wassily. Untitled Improvisation III. © 1985 Museum Associates, Los Angeles Museum of Art. Museum Acquisition by exchange from David E. Bright Bequest. 155: Lawrence Migdale for SBG. 158: Shelia O'Neal/LGI. 163: Patrick Harbron©/Sygma. 165: SuperStock. 169: t. The Bettmann Archive; b. © 1990 Jack Vartoogian. 170: t. © 1992 Ken Francklling/LGI; b. ©Steve Jennings/LGI. 171: t. ©Ron Delany/LGI; b. ©1987 Ken Francklling/LGI. 176–177: Brown Brothers. 180: ©1991 R. Corkery/LGI. 182: © ç. Schmeiser/Unicorn Stock Photos. 183: Charmaine Lanham. 184: t. Paul Rider/Photofest; b. ©Michael James/Sygma. 185: Victor Englebert. 186: LGI. 190: Mike Medici for SBG. 191: Allan A. Philiba. 192: ©1993 Picture Perfect USA. 193: Michael Kornafel/FPG International. 194–195: border Richard Nowitz/SuperStock. 196–197: © 1993 R.T. Nowitz. 198–199: ©Clive Barda/Performing Arts Library. 202: t. Photofest; b. Herb Ritts/Shooting Star. 203: John Dunn. 204: © 1991 Marko Shark/LGI. 205: Culver Pictures, Inc. 206: "Evita" Playbill, Photofest; © Trapper/Sygma. 207: Martha Swope. 210–215: Martha Swope. 217–245: ©1991 Martha Swope Associates/Carol Rosegg; inset on 239 Photofest. 245: t. inset The Bettmann Archive; l. inset UPI/Bettmann Newsphoto; r. inset Archive Photos. 246: Trumbull, John. The Declaration of Independence. Yale University Art Gallery. Photo by Joseph Szaszfai. 247: © Plimoth Plantation. 249: The Granger Collection, New York. 251: Merritt, Susan. Picnic Scene. American, 1826–1879. Watercolor and collage on paper, © 1853, 66 X 91.4 cm. Gift of Elizabeth R. Vaughan, 1950.1846. Photograph © 1993 The Art Institute of Chicago, All Rights Reserved. 253: © D. & I. MacDonald/Photri Inc. 255: The Center for American History, The University of Texas at Austin. 256: SuperStock. 260–261: UPI/Bettmann. 263: UPI/Bettmann; inset © 1990 Paul LaRaia/LGI. 267: © 1990 Martha Swope. 268–269: ©Jean-Paul Manceau/Tony Stone Images. 270: Doug Armand/Tony Stone Images. 271: Richard T. Nowitz. 272–274: ©Robert Young Pelton/WestLight; inset SuperStock. 275: Tanner, Henry Ossawa. The Good Shepherd. Oil on canvas, Hampton University Museum, Hampton, Virginia. 276: Tanner, H.O. Self Portrait. National Museum of American Art, Smithsonian Institution, Gift of Mr. and Mrs. Norman B. Robbins/Art Resource, NY. 278: © Suzanne Murphy/DDB Stock Photo. 287: Courtesy of Panhandle-Plains Historical Museum, Canyon, Texas. 288: Ewing Galloway. 289: NASA; insert ©Elena Seibert/Outline Press. 290–291: NASA. 292: Witwatersrand University Press, photo by P.R. Kirby. This photo by Michael Campbell. 295: A. & M. Sutton/FPG International. 296–297: border FPG International. 296: ©1993 Kit Breen/Picture Perfect USA. 298: FPG International. 299: Photofest. 300–301: © O'Brien & Mayor Photography 1991/FPG International. 302–303: border Merrilyn Ayala for SBG. 302: Ronald Shickey. 307, 308, 311: Photofest. 314–317: border ©William A. Holmes/FPG International. 314–315: bkgd. Tony Stone Images; inset Marie Ueda/Leo de Wys, Inc. 316–317: FPG International. 321: t. Michael Provost for SBG; c. John Bacchus for SBG. 322: l. Michael Provost for SBG; r. Lawrence Migdale for SBG. 325: t. and b. Mike Medici for SBG. 326: t. Michael Provost for SBG. 331: Mike Medici for SBG. 335: Lawrence Migdale for SBG. 337: t. Lawrence Migdale for SBG; c. Michael Provost for SBG. 344–345: Lawrence Migdale for SBG. 346: Michael Provost for SBG. 363: t.l. ©1991 Bruce Talaman/Michael Ochs Archives; t.r. ©Dave Allocca/RETNA Pictures; b. Michael Ochs Archives.

Sound Bank Photographs (in order, top to bottom)

364: Ken Karp for SBG; The Shrine to Music Museum/University of South Dakota; Mike Medici for SBG; Ken Karp for SBG; MATHERS MUSEUM. 365: Ken Karp for SBG; Michael Provost for SBG; John Bacchus for SBG; Mike Medici for SBG. 366: SBG; SBG; The Shrine to Music Museum/University of South Dakota; Mike Medici for SBG; The Shrine to Music Museum/University of South Dakota. 367: The Shrine to Music Museum/University of South Dakota; The Shrine to Music Museum/University of South Dakota; John Bacchus for SBG; John Bacchus for SBG; Terry E. Miller; MATHERS MUSEUM. 368: SBG; SBG; The Shrine to Music Museum/University of South Dakota; SBG. 369: SBG; John Bacchus for SBG; Ken Karp for SBG; MATHERS MUSEUM; SBG; SBG. 370: Jarana–Ann Summa for SBG; Ken Karp for SBG; SBG; SBG; MATHERS MUSEUM; SBG. 371: John Bacchus for SBG; Courtesy Zazhil/Bill Albrecht for SBG; SBG; SBG; Ken Karp for SBG. 372: SBG; SBG; SBG; SBG. 373: SBG; SBG; SBG; John Bacchus for SBG; SBG.